Glass, Paper, Beans

Glass, Paper, Beans

Revelations on
the Nature and Value
of Ordinary Things

Leah Hager Cohen

Doubleday / Currency

New York London Toronto Sydney Auckland

A Currency Book

PUBLISHED BY DOUBLEDAY

a division of Bantam Doubleday Dell Publishing Group, Inc.

1540 Broadway, New York, New York 10036

Currency, Doubleday, and the portrayal of a hand wielding
lightning bolts are trademarks of Doubleday, a division of
Bantam Doubleday Dell Publishing Group, Inc.

Book design by Chris Welch

Library of Congress Cataloging-in-Publication Data
Cohen, Leah Hager.
Glass, paper, beans: revelations on the nature and value of
ordinary things / Leah Hager Cohen. — 1st ed.
p.   cm.
"A Currency book"—T.p. verso.
Includes bibliographical references.
1. Material culture. 2. Commercial products—Social aspects.
3. Commercial products—History. 4. Fetishism. I. Title.
GN450.C65   1997
306.3—dc20   96-19273
CIP

ISBN 0-385-47819-4

February 1997

First Edition

1   3   5   7   9   10   8   6   4   2

To Paul Scherer

Acknowledgments

I am grateful to Brent Boyd, Ruth Lamp, and Basilio Salinas, and their families (those related by work as well as by blood), for letting me spend time with and write about them.

In reporting on glass, I received help from Beth Hylen at the Corning Museum of Glass; Jerry Hersch at New England Store Fixture; and Karl Salmon at Anchor Hocking. In reporting on paper, I received help from Paul Shortall and his family, Pamela Folkins, Beth Brown, Rick Wightman, and Pierre Zundel in New Brunswick; Douglas Dwyer and Godfrey Kauffmann at the *Boston Globe;* Mike Ryan, Doyce Brown, and Madison Paper Industries. In reporting on coffee, I received help from Dave Griswald, Lilith von Foerster, and Francisco Zavaleta at Aztec Harvests; Lindsey Bolger at Batdorf and Bronson; Bill Fishbein at Coffee

Kids; Ana Bazdresch, Holly Benton, Molly Doane, Richard Snyder, and Toni Scribner.

Jill Kasiewiez interpreted far above and beyond the call of duty in Mexico. Jeff Hale, Leigh Ann Dainty, and Matt Kuhn were most helpful at the Someday Café. Lowell S. Thomas, Wendy Yanowitch, Harold Rubin, and Jeff Kaplowitz generously assisted me in the area of commodities and trading.

I am deeply indebted to Wallace Shawn for having written *The Fever*.

Sam Freedman, Eileen Sullivan, Gary Shrager, Lori Taylor, Jay Fitzgerald, and Sue and Oscar Cohen offered important ideas and encouragement. Thanks to Dave Prifti and Erica Seidman, each of whom inadvertently helped trigger the idea behind this book. I am so grateful to Barney Karpfinger, my agent, for his great faith and heart; to Betsy Lerner for editing with a poet's sensibility; and to Robert Fitzgerald for his unending goodness and the birdfeeder.

I love
all
things,
not because they are
passionate
or sweet-smelling
but because,
I don't know,
because
this ocean is yours,
and mine:
these buttons
and wheels
and little
forgotten
treasures,
fans upon
whose feathers
love has scattered
its blossoms,
glasses, knives and
scissors—
all bear
the trace
of someone's fingers
on their handle or surface,
the trace of a distant hand
lost
in the depths of forgetfulness.

—from *Ode to Things*
Pablo Neruda

Contents

P r e l u d e

Someday Café

Here in the Someday Café, I sit at a rickety wooden table on which are laid: a newspaper, Sunday-fat; and a tall glass tumbler filled with steaming coffee.

The Someday Café sports two large plate-glass windows, which look out upon a busy, twisty intersection; and a small, not-quite-square interior, which manages, just, to accommodate six tables, fourteen mismatched chairs, a slip of bookshelf, and the coffee bar. The furniture looks as though it might have been picked up at a fraternity-house yard sale, late in the day. The café is full this morning, as it often is on Sunday mornings. Its clientele appears homologous in a motley sort of way: holey jeans abound, as do thick sandals and thick socks, cracked leather jackets, plaid flannel shirts, and heavy, earth-colored sweaters.

It is late winter and the plate-glass windows, the pastry case, and the eyeglasses on people's faces are all slightly fogged, glazed with a fine moisture signifying warmth and close bodies and the pressurized pulling of espresso shots. Jazz meanders from large mounted speakers. There are hanging plants, and a collection of vivid, juicy-looking oil paintings on the walls. Some of the paintings have objects glued to them: for example, a pair of mittens and a tiny plastic shopping cart. There are almond biscotti and German chocolate brownies and something called Stroopwaffles in the pastry case, and a gumball machine in the corner that dispenses chocolate-covered espresso beans into your palm when fed a quarter. Some wilting orange snap-dragons stick out of a thermos on the counter; beside them, taped to the back of the cash register, is a printed card advising, "COFFEE KILLS." Six feet overhead, a tiny cardboard carton labeled "Suggestion Box" has been masking-taped upside down to the ceiling.

The Someday is so crowded that two men have taken their coffees to the wide, crooked ledge in front of one plate-glass window, where they sit cross-legged on a blanket of strewn newspaper, and other people (and one Irish setter) share tables with strangers, while still others lounge against the counter, waiting for vacancies. I'm sharing my table with a stranger, a woman knitting something plum-colored on long silver needles, whose sound is pleasant, like a pair of aunts chatting in the next room. Our table is away from the door, and I have the good seat, the one facing out. My coffee is creamy and holding its heat, my newspaper satisfyingly thick and splashed with exciting pictures on the front page of every section. I have all that I could want.

But I am not content. I feel obscurely put-upon. It's this dearth of chairs and this constant minute shifting of the people standing around waiting. I feel the pressure of an unspoken entreaty—to finish my drink and relinquish my seat—and I am uneasy. I do not want to give up my seat, and neither do I want to feel like a hog. I'm conscious of feeling annoyance toward the people waiting for tables. I seem to be annoyed with them for being there, and for not having seats. The pressure builds; it has a kind of ungainly moral weight, like guilt.

I look up from the newspaper. Behind the counter a large chalkboard displays—amid intricate and psychedelic depictions of chimps, cowboys, teacups, and hookahs—the menu. *Coffee lg,* it says, $1.25. That's right, I think. A large coffee costs a dollar twenty-five.

I paid that. The expenditure of such a sum, I reason, not only entitles me to the beverage itself and temporary use of a receptacle for it, but also confers on me the right to sit and enjoy it at this table for a reasonable length of time. When I became the consumer of this coffee, my standing was affected in such a way as to gain me that right. I have membership status here, purchased with this drink, which I raise now. The glass is warm against my lips, and I consume some of the coffee that is my ticket to this place, to this little world with its steamy windows and its sagging orange snapdragons. The pressure resolved, reasoned away, I lower my eyes again to the paper.

The text dances, dazzlingly uncooperative. The Someday Café is so cramped it's hard to ignore the bodies, their movements, their smells, their sheer presence. Catching my attention by accident, they have become lodged there. In spite of myself, I look up again from the gray blur of news to the people around me, and this time, with no warning, a strange thing happens to my eyes or to my brain: the people loom up, in odd, alarming focus. Every one of them for a protracted moment seems far more specific, more particular, than any stranger could ever be. The general annoyance I felt toward them a minute earlier dissipates and then completely vanishes in the heat of this vision of each one's absolute singularity. I fix on the pale red rash on the forearm of the woman next to me; the muffin crumbs in the white beard of a tall man; a wince flashing across the face of a young man reading sheet music; a label sticking out of the collar of a well-ironed shirt. And I am flooded by the conviction that I could know them all, the people in this shop—rather, *should* know them. It seems briefly a matter of course.

It's not unlike the feeling I used to get as a child, when, periodically, the object in my hand, be it a spoon or a crayon or a shoelace, would seem in an instant to declare itself, all at once coming to my attention as something with a life that extended beyond my pudding or drawing or shoe. For a moment then I would wake and wonder, Who made this thing? Do I know them? Do they know me? Will I ever meet them? And when that happens, what will we know of our connection? Someday, I imagined, I would investigate all this.

But such prodigious possibilities would spin themselves out in my thoughts for a few seconds only. Then, all too quickly, the eating or drawing or business of tying my shoe would recommence, and I would find myself holding once again a mere utensil, a common thing gone abruptly dull and flat—here only in the service of my own activity, no longer a material link to other lives.

Just as quickly now in the café, noise from the milk steamer fuzzes up the room, blotting meaning from all the murmuring conversations, from the idea that we are all not strangers. My head clears, or it muddles: it returns to its common state. Even as I look from face to face, trying to invoke whatever aspect has just been radiating from them, I'm aware of my focus going soft and general again, of the mystery of everybody's singularity receding, of myself falling back within my own smooth boundaries.

I pluck at the newsprint before me, drink again from the warm glass tumbler. Around me no one else seems to have registered any strange occurrence, any fleeting revelation. We all go on as before, some of us in pairs, more of us separately, with our usual business. Some of us gaze out the window at the caravan of salt-stained cars waiting for the light to turn. Some of us tap fingers against laptops or skate ballpoint pens across notebook ponds. Some of us pick raisins out of scones and feed them to ourselves or the Irish setter. But mostly, I observe, just before I lower my own eyes once more to the black and white, we are reading the paper. It is Sunday, and we are curious about our world.

One

Morning

Every day this happens: we rotate into light. Light meets a band of earth, drapes itself simultaneously across grass and waves and trash cans, awnings and snow and mango trees, gas pumps and basketball courts and steeples and iguanas, gravestones and quarries and billboards and skin. We say of this, "The sun has risen."

Every day this happens, all over the world, for all of our lives. The earth pivots round on its axis, and every moment, from north to south, a great strip of us who have never met, and will never meet, enter the day together. The zones defined by these slices of dawn, these longitudinal coincidences, mean little or nothing to us. As boundaries, as articulations of territory, these strips of light are at least as delineated as any political border, but the communities formed by them are nonexistent. Most maps don't even bother printing such lines; those that do, render them minutely: in gossamer lengths of ink, infinitesimal jottings of number and degree. If we note them at all, rarely is it in relation to ourselves, to our own imaginable lives. How many of us could report the number of degrees and minutes east or west of the prime meridian we live? Of those, how many would identify as members of a community of people who reside along that north–south strip? It is preposterous. We have not been taught to see that way.

Instead, we have nations. We have provinces, states, districts, regions. Some of their borders coincide with natural features of the earth's surface; others flout them. A few borders are made manifest in barbed wire, signposts, tollbooths, gateways; many more are manifest only on paper, in the forms of maps and charters, treaties and accords, painstaking tributes to a collective imagination so strong, so encompassing, it operates as fact. The reification of political borders, of community and kinship constructed around nation and state, is absolute. It feels natural. We have been taught to see that way.

Morning occurs, regardless, in strips: a quietly, chronically subversive occurrence. Like a child who will not abide by game rules, who insists that the floor is *not* boiling lava and steps off the couch, morning trespasses across the boundaries we've so solemnly arranged, and there is nowhere morning does not go.

Plumweseep, New Brunswick
45°43′ N   65°32′ W

The sun's advancing frontier is still somewhere out between Newfoundland and Nova Scotia when Brent
Boyd wakes at half past four, accompanied by neither
light nor warmth. He withdraws from the pine bed his
grandfather built and exchanges twin layers of green-
maple-leaf and wine-clover quilt—the one pieced by
his great-grandmother, the other by his mother—for
the stiff black mantle of predawn chill, whose harsh-
ness he barely registers. This is nothing. This is Atlantic time, the Maritimes, late wintertime. He puts on
his boots, goes out to start the half-ton.

The half-ton, a red-and-white Ford, sits in the
driveway and heaves plumy exhaust into the air. A diesel fuel tank, glistening with frost, looms broadly up
out of the truck bed. Along the side of the house, the
dusky shapes of the shrubs he put in this year—mocha
pine, baby princess, hen and chickens—are mottled
with remnants of snow. Alone on the lawn, the little
Pumpkin Sweet apple tree—also planted just this
year—stands black against a less black sky. No lights
show in neighboring houses.

He leaves the engine running and goes back in
through the garage doors to gather an armload from
the pile of wood there—a gift Grampy Boyd makes
from his own woodlots to his children and grandchildren every year. Brent carries the load up a short flight
of stairs from basement to den and deposits it by the
woodstove. It is enameled dark green, with gold trim
and a glass door; the darkling glow of embers from last

night's fire lingers inside. He gives these a stir, adds crumpled newspaper and then bits of wood, coaxing up flame, and now he switches on TV—Channel 29, the Weather Network—curious about the roads. Satellite pictures and computer-generated maps appear on the screen: alternating images of vast, curved segments of globe and intimate, cookie-cutter juttings of coast; the gray perambulations of cloud patterns, swirling jerkily across the continent, like curdled milk on the surface of coffee.

Crouching near the woodstove, Brent continues to stoke the fire, which crackles and swells, begins again to distribute heat. In a few minutes he will leave, headed for the forest and his day's work of cutting down trees. The fire's for the two he's left upstairs, his wife and his daughter, one under maple leaf and clover in the big pine bed, the other in her little white bed across the hall.

Lancaster, Ohio
39°40′ N   82°35′ W

One time zone to the west, Eastern time, one hour later, Ruth Lamp's workweek ends. She takes a last swallow of cooled coffee and crosses the boxcar-shaped sluer office. The office, which oversees the glass factory's Select and Pack department, is small and hardly well-appointed, but it does boast a small metal sink. Ruth rinses her mug and, with a satisfied little thonk, sets it upside down on a folded sheet of paper towel, where it will remain untouched for four days.

No bell rings to signal the completion of her twelve-hour lock shift. No machine shuts down, no motor hushes. No sign of dawn seeps into the sluer office, whose three rather bleary windows look out, anyway, on the plant floor, awash as ever in the canned glare of fluorescent lights. The line workers are on an eight-hour rotation, and the current shift didn't come on 'til eleven last night, so Ruth's departure does not even get marked by a collective mobilization, a comradely gathering up of sweatshirts and purses and empty Tupperwares, a group tromp down the ramp to the gatehouse and employee lot.

She jiggles her black pocketbook for the sound of keys, fishes them out, and hoists her bag over her shoulder. On her way out, Ruth gives a wave to her day-shift replacement, already well installed at the desk they share, phone pressed to her ear, rumply-edged pages of logbook between her fingers. The replacement closes a palm over the mouthpiece, hoarse-whispers, " 'Night, Ruthie."

"Have a good one."

The other woman rolls her eyes and cracks some gum into the phone.

Across the plant floor Ruth scrupulously follows the red-painted path that marks a safe passage among the moving tow motors. It forces her somewhat out of her way; she has to loop backward, toward the annealing room, before cutting over and heading for the exit, but it's a safety precaution everyone takes seriously. Around her now the tow motors maneuver sluggishly, lifting and conveying pallets of ware, their perpetual whistling pulses sounding haggard and sorrowful. But maybe it's just her, maybe it's just a projection of the state of her own self at the end of a four-day, forty-eight-hour workweek.

Morning has come to her, but when she reaches the bottom of the ramp, the sky is still dark, with steam from the plant stacks billowing high and white against it. She locates her turquoise Ford Ranger, starts it up. Now for four days she will not think of work. She'll go walking in the woods with her wolf, drink water from her spring, see her children and grandchildren and great-grandbaby. Do some cooking and cleaning, gardening and mowing. Maybe burn some more of that brush along her road. But first thing she'll do is sleep. If she doesn't dawdle over the back roads, she should be able to beat the sun home.

Pluma Hidalgo, Oaxaca
15°54′ N   96°23′ W

Two hours later, six A.M. Central time, the sun and the fog are flirting madly high in the foothills of the Sierra Madre del Sur. The fog likes to pretend to give in; it gets shimmery and faint, coupling with the sun, transporting itself as it lifts submissively toward the heat— and then suddenly it is traipsing back from the other direction, as insouciant as ever, in wavery columns like ghost milk. They might keep this up, the sun and the fog, well until noon, when the sun will have its way at last. That is the nature of this place, this altitude. The fog lingers so longingly, for so many hours of the day, that the people who live here call it a baby cloud forest.

Above a long embankment, where the forest gives way to a small cemetery, the sun creates a stronghold. It seems to kindle among the sparse stones and the wooden crosses, painted candy colors and decked with bunches of wildflowers. The fog slinks lower, rolls down the embankment and across a dirt road to the single house standing at the eastern tip of the cemetery. It wraps its moist self around the pitched tin roof, noses through gaps between the knobby wooden slats that, nailed together, form walls, and tarries over the eight people sleeping within.

The figures lie on mats of woven palm. The mats lie on earth. The earth in here is swept daily and has been pressed so firm by generations of feet that it resembles rock and rarely ever yields to the elements, except in rainy season. The fog circles the room, spreads out, fills it with a kind of palpable, inaudible sigh. For a moment the peace is unbroken by anything but the roosters, burros, fowl, and dogs, which have been carrying on more or less all through the night at this and neighboring homesteads—sounds as familiar and inappreciable as heartbeats or wind. Then sun comes gliding triumphantly through the openings in the walls, slicing the fog with planes of gold, and wakefulness conquers sleep.

This occurs first and most volubly in the babies, whose respective mothers arise quickly to their cries. The children wake next, and then come the men. The last up is Basilio Salinas Martínez, at twenty-six the eldest and the head of this household, which comprises a burro, two roosters, some chickens, a big black turkey and several feathery little poults, a ravaged-looking, nameless dog, and eight people, who make up either one or two families, depending on how you count. Truly, in Pluma, it is not always easy to say where one family leaves off and the next begins. Rather, there are many ways of saying it, a variety of equations for determining kin, and the equations overlap, so that all through this mountain town the threads between families are spun from house to house. If you ask Basilio to introduce you to his family, he will blink his brown eyes consideringly a few times before asking what you mean by that word.

In Australian mythology the sun was created when men tossed an emu's egg into the sky. Hopi myth says it was created by a bright shield comprised of buckskin, fox skin, and parrot's tail. Oceanic myth says the object in question was a snail, and Tartar myth claims it was created from a sword dipped in fire.

Norse myth asserts that the sun is a spark from the sacred realm of fire, chased daily around the sky by a supernatural wolf. Ancient Egyptians believed in a golden egg laid by the chaos goose, Qeb. The San people tell the legend that the sun was once a mortal who gave out light from under his armpit; in order to make the light bigger, some children threw him into the sky, and there he grew round and shone for everyone.

The sun has been symbolized by an apple, a white horse, an ax, a chariot, a bow and arrows, a cock, an eye, a buttercup, a monocle, a wheel, a hoop, a daisy. It has signified creation, faithfulness, free will, purity, and life; also destruction, faithlessness, enslavement, poison, and fury. It has been characterized as a shepherd whose flocks are the clouds and winds, as a phoenix, as a golden boat sliding across an ocean of sky, as a protector of financiers and sultans, as the eye of God, as a spy for the gods, as a dying god that must be resuscitated each morning with an offering of human blood. It has been identified with the number 20, the Hebrew letter *resh,* ethical goodness. Birds are its messengers.

The desertion and advent of the sun have occasioned interpretations of their own, with eclipses generally feared (although some North American Indian nations said eclipses signified that the sun was holding its infant in its arms) and dawns generally celebrated (although the ancient Sumerians perceived the sun as an all-seeing, stern, and vengeful judge of humanity). Ancient Egyptians believed the sun got swallowed up every night by the sky mother, to be reborn each morning from between her thighs. Ancient Persians believed the sun was a demon chaser, purifying the earth each time it rose. According to certain aboriginal tribes, the sun is a woman whose lover resides with the dead. Every night she travels under the earth to lie with him, and every morning reascends clothed in her lover's gift: a red kangaroo skin. According to scientists, the sun is a more or less stationary ball of gas about 865,000 miles in diameter burning 93 million miles from the earth; morning occurs as a result of the earth's rotation, at the moment when the sun becomes visible on the eastern horizon. Mystics associate early morning with the musical note A.

All over the earth, the morning sun has been greeted by prayers, hymns, kisses. Some names of sun deities are Mitra, Varuna, Shamash, Ninurta, Marduk, Nergal, Baal, Hvar-Khshaeta, Savitri, Surya, Babbar, Utu, Ra, and Helios. Heliolatry, or sun worship, has been practiced for as long as anyone can tell, among as many groups as anyone knows to have existed. Neanderthals buried their dead according to east and west. Pagan ritual bonfires were held to strengthen the sun's power at each solstice, and at Inca winter solstice festivals all fires were relit by a piece of cotton kindled in the sun's rays. Sun chariots have been found in Denmark and India; temples to the sun have been built in China and England and Peru. The Bible begins with an account of the creation of light, and traces of sun or light worship crop up in the contemporary appearance of candles and halos in Judeo-Christian symbols and rites. As recently as the end of the last century, the belief that the sun danced for joy on Easter morning drew British countryfolk to hilltops on that day to watch it rise, leap, wheel about, and change color.

Everywhere morning comes to people, people tell themselves stories about morning.

We tell ourselves stories, too, about beans, glass, and pulp, the goods that bring us our daily cup of coffee and newspaper. They come with morning, these things, customarily; they are rites of morning in a country short on rites. Here we do not kiss the first spot the sun's rays strike, or kneel in the direction of the sun and pray, or climb to the tops of hills to watch the newly risen orb wheel about the sky. Mornings in this country bring coffee and the paper: a liquid brown drug and a smudgy pack of stories we toss at the end of the day.

In the Someday Café a large coffee costs a dollar twenty-five. It is worth exactly one hundred and twenty-five cents. That is one story I could tell myself about coffee.

The Sunday paper costs a dollar fifty; the daily paper, thirty-five cents. It is equal to, interchangeable with, thirty-five cents. Its value is less than a third that of the cup of coffee. That is a story about the paper.

I do not think about the worth of the glass tumbler. After all, it is not for sale; it has use but not exchange value. Lacking a visible price, the glass is storyless.

This tendency to regard objects as though their essence and their monetary worth were one and the same is sometimes called commodity fetishism. A commodity is a thing with a price. A fetish is a thing with a spirit. Commodity fetishism is the habit of perceiving an object's price as something intrinsic to and fixed within that object, something emanating directly and vitally from that object's core, rather than as the end result of a history of people and their labor.

In the Someday Café a large coffee is a modest order. It's neither a show beverage, like the multihued macchiato; nor a baby candy drink, like a latte with a caramel flavor shot; nor a New Age brew, like World Peace or Haiku tea; nor is it hard-core, like the four-shot headbanger. It is simple, a little blunt, unpretentious, adult.

The *Boston Globe* is the local paper of record. Reading it is more highbrow than reading the *Boston Herald,* but less so than reading *The Wall Street Journal.* Each morning I buy it I become one of many; I participate in a peculiarly communal act. On the street, on the subway, I see strangers and we are all performing in common, holding to our bodies, clutching under our arms, identical words and pictures we will later ingest in separate rooms.

The glass tumbler flares gently at the top and is just

thick-bottomed enough to make a neat sound of authority when set down full. I keep my hand cupped around it even when I am not drinking, partly for the way it conducts warmth and partly because its circumference is the perfect size to fill up the socket of my C-shaped hand, and this feels good, this smooth, hard nestling.

Those are some of the other stories we might tell ourselves about this trio of objects. This latter group of stories has to do with a missing, noneconomic side of commodity fetishism, a different kind of layering that has more to do with subjective associations and less to do with exchange worth. But it, too, paves over the connections among workers and products and consumers, obscuring the links between people and things, people and people.

Once upon a time, to fetishize something was to believe in its magical or charmed essence, to deify it or link it to a deity, to see in it something beyond its material self. Bits of carved wood, stones, certain metals and plants; locks of hair, pigs' teeth, and chicken bones; mountains, trees, and rivers; albinos, dwarves, and hunchbacks; bread and wine, scrolls and shawls; comets, thunder, the moon, morning—all have been fetishized in religious or sacred ways; all have been vessels of faith. Today there is little that doesn't get fetishized, but as a commodity. Almost everything can be seen in terms of exchange value; we look to a thing's price to gauge, even decipher, its meaning. We commodify things that seem inappropriately included in that sphere: advice, sex, adventure, babies, time, nature, safety. Our greatest expressions of adoration and rejoicing seem tied today to the market value of a given thing, to exalting it as a commodity. Not even dawn is exempt from this strange progression. Where once sunrise occasioned the singing of religious hymns, in the musical *Oliver!* the title character, an innocent-hearted orphan, praises the event by singing, "Who will buy this beautiful morning? . . . Who will tie it up with a ribbon, and put it in a box for me?"©

Today we want, and get, most things boxed and beribboned—sealed off from their origins, ensconced from their own true stories, which are the stories of people, of work, of lives. Once, this kind of ignorance would not have been possible. Once, we could not help but know what piece of earth the potato on our dinner plate came from. We knew whose hands shaped and fired the plate. We knew who cobbled our shoes, and whose cow was slaughtered to provide the leather. We knew from which spring, or well, or rain barrel our water was dipped. In many parts of the world people still know these things, but in what we term the developed nations of the earth such facts have gone hazy, have taken on the properties, almost, of fairy tales: the notion of connections seems charming, but not quite real. Real is only the coffee, in and of itself, on my table, in my mouth. It belongs to me, it exists for me, exists within the sphere of my ownership. Charming is the sun, unpurchasable, unfathomable, dropping as it pleases in funny shapes across my table, into my cup.

Glass, paper, beans. Snapdragons, candles, incense. Caramel syrup, jazz, mittens. Irish setters, plaid flannel, road salt, sheet music, knitting needles. It does not matter that this book is about coffee and a newspaper and a drinking glass. It could have been about a shoelace, a nail clipper, jam. A postage stamp, garlic, an ice cube tray. It could have been about the electricity that flows to your wall sockets. It could have been about a square of sidewalk cement. The water that runs from your tap. All of these things are commodities, and they all contain stories encompassing geography and time, supply and demand, raw materials and market forces, and people. People with names and toes and sores and wages and fancies and parents and memories. I look at the thing I touch: a doorknob, a can of soup, a ticket stub, a raisin—very small things evoke the question most liltingly—and I think, Did someone's hands touch this thing, did a worker's hands hold this?

Plumweseep

Brent Boyd does not call himself lumberjack. Neither does he say logger. Nor woodcutter, woodsworker, harvester, timberman. He doesn't think of it in terms of a noun at all. This is Brent's phrase about himself: "I work in the woods."

He works in the woods in the province of New Brunswick, all day long among black pines, red pines, jack pines, whites; among cedars, balsam firs, white and yellow birch, red and white and black spruce, poplars (called popples here), and larch (called tamarack or hackmatack); among maples and oaks and alders and cherries and hazelnuts; also willows and dogwoods and ferns and raspberries and moss and woodpeckers and partridge and deer and moose and fox and rabbits and bears and coyotes ("ky-oats").

To do his work he sits inside a sort of large glass

bubble—the cab of his FMG Timberjack 990 single-grip harvester. On a hot afternoon, with gold light careering through the cleared area at his back turning the cab into a solar baking dish, he might scrounge a hammer from the jumble at his feet and use this as a wedge to prop open the door (he has somchow never managed to keep the air conditioner up and running, and the little built-in fan churns only so much breeze); but in winter he is enclosed, sealed off from the elements, sealed off from the woods through which his machine trundles. He barely hears, over the motor and the radio, the boughy crash of the trees falling when he cuts them. He does not smell their sap. In the upper-right-hand corner of his cab dangles a bouquet of air fresheners, each one a piece of cardboard cut in the shape of a Christmas tree.

Brent is thirty-two. He wears glasses and a wiry brown beard, and his voice has a nice easy springiness to it, like a pink Spalding ball. He has lived all his life in the general area of Sussex, which is known as the dairy capital of New Brunswick and also, according to signs posted at the outskirts, as the friendliest town in the province. It lies smack between the province's three largest cities: Saint John to the south, Fredericton to the west, and Moncton to the east. North of Sussex the towns get smaller, sparser; the forest, thicker. The major routes leading into town are called Highway 1 and Highway 2. A few miles before the Sussex exit on Highway 1, a sign advises motorists, "Be Sure Your Sins Will Find You Out." A similarly situated sign on Highway 2 hails, "Remember—After Death The Judgment."

On all sides of town, land ripples out over gradual

humps and dips in the earth, broad stretches of field and pasture broken up by furry tongues of forest. Brent lives just north of the town line, across the railroad tracks on Smith Creek Road, in an unincorporated area called Plumweseep. It's not a town or village; no mail gets delivered there; it has a name but no official status. Everyone pronounces it "Plumsweep." People figure it's a misspelling of an old Indian name. Plumweseep Cross branches off Smith Creek Road opposite the Salmon River covered bridge, and just beyond a low cow pasture Brent's street branches left. The sign says, "Rue Valley View Cres." Sussex itself is staunchly Anglo-Saxon, but it lies in the heart of Canada's only officially bilingual province, and each of its street signs echoes French with English, like an image reflected in a trick mirror.

Brent's house is a split-level in four sections, the color of buttermilk, with garage doors painted a surprising, bold jade. Brent has lived in it for three years, with his wife, Joy, and now their daughter, Ellen, who turned two this past fall. The house is one of a few dozen like it sprinkled in neat rows throughout the compact development called Fennel Subdivision. It is not Brent's dream house but it has some woods behind it, and a half-mile path that climbs through them and offers wild raspberries and blackberries. The land is not his; in wintertime when the Boyds go strolling back there, signs of human activity stand in relief against the crusty snow: dark planks of old lumber, rusty metal plow parts, a plastic jug from which have bled deep pink smears of antifreeze across the dead, white ground.

Fennel Subdivision comprises four streets linked up

in the shape of a capital E. The way that it is situated neither smack in town nor miles out on some potholed country road reinforces its nebulous condition. It's like an ecotone poised on a hillock, a transitional zone between ways of life, new and old. The dairy farmer who owns the bit of woods behind Brent's house has been harvesting trees from it this month in the old-fashioned way, hauling logs out of the woods by horse and carting them the mile and a half to the mill on a little rubber-tired wagon. And everyone in the subdivision's been getting a kick out of that, the novelty of seeing a horse-drawn wagon trundling past all the split-levels and the Land Rovers, the swing sets and the satellite dishes.

When Brent leaves his house in the morning, he sees all of this but barely, only a curve here, a sloping plane there, abstracted geometric shapes in the thin white bath of the half-ton's headlights. He drives first to the Four Corners Irving station, just a mile past the covered bridge. It glows like a small space station in the darkness, its insides humming quietly with the interactions of truckers, coffee, sundries, newspapers, clerks, cash. Brent himself has never cared for coffee, and the paper he favors is the *Kings County Record,* published right here in town once a week, technically on Wednesdays, though more often than not it's available for sale by Tuesday, Sussex naturally being on the cutting edge of things, or as Brent likes to put it, with one of his soft, springy chortles, "In Sussex, you're always more than up to date." He pulls in for gas only, diesel fuel, not for the half-ton but to fill up the tank that rides perpetually on his flatbed.

He does this bare-handed. His only head covering is

a grease-blackened baseball cap. Instead of a coat he wears a pair of heavy orange coveralls that zip up the front and say "Cape Breton Development Corporation" over the left breast pocket. They're standard issue from the coal mines out there at the curving tip of Nova Scotia; Joy's dad worked down in them thirty-five years before getting moved to an office job in heaven, which is how the miners refer to sea level. The union contract stipulates he's still entitled to company coveralls, so now he sends them on to Brent; they make good work clothes for him and serve a double purpose in hunting season, when it's the law to wear this color in the woods—miner's orange, hunter's orange, safety orange: what you call the color depends on where you're from.

He sticks his Irving credit card in the machine, then leaps up into the back of the truck to fit the nozzle into the tank. He jams his bare hands in his pockets while he waits. The next island over, a Shur Gain feed truck is filling up. Around the other side of the gas station, a couple of eighteen-wheelers are droning in the wintry air, idling while their drivers stop inside for refills of coffee, prewrapped sandwiches from the refrigerator case, a trip to the washroom. There is a marigold truck carrying chips, and a green and white one with a load of sawed lumber. They'd be common sights nearly anywhere in the province, but are especially so here, two tenths of a mile down the road from the mill. The mill is owned by Irving, as are the marigold Sunbury trucks and the green-and-white Midlands, and also this gas station and the fuel it dispenses and the convenience store attached to it, as well as the province's four largest daily papers, three of which are for sale inside. Most of the wood Brent cuts down becomes Irving's, too.

He finishes pumping fuel, replaces the hose, and repockets his Irving card. Then it's back in the half-ton, and the door slams with that frozen metal sound, and he's pulling away from Four Corners, heading toward his stumpage. And on any given day that would ordinarily mean heading out now for a half-hour or an hour or an hour-and-a-half drive to the block he's working on, driving past darkened farms with their waking dairy herds and beef cattle and morning smoke beginning to twist out of chimneys, and he'd mark, without really thinking about it, the names of the inhabitants he knows, and little identifying facts about them, like whose stone farmhouse is so old it's got a slave tunnel built into it, and who lost his arm to a tractor accident, and which place was Wes Alcorn's blacksmith shop before the piano tuner moved in, and who ran a boarding house for the men who worked the river drives before the logs started going to Saint John by truck. And he'd know in his head the names of the invisible surrounding areas—Poodiac, Vinegar Hill, Mechanic Settlement, Kars, Parleeville, Joliffs Brook, Peekaboo Corner, Beulah, Browns Flat, Woodpecker Hall, Dickie Mountain, Jemseg—all these place-names like the names of older relatives who've known him since before he was born.

Brent grew up in one of these places, a community called Hatfield Point twenty miles southwest of Plumweseep and perched right out over Belleisle Bay. It was here that, as a little boy, he had his first job in logging: he and his brother and sister used to earn a nickel among them for each stray log they fished from along the banks during a river drive. It was here at Hatfield Point that Brent learned firsthand what a valued commodity New Brunswick's forests are, for his father, Howard, trucked tens of thousands of loads of their lumber to points all the way down the Eastern Seaboard. And it was here at Hatfield Point that Brent learned what it meant to go into the woods, at the side of his father's father.

Everett Boyd is seventy-nine and he does refer to himself as a lumberjack. Actually what he calls himself is an "old-time lumberjack." By this he means everything: the pike poles, picaroons, twitching dogs, whiffletrees, bucksaws, crosscut saws, river drives, booms, dynamite, scarred hands, missing fingers. He means pit-baked beans and raisin pie, mouth organs and step dancing in a log shanty at night, and the smells of the bodies of two dozen men sleeping side by side in wooden bunks, their socks and gloves steaming around a central oil-drum stove. He means teams of horses hauling pulpwood, teams so good they'd lead the way into the woods in the morning and follow you back to camp at night, some so smart you could speak English to them and they'd understand. One, a mare named Lark, smart as a dog. He also means staying away from home for months at a time, rising before daylight and having your breath turn to ice crystals soon as it hits air, working with axes and crosscut saws. Sap in your hair and on your jacket. A dollar a day. Back when you touched the trees with real human hands.

Everett still lives just down the road from where Brent grew up, in a century-old house on a hill. A glassed-in sunporch faces the main road. Whenever

Everett and his wife, Elsie, are sitting there and a car or a truck comes round the bend, they look to see who it might be, responding to the driver's near-inevitable wave with nods of recognition and lifted hands of their own. A square of printed cardboard hangs in the window. One side, formerly crimson, barely reads, "Perfection Milk." The other, gray, says, "No Milk Today." Used to be they got their food delivered, too. They'd see what they wanted each week out of the rear of Don Gray's grocery truck, and he'd reach his pole back and scoop it down. No more.

They haven't got a doorbell. A large black bell with a clapper hangs in its stead on the sunporch, beside the main door leading into the rest of the house. More often than not, a visitor will disregard the bell altogether and simply step one boot up on the threshold, poke his head into the kitchen, and call. More often than not, the kitchen will be smelling of pie, or lemon tart, or raspberry jam gems, or ham, and that visitor will be waylaid on his errands by such smells and a gentle but ironclad invitation to partake in these pleasures.

Behind the house stands a cluster of cedar-shingled sheds, at somewhat rakish angles effected by gravity and time. Some of their boards are held together with square nails, and curve a bit, having been hewn with a broad ax rather than sawed. One appears to be in the act of dipping a very slow curtsey, from which posture it will never manage to rise. The sheds house tools, all manner of old and not-so-old side by side—adze by grinding stone, maul by chainsaw, oil lantern by extension cord—all more or less in use, nothing quite retired, nothing packed or set away.

Everett Boyd's right hand is without an index finger. One day when he was six and his brother seven, each had wanted a turn splitting wood. They argued over who would get to use the ax first. Everett, losing out, said, "You're not going to cut that log," and placed his hand stubbornly across the chopping stump; his brother brought the ax down on it.

Another time his left hand was carved clear through between the middle and ring fingers, several inches toward his wrist, with a chainsaw while he was working in the woods. The doctor did a neat job of stitching it up, but it's a thickish, stiff hand now, the muscles and range of motion not what they were.

Some time after that, his foot got split open with an ax; the doctor stitched that up, too, but a week or so later Elsie noticed it wasn't healing properly. She pricked it open with a sewing needle and the wildest corruption came flowing out, along with a piece of sock the doctor had closed up inside the wound.

All of these extremities remain nevertheless in use. Their owner, solid and spry, continues to take home the trophy for the crosscut sawing competition every summer at Fun Days in Sussex; he keeps them on his bedroom bureau. He continues to carve ducks and loons, make beds and chairs and rocking horses for his children and grandchildren and great-grandchildren, cut fuel logs from his own woodlots. And he continues to go to the woods. He started working as a lumberjack at age thirteen, cutting beside men and earning a man's wages. Nowadays when he goes out, it's usually with his grandson, the lone grandson who works in the woods—although it's all different now; the phrase means something else altogether. Everett Boyd, amazed and proud, goes along and watches Brent operate the Timberjack. He perches up in the cab behind Brent and watches him work the levers and buttons of that great machine.

The FMG Timberjack 990 single-grip harvester and its sidekick, the porter (a truck with a boom arm and clam grip that loads the cut logs and totes them out to roadside), are like Brent's babies. The porter's gas tank needs filling every day; the harvester, with its five-hundred-liter belly, can go two days without needing a hit; together they suck up about fifteen hundred dollars' worth of fuel a month. With its daily minor ailments (and occasional major ones), the harvester in particular demands extra shows of care and devotion. In return it carries out his most intricate instructions, responding to the subtlest pressures, the finest movements of his fingers and wrists.

In 1990 Brent became the first person in the Maritimes—the fourth in all of North America—to own a single-grip harvester. The machine resembles nothing so much as a small brontosaurus, rolling through the forest on six huge tires, munching tranquilly but tirelessly anything in its way. At the end of Brent's armrests within the cab lies an assortment of buttons and knobs. With precise, fluent delicacy, he uses these to control the beast: propelling it forward, extending its long neck, hugging its metal jaws around the base of a tree, slicing its steel blade straight across the trunk, then rotating the severed tree until it's parallel with the forest floor and shooting it through two cleated wheel drives while five hidden knives trim away every branch in a lightning act of mastication, and finally bringing the blade through once again at exact intervals to plunk out naked, measured logs, bones picked clean. The whole spectacle is a pastiche of cumbersome and graceful motion, like a very heavy person dancing a neat and articulate jig.

Brent bought the harvester and porter at the same time. Together they cost six hundred thousand dollars. Brent put in some money and the bank put in some money and then Brent set out to see if those machines would return the investment. Five years later, he's still undecided.

A single-grip harvester is designed for selective harvesting. Supposedly, this is the new trend in forestry. The older method was to clear-cut, which is just what it sounds like: everything within a given block of woods comes down. In a full-tree operation, trees are skidded to roadside, where their branches and crowns are cut off and burned. The patch of former forest, now stripped, may get burned, too, in order to eradicate any remaining undergrowth, so what's left is a stubbly, razed expanse, what Brent calls a moonscape. He should know; he once worked these kinds of operations. They'd wait until the wind was right, then go around to the mounds of brush and torch them, the smoke turning the air so gritty and black you couldn't see your hand in front of your face. The cleared land could then be planted in rows with saplings of the most desirable species, to be harvested again in twenty or so years.

Selective harvesting, sort of the opposite of, if not exactly the antidote to, clear-cutting, is just what it sounds like, too: only select trees come down. Various criteria determine selection. Genetically inferior as well as older trees (more susceptible to disease) get selected for harvesting, affording more space to new saplings and genetically superior trees. Crown cover is considered: if the crowns of several healthy, maturing trees have grown so dense and close that they choke off sunlight to the forest below, some of them may come down. Species may matter: someone might decide to harvest a mixed stand exclusively for hardwood because the price for fuel logs in the States has just jumped; another might want a stand of cedar untouched because he knows deer like to winter there and he's an avid hunter. In general, though, selective harvesting is envisioned as a tool to increase the sustainability of the forest: to work with the natural life cycle of trees, improve their gene pool, and minimize the disruption to wildlife and watershed. It's seen as more environmentally sound, as well as more potentially profitable over time, but less so in the short term.

The whole purpose of Brent's single-grip harvester is to cut selectively. It's much smaller and lighter than the massive feller-bunchers and skidders used to clear-cut, so it does less damage to the forest floor. It weaves more nimbly among trees left standing, reaches with precision around one to grip another, and because it delimbs right there in the forest, all the unused branches and crown are left behind to enrich the soil for regeneration. Its computerized complexity and delicate range of motion become pointless when applied to a clear-cut operation, where the object is basically to rip everything down anyway. It's like using a laser to cut out a coupon. But how a lot is to be harvested gets determined by its owner, and Brent'll cut to any specifications, whether he approves of the method or not. He's got over half a million dollars standing between him and the freedom to pick and choose.

When Brent, at twenty-seven years old and a week before his wedding, decided to trade in the skidder he'd been operating and pour all his savings into this novel machine, it was—okay, yes—maybe one part hubris, a desire to test himself, to increase the stakes of his business and discover how far he could go with it. The idea of taking a risk, of being an adventurer trying something new, appealed to him. Mostly, though, the decision just made sense, environmentally as well as economically. Silviculture was the new buzzword, sustainability the wave of the future, and everyone anticipated an increased demand for selective harvesting. The investment seemed at once progressive and pragmatic.

The first year, about twenty-five percent of his work involved selective harvesting. The next year, recession hit; it dropped to ten percent. Over the next few years, a series of natural disasters in the States—a hurricane in Florida, an earthquake in California, and flooding in the Midwest—increased the demand for building materials, thereby boosting lumber prices and enabling more woodlot owners to try selective cuts at lower yields. But the shift has been gradual, and the volume of selective harvests Brent does is still a far cry from what he'd hoped, from what he'd banked on. If he's lucky he'll get another five or six years of work out of the harvester, but whether or not it will be worth it in the end, it's too soon to say. What is certain is that right now, for four fifths of the work he's called upon to do, he might just as well have stuck with the old skidder and chainsaw.

This morning Brent has more pressing concerns, however. The tail end of winter's edging into spring, and once thaw sets in he won't be able to harvest anything for about six weeks. Winter, for all its pitch-black commutes, its slippery roads and finicky engines and bitter cold when he has to climb out on the machine to do some numb-fingered repair, is hands-down Brent's favorite time of year to work. For one thing, it's sort of beautiful, and easy to see what you're doing with the hardwoods all naked and black against the white, but the main thing is how well the machines move across the frozen ground; it buoys them, frees them. The rhythm of winter is smooth and high.

Come thaw, woods operations mostly halt, for two reasons. All the smaller roads (that's everything but Highway 1 and Highway 2) become off-limits to heavy rigs, which would damage the pavement with the ground so soft underneath, meaning there's no way to get the wood to the mills. The other reason is that the soft, wet earth won't support most heavy woods equipment; it'll sink into the mud and get stuck.

That's the reason Brent isn't heading out of Four Corners this morning for an hour's commute along miles and miles of cambering blue-black road to some lonesome grove where it would have been just him and his machine all day, and the trees coming down one after another like dominoes. This year Brent managed to line up a job for the end of winter that's almost embarrassingly well-situated—right here in Sussex, about a minute from the mill. He got stumpage rights to an eighty-acre black spruce swale tucked in between

Four Corners and the government road-salt shed down the road. It nearly abuts the drive-in, Sussex's only movie theater and closed now until summer, and it's actually visible from Fennel Subdivision, though not from Brent's own house. But many of his neighbors' views include the swale, and Brent doesn't think they're desperately keen about his harvesting it. The land was bought by a trucking company; their plan, as far as he knows, is to take out all the black spruce, root-rake the whole thing with a dozer, and fill in the wet ground with gravel. He's heard something, too, about their building a big dome for stockpiling locally mined potash. All he knows for sure is he's been asked to do a clear-cut.

Selective harvesting wouldn't be an option here anyway, with the ground too wet and unstable to support the remaining trees after more than a few have been taken down. Harvesting in a swale's kind of like playing a game of pick-up sticks; in some places, all that's supporting you is a mass of intertwined roots floating on a bed of water. That's not so bad when the ground's frozen, but Brent knows he's working on borrowed time. He bid for the block when he first heard about it a fortnight ago, won stumpage rights, and began harvesting it not quite a week ago, and already he's felt a change in the ground, a deep softening taking hold beneath the bogies of his harvester, each day a touch more conspicuous. He won't finish it this season.

He'd like to see how much he can squeeze in, though. That's why he rose as early as he did this morning, not to allow for any commute, as he usually must, but in order to beat the sun, to take advantage of what darkness has done to the ground: stiffened it up, made it solid again. Soon it will be time for Brent to tip his hat to spring, to watch the sun turn the land wild and runny, to perform his own springtime rituals. In a few days, a week if he's lucky, it'll be time to take a rest, to pack things up for two months, drive down to Moncton and get tune-ups and repairs on all the hydraulics, and also cut up his firewood, and go out and walk his upcoming blocks, the ones to which he's lined up stumpage rights for the fall. And while he's doing this, spring will be edging itself nearer to summer, and the same sun that turned the ground unstable will be baking it back to firmness, and the trees that haven't been cut down will be extending their roots into ever knottier entwinings, and the trees that have been cut down will be turning into pulp and paper and Popsicle sticks.

But for now Brent still has time. He brings the half-ton over to the side of the road and turns off the engine. Ahead stands the sleeping dinosaur figure of his harvester, moonlight glancing off its metal hide. Beyond it, through a scramble of boggy brush and hardhacks, he can see the stripe where he left off last night, the place where cleared area meets the edge of the woods, the place where he is bound.

Lancaster

Ruth Lamp's job came to her entirely through the grace of God. She is so clear about this fact, still, after fifteen years, so matter-of-factly awake to the wondrousness of it, that there is something oddly clarifying about being in her presence. She is tall, with thick, cropped hair that goes from charcoal to silver-gray as it ascends, and a face like a small elliptical loaf of home-made bread: warm, baked the color of toasted almonds, crosshatched with some faint, some bold markings. Above her upper lip time has wrought a strong horizontal crease, which curves into a kind of breve symbol whenever she smiles. The highest compliment she can pay a person is to call him "common," to say of someone she's "just plain people."

One of the reasons Ruth looks upon her current situation as a kind of miracle is that she was already forty-four when she got hired by the Anchor Hocking glass factory fifteen years ago, after having been laid off from her last job, assembling Riviera kitchen cabinets. She'd been let go after only three months working the line (not that she'd taken much satisfaction in that work; it had always seemed a shame to her, when you looked at what they charged in the stores, how shabbily those cabinets got glued and stapled together). That had followed the layoff from Ray-O-Vac, where she'd packed carbon pieces into plastic battery casings, turning her fingers so black she'd go home at the end of her shift and scrub them with bleach to get the residue off. Plus, she had kids to support; two of her sons were grown but the twins were in grade school, and though it was before her husband died, she was essentially raising them alone. But it wasn't only how much she needed a job that made getting one seem so marvelous; it was also that out of seven new hirees, she was the only one who didn't have a family member already working at the plant, the only one called in straight through the unemployment office. At the interview she told them she'd made three twenty-five an hour at her last employment, and that if she could get a job here, she guaranteed they wouldn't ever be sorry.

It was months before she got word she could start. She called the plant every week in the meantime, to make sure they didn't forget about her. March 4, 1980, was the date she finally reported for work over at Plant 2, on the east end of Lancaster. One thing is certain: no one will ever know the pride she felt the first time she passed under that sign that reads, "Through these gates walk some of America's finest glassworkers."

Ruth doesn't actually make glass. Actually, no one at the plant exactly makes glass. Machines mix up the raw materials, and machines blow and press the molten glass into ware. Machines cool and reheat and recool the ware. Machines do the decorating, applying decals to the glass with sprays of colored ink. What the people do is tend the machines. This is the case most everywhere except in one department, Select and Pack, of which Ruth is a supervisor. In this department, people tend the glass. They look at it, they pick it up, they handle it, label it, lower it into cardboard compartments. Sometimes they chunk it down a chute where it smash-lands on a conveyor belt heading back toward the furnace room. Sometimes they burn themselves a little on a piece of fresh glass. Sometimes they cut themselves a little on a shard of broken glass. Sometimes they remember to wear gloves.

Ruth came on as a line worker in Select and Pack. Plant 2 mostly produced ovenware. Her job was to weed out the odd lopsided casserole or fractured pie dish coming off the line and pack the others into cardboard boxes. Pick them up, look them over, stick on bar code labels, tuck them into square brown nests. Anywhere from two to five men and women would stand together at the end of a line and work in steady syncopation. Pick up, give the once-over, label, lower. You got a ten-minute break every hour, plus a half hour for dinner once a shift. Lift, check, stick, pack. You didn't have to keep silent on line, but the machines made it noisy to try to hear people, and the earplugs you had to wear didn't make it any easier. Also, Ruth is a person who likes to use her hands when she talks, likes to train her eyes solidly on the person she's in conversation with; having her hands and her eyes necessarily preoccupied rendered her mostly quiet. That was all right, too. She was glad to be there, stationed at the checkpoint as it were, guarding the frontier between the chance piece of faulty ware and the consumer. Glad to be making eight twenty-five an hour, good golly, more than she'd ever made in her life. She bought herself a house over on Forest Rose, a squat white box with two black shuttered windows downstairs and two dormers jutting like cocked eyebrows above, as if the house were as shocked at Ruth's boldness in making such a significant purchase as she was herself.

But there have been so many little miracles. Going from selector and packer to quality control technician, from hourly worker to salaried—these things were beyond Ruth's fondest dreams. And when they shut down Plant 2 and laid off near about everyone, including Ruth, the company not only rehired her a few weeks later down at Plant 90 in Clarksburg, West Virginia, but paid her moving expenses as well. And then when the Clarksburg plant shut down ten months later, not only was she one of just a handful of people to get work back up at Plant 1 in Lancaster, but she was brought back as a supervisor.

Last winter she surprised herself again, she just did, acting almost in spite of herself, as if an invisible wave had come and lifted her up, without her having any say over where it brought her. She left her little house on Forest Rose (which was close enough to the plant that on a summer's day, with only screens in the windows and the wind blowing right, she could hear workers being paged over the loudspeakers at Anchor Hocking). She'd grown a hunger for unbroken quiet, and space, and, frankly, distance from neighbors whose lawns lay neat and regular as squares of felt and who looked askance at a woman her age climbing out on the roof, washing windows, running the mower, doing a man's work. So she sold the orderly saltbox on Forest Rose and bought a haggard old farmhouse that lay twenty minutes south of town on its own nameless dirt lane branching off Eaton Hollow Road. It had holes in the roof, missing windowpanes, and an acre for every year she'd lived, which was fifty-seven.

Ruth heads home now from work along Route 22 and Boving and Hamburg roads. She slows when she reaches the bumpy bends near Oil Mill Hollow, ambling past the still pearliness of very early morning, past hoary meadows, and past two black ponds where a heron might be standing tall, or, lately, Canadian geese, returning as they cannot help from doing every year to nest for a while and multiply. This morning she sees deer. Her eyes, the color of faded blue jeans and round behind her large glasses, fasten on them and she brakes, waits awhile, idling, watching their brown bodies move in and out of pawpaw and witch hazel and wild plum. Twelve hours of factory recede from her brain in the immediacy of their perfect, thoughtless motion. She rewards herself in this way after work, slowing where the road, meandering, seems also to slow; she rewards herself with the things she sees.

Fairfield County lies in not-quite-the-center of Ohio, where Appalachian highlands lap over into central lowlands, and the landscape here is soft and mild, devoid of obvious extremes. The plains are rolling, the soil fertile. The crops are corn and soybeans, hay and winter wheat. The seasons come and go with decorum, each one full in character, yet none commandeering for itself more space than the calendar allots. Ruth grew up on farms throughout the area, living on two dozen of them by the time she was ten, all of them other people's, and never thinking to dream she'd one day have her own. The motto here in the Buckeye State is "With God all things are possible," and truly she has seen that demonstrated time and again.

She calls it her teacup, the farm, her little teacup. By the time she swings her turquoise truck off Eaton Hollow and onto the yellowy dirt road that sweeps a quarter mile past a bramble-choked gully to her house, she has shed all thoughts of the plant. She does not think about cold molds, shadow cracks, quarantined loads, tray partitions, or culleted stemware when she is here, tucked into her little teacup. Named for the way it's nestled on the snug side of a slope and graciously ringed by trees, the teacup is protected from winds, invisible from the main road, and almost fancifully peaceful. The deepest cavity in her fifty-seven acres is the great gully that dips down where a front lawn would ordinarily be. Her sons have been after her to dam up the creek that trickles through the gully and make a pond of it, but Ruth is afraid of a little child falling in and drowning, or one of the older ones careening back to the house after dark with a bellyful of beer and plunging off the road into deep water. She herself does not swim, as a child went only mud-crawling—wading and splashing through armpit-high shallows. She has, however, started tidying up the gully, burning off the tangly thickets of brush along the side of the road, and the palest of grays illuminates the burnt patches now as she winds around toward the house, still ahead of the sun itself, if being overtaken by its heralders.

She parks between the house and the barn, on whose outer wall are mounted three sets of deer antlers, shiny with dew and gleaming faintly in the thin light, and looks to see whether Robert's '72 Chevelle Supersport is there. The twins are twenty-two and Robert, the younger by seven minutes, has a bedroom here but frequently spends the night with friends. Chris, the other twin, has been in the marines a little over two years; he's recently back from Korea and stationed down in Camp Lejeune, North Carolina. Timothy and Mark, the older two, are in their late thirties and have families of their own, Timothy's in Columbus and Mark's in a little prefab house just three miles from Ruth's farm, which she has to herself this morning, the Supersport being absent. Birds are already singing as she walks to the door; soon finches will be gathering in the walnut tree outside her bedroom window where a ball of suet mixed with peanut butter hangs. Attracting the birds, it's true, is not necessarily conducive to sleep, but she likes doing it, and also scattering corncobs through her woods for the wild turkeys to come feed on in winter, and she does not even mind when the deer come to her apple trees in autumn and wake her with the sound of their night-time crunching.

Waiting inside the dun-colored house for Ruth is Shenandoah, her ninety-eight-point-six percent hybrid wolf. Ruth got her as a pup last summer from a kennel ten miles away, down in Lucasville, where a woman breeds them specially. Shenna has the look of a big sun-bleached German shepherd; the only thing espe-cially wolfy about her appearance is a short, stiff tus-sock, like hackles permanently raised, which streaks from her nape down her back. Ruth calls this a cow-lick.

She wanted a wolf originally for protection. Her farm lies about a mile from a minimum security cor-rectional facility; the area around it is largely wooded and sparsely populated; and Ruth is not blind to the twin vulnerabilities of her age and sex. Her boys urged her to get a gun; they bought her a .38 police special, which she keeps on her night table, loaded; she has practiced some and could shoot it if she had to, but she does not like the gun. She prefers the security of just her wolf, who protects her from snakes, the one ani-mal Ruth loathes, as well as any potential human threat. And of course Shen has become far more than peace of mind. In the night, when Ruth can't sleep, when her body gets up, its internal clock discombobu-lated by twelve-hour lock shifts and four-day rotations, by nights spent under the unrelenting glance of fluorescent lights and mornings spent trying to ignore the sun, it's Shen she talks to, sitting in the moonlit kitchen in her robe, eating a bowl of oatmeal at the small round table under the window, whose long blue curtains wave in the currents of the hot-air register, Shen who is her company and confidante.

Shen and the farm. Her teacup and her wolf. These are her life. So much to be amazed at, so much to be thankful for. No, she does not think of the plant when she is home on her farm. But Ruth believes the plant has made possible all that she now has in her life, and she is ever mindful of that, and constantly, quietly grateful.

Anchor Hocking has deep roots in Lancaster. The company has been making glass since its beginnings here nearly a hundred years ago in an old carbon factory, which everybody used to call The Black Cat, and which eventually burned down and got replaced. Anchor Hocking was originally called Hocking Glass Company, named for the Hocking River near which it stands. The river got its name from the Wyandot Indians, who arrived in Ohio from Canada around 1700 and called the river Hockhocking, which was their word for gourd or bottle, whose shape they saw in a waterfall on the upper part of the river. The anterior part of the company's current name resulted from a merger with the Anchor Cap and Closure Corporation, which derived *its* name from the slogan "Anchored for Safety." By its seventy-fifth anniversary, Anchor Hocking had forty-one manufacturing plants and distribution centers in the United States, Canada, the Netherlands, and Puerto Rico, and its ware sold in over one hundred twenty-five countries. It had eighteen thousand employees in twenty-five divisions and subsidiaries, and produced glassware, plastics, earthenware, stoneware, ceramics, cabinets, and decorative hardware. It had its own trucking fleet and a jingle that went, "Anchor Hocking sets the table / We're America's number one / Invite us over, we know just what to bring / We make most everything."

Then, in the eighties, the company fell into rapid decline. It had a hard time competing with companies whose glass was manufactured in parts of the world where people would work for much less money. It had terrific overstock in its massive distribution centers. It was losing money. Operations began to be curtailed. Ruth, as a new hire in 1980, arrived at work several times, only to be informed she was being laid off for the day, or for a few days, or for a week. Then in 1987, Plant 2 shut down altogether and Ruth was laid off again—permanently, she feared, until one of those little miracles occurred and she got offered a position back at Plant 1.

That was also the year that Anchor Hocking was bought for 350 million dollars by Newell, a publicly traded conglomerate with a reputation for acquiring companies that are losing money and turning them drastically around, something it has accomplished with thirty-one companies in twenty-five years. Some of Newell's methods include pruning inventories, stopping the manufacture of less profitable ware, closing plants, and laying off workers. In Anchor Hocking's case, each of these strategies was used, and within three years the company was posting net profit margins of fifteen percent. Now, only one other plant besides the original still operates—number 44 out in Monaca, Pennsylvania—and the company is back to concentrating on glass table- and ovenware, for restaurants and cafeterias as well as for domestic consumers. But locally Anchor Hocking is still the biggest employer, with a reach that sometimes seems as broad and intractable as a family tree. Ruth herself has a daughter-in-law and a cousin at the plant right now. Her own mother even worked there briefly, once.

Long ago, when Ruth was ten and could sit on her hair, her father announced to the family one Saturday afternoon that he was leaving and this time would not be back. His name was Frank Jeffers. He was a tenant farmer who seemed constitutionally unable to tenant any one property for any length of time, and who came to be regarded as the town drunk wherever he went. From the time Ruth was born, up in Champagne County, her father moved the family around continually, sometimes as often as every three months—sometimes, Ruth recalls, so suddenly that she would head off to school from one farm in the morning, only to be met at the school bus and told to come on home to a different farm that afternoon. After he left, her father got sent to the work farm in London, Ohio, for a while; the family knew this to be the case because for the nine months he served there, he was made to send support back to his family in the form of twelve dollars a month. After he was released and the money stopped, they knew nothing of him for nine years, at which time word came he'd fallen into a cow pen and gotten trampled; he died a slow, painful death in a hospital bed while the nerves in his spinal column corroded and decayed.

Frank Jeffers was part Cherokee. Ruth sometimes

wonders whether it could have been his Indian blood
that made him restless, the blood of the dispossessed
that made it so he couldn't stay put. Also, both his
parents had died when he was a boy, and Ruth sometimes wonders whether *that* could be the reason he
roamed, that he was searching for something he knew
he'd lost long ago.

When he took off for good that Saturday afternoon,
he left Ruth's mother with four children, no land, and
no money but the twenty-five dollars a week she
earned herself doing other people's laundry and house-
cleaning. There was no welfare; instead, the family was
delivered from its plight by the Apostolic minister and
his wife, who arrived at the door of the farm where
the family had been lingering on and offered them a
little house out in Carroll, where the rent was only
fifteen dollars a month and where Ruth's mother,
working for a brief while at Anchor Hocking and then
as a nurse's aide at Lancaster Fairfield Hospital, managed to scrape together just enough to keep the family
intact and fed.

Ruth's mother was born Charlotte Lee Calle. People called her Lottie. She'd been a devout member of
the local Apostolic congregation since before it even
had a roof over its head, joining when it was first
forming, back when Ruth was a baby. For as long as
Ruth can remember, her mother has tithed to the Apostolic Church. Even in the days when they were their
poorest, she remembers her mother counting out two
or three dollars and a scrupulously exact number of
cents, whatever amounted to ten percent of her
weekly earnings, and setting it aside for the church.
Ruth's mother is from German stock, and Ruth won-

ders whether this isn't what made her such a strong survivor.

Ruth thinks of her own self as a kind of Heinz 57 sauce, with strains of varied ancestry blended in her blood—the German, the Cherokee, some Irish, whatever else her father's family may have been—and yet she somehow manages to view each of her parents— her father in his roaming, drunken weakness; her mother in her radiant tenacity—in bold, single-hued palettes informed largely by ethnicity, by stories people tell of Germans and of Indians, of what each are like, of what those names mean. Perhaps this is particularly easy to do here in Ohio, where East and West slosh over into each other, where industry and agriculture meet and mingle and even the landscape seems tempered, a place where the whole seems to swallow the parts, digest them into uniform pieces, a place where the highest approbation may be reserved for commonness. Perhaps here stories of difference have a peculiar salience: like talismans or ciphers, like parables or myths.

If her father has become something of a cipher to her, though, her mother is hardly that. Ruth would be hard put to think of her mother in such abstract terms when she visits her every second day. Lottie Jeffers is ninety. She is small-boned and luminous, like a silver bird, and lives alone on the first floor of a small brick building right in town, on South Broad, in an apartment that has changed little since she moved there in 1956. Color pictures have been added to the black-and-white ones along the top of the bookshelf as Lottie's grandchildren have had children and grandchildren of their own, and the television has been hooked up to a VCR (ever since she fell and broke her pelvis last year, she has watched her weekly sermons on tape instead of from the pew), but her faith is in a religion that proscribes worldly things, and within this small apartment the air, the couch, the stove, even the bowl of fruit, have a serene, everlasting quality that seems to stand in blithe disregard of changes that have occurred without.

The changes without are significant, nevertheless. Downtown Lancaster seems virtually to be disappearing. Even Thimmes's Grocery, which had been run by the Thimmes family in the front half of Lottie's building for five or six generations, closed down a couple of years ago. While certainly sad, this was hardly surprising, what with the way everything downtown has been fading, turning into scraps and dust. Once, businesses stretched out all around Zane Park like spokes of a lively wheel, and you could get all your shopping done right in town. There were Woolworth's and J. C. Penney, Betty Gay and Jean Frocks, Luckoffs and Joos Shoes. There was Gallagher's Drugstore with its soda counter, where Ruth and Lottie would share a bowl of homemade noodle soup for a special treat; and Kresge's, where Ruth would indulge in thirteen-cent bottles of Blue Waltz perfume to use on her dolls.

Not one of these businesses remains. Some have been reborn in the River Valley Mall or elsewhere along the commercial strip that now lines the main route into town, where billboards and plastic signs fairly jostle one another in their zeal to claim the attention of an endlessly streaming parade of consumers. Others simply closed their doors for good, leaving sudsed-up, darkened storefront windows or a succession of ever-humbler retail outfits to try, and fail, in their places. And Lancaster's wide streets and wide sidewalks look even wider now in their relative bareness, and litter of no particular shape or color blows and settles along the curbs. This is not how Ruth remembers the town from her youth, but times change, as people do say, and how could anyone expect a Thimmes's to compete with the mammoth grocery store chains? And how could anyone expect streets to be swept on a block where money isn't spent?

Ruth herself in fact relies on Big Bear and Kruger's, both twenty-four-hour supermarkets, to do her shopping when she gets off work on the fourth day of her rotation. Their parking lots at five A.M. are vast oceans of macadam; their aisles vacant, hospital-bright speedways; but with Muzak piped continually into the air, and the products costing and tasting the same at any time of day, Ruth hardly notices the hour. Although the butcher's counter is dark, even Shenna's bone may be had; gleaming, prehacked, plastic-wrapped soup bones are laid out for the taking; Ruth always throws one in her cart. And ground beef, too, a neat mound of it, from which she'll tear small pink wads, rolling these into balls to slip in Shen's mouth.

All a person could want seems available here. A peacock mosaic of cardboard boxes and metal cans, like thousands of sirens, croons mutely to Ruth, who rolls past with her cart like the captain of a metal ship. Some of the cartons say Anchor Hocking; they're printed with pictures of beverage sets and baking dishes, and information about their contents in three languages, a reminder that these wares are also for sale in places remote from Lancaster. Ruth stops to pull a can from one shelf, a large-size Folger's. She won't actually brew any until she's slept and woken up again later in the day; then a few cups will help restructure her body clock in opposition to the sun. At the check-out counter she glances at but does not pick up the *Lancaster Gazette;* she never bothers with the daily, although she peruses it two or three times a week over at her mother's, keeping an eye out for local stories and obituaries involving any one of the several hundred people she knows through working at Anchor, as well as noting what's for sale: land, farms, equipment. She has a weakness for old tools, the odd sickle or knife picked up at a yard sale, but mostly she just looks out of curiosity, interested in knowing what's available, what's being offered for exchange.

Ruth, bags in arms, crosses back over the store's electronic threshold, and glass doors shut automatically behind her, sealing off the rarefied air, where time and weather are suspended, from the cold, blooming silveriness of the parking lot. Without stores like these, her artificial evening would be less easily conjured. With them, it's downtown that's becoming ghostlike, mythical; morning and night that have been made swappable, illusory. With them, Ruth may work and buy at any hour; hours slide off their stations on the clock; they scatter like pages shaken loose from a book; all through the night the stores stock their shelves with worldly goods; the sun comes up and Ruth goes home, gives the wolf a bone, slides between the sheets.

Pluma

The land is not a thing that Basilio Salinas works in order to earn a living; it is the source of life. And cultivating coffee is not the means by which he has chosen to support a family; it is the force of gravity around which revolve his and his family's lives. And when he wakes in the morning, when he rises from his *petate,* his mat of woven palm, into the air variegated by sun and mist milling cocksurely through his house, he wakes into a world where no boundary separates work from life, job from family, coffee from home. In his own house now and in thousands like it, the women are making breakfast fires, and the men are preparing to go out among the trees.

Ten thousand families live clustered in or scattered around the mountain village of Pluma Hidalgo, and virtually ten thousand families grow coffee. Well, seeds and earth and rain and sun grow coffee; people help, and people harvest, and people pulp and dry and sell the beans, and people roast and grind and brew them and drink the brew. Basilio does not strictly own the coffee he sells, or the land the coffee grows on. He, like most of the ten thousand families, looks upon land from the traditional Zapotec perspective, which is communal. But he has use of three hectares of good coffee-growing land; it passed to him through the father of his wife; it has a house and a stream and its own name, El Corozo. This *parcela,* like any other, has been called the same thing for generations. The name of each *parcela* comes to it from the land, in this case from the type of tall palm tree that adorns its steep slopes so abundantly. Basilio no more named this land than he owns it, but there it is: his to work and live on for the time that he is here.

Basilio married and came to El Corozo when he was twenty. He moved all of a half kilometer or so from the place where he grew up, Los Naranjales (The Orange Groves). Los Naranjales is larger than El Corozo. It has eight hectares, a poured-cement patio for drying coffee, and a large yard of rich red earth upon which smack small hard globes of orange fruit when they are ripe, but Basilio's parents still live at Los Naranjales, as do some of his brothers, a sister-in-law, nieces and nephews. His wife's parents, on the other hand, have moved to the coast, to work at the coffee mill down in Rincón Alegre, leaving an empty house and all the coffee plants to be tended at El Corozo, and this was the mantle Basilio assumed six years ago, when he married Genoveva Cortés Santos at the big pink church in *el centro,* the village square.

Now they share the *parcela* with Genoveva's younger, adopted sister, Isidra, and Basilio's younger brother, Lucío, who is married to Isidra—and of course the children. Basilio and Genoveva have three: Silvestre, Yolanda, and Juan Diego, aged six, four, and two; and Isidra and Lucío have one, a moon-faced baby named Enriquetta. All except the littlest two help in some way with the coffee, with the fertilizing, pruning, planting, harvesting, pulping, drying, raking, and sacking. When the beans are ready, they get sent to be milled at the coast.

Pluma Hidalgo is only thirty kilometers as the crow flies from the southernmost dip of Oaxaca's coast, but the trip can take two or three or more hours, depending on whose truck you are hitching a ride in, and whether or not it has rained, and whether or not you break down, or detour to let off passengers, or stop in Candelaria to relay a message or swig a pineapple soda in the shade before returning the bottle to the vendor and getting back in the truck. The twelve kilometers that connect Pluma to the main road alone take, barring unusual conditions, nearly a half hour of laborious edging along a narrow, unpaved passage that hugs the side of the mountain. Every so often the road swings out to what feels like one edge of the world, and then the sea can be spied far away, ash-colored and glimmering like a mirage. Also, on occasion, partway down the mountain, a dull ochre square interrupts the dense forest: evidence of a *finca,* a plantation-like coffee farm, some as large as three thousand hectares, where hired workers rake the golden beans out to dry on huge cement roofs.

A hundred years ago there were no *fincas* here. Basilio's and Genoveva's Zapotec ancestors had always worked the land they lived on without deeds of ownership. Communities and families shared land, and they passed on land, but they did not buy or sell it.

Then, around 1895, people from the city began to show up in Pluma and the areas around it, as well as in rural areas all over the country, waving pieces of paper they called land titles. According to these pieces of paper, the people who had been living on and cultivating the land for generations did not own it. As, of course, they had never claimed to. But also according to these pieces of paper—scripted so elegantly in the Spanish language and backed up with governmental flourishes and seals—other people, people who held land titles, could claim to own the land, and could do with it what they liked. They could establish huge *fincas* where many families had been living, and those families could then either stay and work for the new *patrones,* or get off the land. Indigenous people who resisted were transported or shot. Stories are told of some who were buried to their necks in the land they attempted to defend, and then galloped over by men on horses. By 1910, more than ninety-five percent of Mexico's population held no land.

Then came revolution, and in 1917 a new constitution, and written into it, the promise of land reform. Which, over the next several decades, was carried out, sort of. What land did get redistributed was handed back slowly, in small parcels, with lengthy delays— sometimes fourteen years between the time the land was officially expropriated and the time peasants were allowed to move back. Much of the redistributed land was unarable. Families that managed to get land allocated to them generally still lacked seeds, fertilizer, farm tools and equipment. And a great deal of land never quite made it back into the hands of the people it had been taken from, thanks in part to changes in the official definition of small landholdings; to large plantations that appear on paper as several small tracts owned by different people; and to the lengthy process of settling land disputes, which go on to this day.

Throughout the country, indigenous people, whose numbers have dwindled to less than ten percent of the overall population, have tended to fare worst in re-obtaining land. Oaxaca's Zapotecs and Mixtecs comprise the largest indigenous population of any of Mexico's thirty-one states. Today, three quarters of a century after land reform was constitutionally mandated, out of Pluma Hidalgo's ten thousand families, thirty-five own eighty percent of the land. These, then, the holdings of the thirty-five, are the *fincas* that appear, from certain overhangs, as dull gold tiles glinting strangely and sporadically amid the dark and curly green of the forest, and although they cannot be seen from such a distance, everyone knows there are Zapotec and Mixtec men down there, picking and pulping and raking beans, and everyone knows it is a misery what they are paid: eight or ten or twelve pesos a day.

Not much else is visible from this road: a tiny mountainside shrine where people have left offerings of red candles and dried flowers and shiny metallic paper cuttings for the Virgin; eagles and vultures coursing seamlessly overhead on unbroken currents, their wingtips carving soft black scallops against the sky; perhaps the tops of a few women's heads, barely visible below the road, where the mountain's slope is more gradual and a stream runs wide enough for washing clothes. Should a truck happen to be coming the other way, you or they will have to look for a lateral bulge large enough to serve as a turnout—perhaps one of you will have to back up for several minutes before coming to one—and then the inside truck will scrape past while the other clings hard to the slight widening on the sheer edge of the mountain. Eventually the road winds itself into the village of Pluma Hidalgo. Here it becomes paved, at least for a stretch: the poured cement halts abruptly fifty yards beyond *el centro,* where "Solidaridad 1994" has been gouged across the grainy surface of the final block—a reference to the group of local people who built the road and the date the cement ran out.

Everything in Pluma that is not made or grown here must travel these twelve kilometers from the main road. Every corn husk, every can of beer, every painting of Jesus Christ, every bottle of medicine, every schoolbook and pencil. Many things barely make it to Pluma; electricity, for example, arrived less than a decade ago, and still not every house has it; almost no one has running water; there are only three telephones, and no newspapers at all—well, some newspapers, but only a few much-dated pages at a time, which arrive in the form of wrapping for some other, more useful item, candles, say, or cheese.

Things that come from outside Pluma, then, hum a bit, if inaudibly, or shine, invisibly; they are in varying degrees marked and special. The knowledge of a journey lies encoded in them, whether simply from the coast, as with a corn husk used to cook a tamale, or, as with a picture of John F. Kennedy torn from an old calendar and stuck to the wall of a house, from another country, another culture, even another era. Basilio's favorite items from outside Pluma are a couple of birds' nests that came from the coast. They hang, droopily long and twigged, like ragged cornucopias, from nails outside his house, where anyone can see them and marvel at their singularity: nests like these cannot be found up in Pluma.

Little else at El Corozo is remarkable in this way. The breakfast fire that Genoveva makes is fed by wood she and Isidra and the children gather from around the *parcela*. The palm *petate* that Basilio now rolls up and stores in a corner of the room is the same sort being rolled up and put away just now in houses all over Pluma. The hammock outside the house, in which Enriquetta is now being gently rocked by Yolanda, is the same sort of hammock, woven by local hands, that swings babies all over the mountainside. The sweet corn *atole* Basilio will drink for breakfast, the tortillas kept over from last night and toasted to go with it, are the same foods that will be consumed by families living throughout the Sierra Madre del Sur, as they have been consumed by the people living in this region since hundreds of years before the birth of Christ. Even the dog, the nameless little dog whose bald, diseased neck hangs like a florid wattle, is the same sort that has always straggled throughout the village in scrappy, bickering, inbred packs.

But the nests are something different, something rare. Basilio found them himself, on a trip down to Rincón. He gave three to his mother, which she has hanging outside the house at Los Naranjales, and brought two back to El Corozo, carrying them carefully the whole joggling ride up in the back of a truck. The little one, he thinks, was once a hummingbird's.

In the morning, after eating, Basilio takes his leave from the family. Soon Lucío will go down the mountain path to the coffee, Genoveva and Isidra will make the day's tortillas, and the children will go to school. For now, Yolanda, in a white slip but not yet a dress, has made a game of fanning flies off her baby cousin, and Juan Diego, tootling around in nothing but a cloth diaper and splotches of dried *atole*, thinks perhaps he's assisting. Silvestre, or Chive, as they call him familiarly, and the wattled dog follow Basilio across the dirt yard to the edge of the road and stop there, where the child, bare-chested and sweetly mannish with his heavy shock of dark hair and wide, impish eyes, belts *"¡Ciao!"* after his father, and the dog becomes interested in a lizard.

Basilio, walking away beneath the colored crosses and viny growth of the cemetery, grins slightly behind the heavy droop of his mustache. Chive at six is already like his mother: forthright, brimful of personal authority. Basilio himself has a more constrained air, as though in spite of his agile, wiry build he is forever weighted down, yoked by the not unpleasant burden of his manual labors, for which he reserves his energy. When he speaks his lips part but barely, revealing two top teeth neatly framed in silver, and his voice skitters out like beans down a wooden chute, small and rapid and dry. When people speak to him, call out *"¡Chilio! ¡Buenos, Chilio!"* as he goes through the village, he responds with apparent diffidence, a heavy clump of hair partly obscuring his eyes as he dips his head in greeting. Right now, though, it is too early for anyone to offer salutation. He moves in solitude through the plumy broth suspended over the road, going to his duty.

Every other morning Basilio heads off not to work on his own *parcela* but to tend La Palma. La Palma is nearby, a fifteen-minute walk up the hill past the cemetery and then curving back down by the *secundaria,* where the older children go to school. The drop of the land here is so sudden and revealing that the distance between Pluma and the Pacific seems telescoped, negligible. This morning the effect is heightened by the fact that it's much too misty to make out the coast, but scores of lower peaks in the interim look just like waves on some frozen ocean, whipped up and blue, with Pluma alone seeming landed.

The road is quite bare this early. Basilio hears only the foghorn plaint of unseen burros, the scrabbling of chickens and turkeys at houses nearby. He smells the smoke of people's breakfast fires steeping the village in its good, slightly bitter aroma, like the charred skin of roasted bell peppers. Smoke weds mist; in their union they brush and curl against him, fragrant and dank, unwhite as bones. Pluma Hidalgo, some people say, got the first half of its name from the feathery lengths of near-perpetual mist that patrol the village and forest like extremely tall ghosts. Pluma is also the name of the kind of coffee grown in this region, and by no coincidence do the coffee plants thrive on the mist. Basilio cuts into the woods behind the *secundaria,* follows the path to the right at the ancient mango tree (whose massive roots provide any number of perches for smallish bottoms and, thus, a popular meeting spot among the schoolchildren), passes the long shack where bagged coffee gets stored before going to the mill and where pickers who have traveled far from home may sleep, and emerges onto the basketball court at La Palma.

Basilio does not think of La Palma as his, although in a way it *is* his. In all of Pluma Hidalgo, La Palma is unique. It was purchased only one year ago and yet the ground here feels like the oldest, most traditional land in the village, because it belongs not to any one person but to them all: this is the *parcela* of UCI.

UCI stands for Unión de Comunidades Indígenas, but everyone calls it by its acronym, pronounced "oo-see." It was formed fifteen years ago by indigenous people around the state of Oaxaca, at the same time that a number of similar organizations were being formed in rural areas around the country in order to improve living conditions. These organizations began with the chief function of bringing government surplus goods into remote, impoverished communities and selling them at wholesale prices from community-run stores.

The community-run store that serves the people of Pluma Hidalgo is named, in the doggedly utilitarian fashion of its sibling stores, Tienda Rural No. 11. It's located two hundred meters up the mountain from *el centro,* in the tiny colony of La Pasionaria, where UCI has its local headquarters. For a while, people at these *tiendas rurales* around the country watched while government trucks heaved over rutted roads into their remote villages, jettisoned loads of cornmeal and dried beans, soap, and lollipops, and drove back again, quite empty, to the cities. Before very long the rural people saw the imperfect logic of this system, and the organizations' second purpose evolved: to export produce from these areas in a way that would ensure the local small farmers more control over, and more of the profits from, their sale.

Previously, small farmers in Pluma, cut off from direct access to the market, had no choice but to sell their coffee at low prices through intermediaries, who would sell it to huge multinationals for great profit. The idea was that UCI, by assuming the functions of the intermediaries, would be able to direct a greater share of the profits back to the farmers and their communities. Naturally, this was contingent upon there being profits; itself contingent upon there being a mar-

ket, of which, the leaders of UCI and similar cooperatives soon discovered, there was in fact very little:
Mexican coffee simply did not have much of a reputation in the world market, and even less of one in the
gourmet coffee market. Yet Pluma's coffee, grown organically and at high altitudes, made it suitable to position in the "specialty coffee" market. This realization
led to the invention, in 1989, of Aztec Harvests.

Aztec Harvests is the brand name under which
Pluma's beans are sold in the United States. Really, of
course, the coffee is harvested by Zapotecs, but to
most people in the United States, Zapotec Harvests
would mean nothing. When an American working in
partnership with the small farmer cooperatives suggested Aztec Harvests, the Mexicans agreed to go
along with it. The name has been around for only a
few years—it was 1992 before Aztec formally incor-
porated and began to sell coffee through the U.S. specialty market—but already Ben & Jerry's ice cream has
named its new coffee flavor after the collective, choos-
ing Aztec Harvests beans at least as much for their
social significance as for their taste. The company's
literature stresses the fact that its shareholders are the
farmer-members of the cooperatives; that the farmers
are largely indigenous people, practicing traditional
methods of growing and processing beans; and that the
coffee is organic. Gradually, the invented name Aztec
Harvests is growing to signify something, to rouse an
image, an identity.

In Pluma Hidalgo, though, the name remains a bit
of a puzzle. Several of the farmers do not even realize
that their beans are being sold under the name Aztec
Harvests; those who do, don't think of the term as

referring to themselves; they think of it, if at all, as the product of American whim, inexplicable but after all very far away and of little importance to themselves. What is important to them is the changes UCI has wrought. Now the farmers are able to sell their dried coffee beans at market rates; receive training and information on techniques for planting, fertilizing, cultivating, and harvesting; and apply for UCI credit at an interest rate of two percent, which they may pay back at harvest time in the form of beans.

Pluma is one of about a dozen coffee-growing communities in which UCI has local branches. Over a thousand farmers throughout the Sierra Madre del Sur now send their coffee to UCI's new main headquarters and mill at the coast, in Rincón Alegre. There it is processed, packaged, and shipped directly to buyers and roasters in the United States and in Europe (where it is sold as Pluma Harvests). One, rather double-edged, measure of UCI's success may be found in the fact that its original mill and headquarters were burned down a few years ago under mysterious circumstances (a government investigation into the matter announced its findings inconclusive, which failed to shock anyone at UCI). Another measure may be that the local intermediaries are now offering farmers higher prices for their coffee—also somewhat double-edged in that Aztec, as a small company still working to establish itself, has not yet managed to prove itself to its member-farmers in the form of dividends, and risks losing their loyalty, as well as their beans, to a higher bidder, a more generous *patrón*.

The fact is that the indigenous people here have been subject to a real or ersatz feudal economy for so very long, many of the small farmers cannot help but look upon UCI as yet another boss—one which is perhaps unusually benevolent, and whose leadership comprises people of similar ancestry to their own, but which in the end must be no different really from the Spanish conquistadors, the noblemen with land titles, the owners of the *fincas,* the corrupt government officials, the foreigners with their multinational corporations. The idea of communally owned land may be rooted deeply in Zapotec culture, but the idea of a collectively owned business is foreign. Business still conjures notions of *patrones* making big profits while the workers earn little, and because most of the small farmers who are members of UCI do in fact still earn very little money, it is only natural to plug UCI into the role of *patrón.* Many UCI members are unaware that it is they who own Aztec Harvests. Many have no idea where their coffee goes when it leaves the mountains, in which countries it ends up, under what names it is sold and for which currencies.

The farmers' appreciation of UCI's role and the whole journey their beans take is slowly changing as more of them come down the mountains to Rincón Alegre, to visit the mill and attend seminars on growing or fertilizing techniques; and also as more of them take advantage of UCI credit to develop their *parcelas.* And perhaps one day there will be real profits to distribute, real dividend checks, wads of bright, crinkly pesos to press into hands and pockets. Perhaps that will convince the farmers at last that Aztec is theirs, that they are its owners. That, then, will be the greatest measure of success: not the pesos themselves (well yes, the pesos themselves), but also what they will mean, the story they will tell, the story that begins, *You alone are the boss of your self.*

Basilio emerges onto the basketball court at La Palma, and the dogs raise their eyebrows but do not come to him. The pack of dogs that resides at La Palma belongs, like the dog that resides at his own house, essentially to no one, and these, like the wattled mutt, are without names, except for one, whose name seemed to spring from it rather than getting bestowed from without; it is called Tigre, not because it has stripes but because it has such a snarling high opinion of itself. Today it looks over its shoulder at Basilio with its mouth open, saunters directionlessly around the court, in and out of the thinning plumes of fog, then disappears down the mountain, followed after a bit by all its mates except the lame one, which stands apologetically in the shade on its forever quivering haunches and licks its chops. Basilio takes no notice.

The basketball court at La Palma is not foremost a basketball court, although it does have two netless hoops, fixed to wooden backboards that are mounted on thick columns of cement, and although the men and boys of Pluma widely love this sport, and will play it even with a flaccid red ball pinched by one of the students from the *secundaria,* or a tennis ball, or even with a lime as the sun is going down. During the hours of heat and light, however, in the seasons of harvest, this apron of cement must function first as a drying patio. Heat and light are beginning to burn definitively through the mist as Basilio crosses the patio to drag out the burlap bags of *pergamino,* depulped beans still wearing their fine skins of parchment; they must be dried and raked for days before they are ready to go to the coast.

UCI purchased this *parcela* little more than a year ago, from a *patrón* who'd given up on it and moved to the city when coffee prices plummeted in the late eighties. La Palma, with fourteen hectares, although tiny by the standards of any *finca,* is large for UCI; no member's *parcela* has more than ten. Most of the land here is harvested for coffee, but a wide, shady section where the mountain grows temporarily level was converted seven months ago into a tree nursery, and near it, in two huge cement tubs, organic fertilizer marinates. During the past year UCI has brought an agricultural engineer to Pluma to spend time with members here at the communal *parcela,* help them build this nursery, and teach crop-improvement techniques. Just two months ago UCI members completed work on a brand-new palm-and-cement bunkhouse at the edge of the basketball court, with glass windowpanes, stitched curtains, tiled floors, and a big, plush pomegranate-colored couch in the central room, where meetings can be held around a wooden table. High above the table, framed under glass, hangs a poster of a blue-plumed eagle with a coffee bean in its beak over the words "Pluma Harvests." Everything about the bunkhouse feels like a promise: clean and unused, poised to come true.

This fall Basilio volunteered and was selected to be the official local UCI agricultural expert, which not only has entailed extra trips to Rincón for meetings and seminars, but also means he has responsibility for overseeing things at La Palma: tending the nursery, mixing the fertilizer, seeing that the coffee gets dried properly before being sent to the coast. The day workers hired to pick beans have not yet arrived when Basilio drags the burlap sacks out from under the overhanging roof of the bunkhouse, unknots the nylon ropes round their openings, and upends them gently to spill *pergamino* in serpentine curves on the patio. It is a lot to take on; if he feels yoked, it is no wonder, having added his responsibilities at La Palma to those he already has at El Corozo, and with UCI still to determine what sort of compensation he will get. As yet, Basilio is working on faith.

He takes the *pala,* a sort of toothless rake or flat-edged wooden paddle, from against the wall of the oddly grand bunkhouse and begins to smooth the beans out against the cracked plane of cement. The scraping song it makes is slow and rhythmic as surf. Wood and beans knock together. Tops of trees turn gold. The last threads of mist suddenly wriggle high and vanish. Basilio spreads the *pergamino* back and forth, rolling it into a single layer, exposing each bean to the sun, which has finally come.

Interlude

Object

In the studio the drama teacher disallows her beginning students language. The big words, especially. Under no circumstances may we utter *mother,* or *heaven,* or *betrayal,* or *desire.* We will have to earn the right to use every word from scratch. She starts us on an easy one. One at a time we must learn to say *bottle.*

I am seventeen, not unfearful. We are all a little desperate to show her we understand.

One at a time we rise to our feet. We try to describe bottles—beer, milk, soda, baby—sketching them from memory or imagination. One at a time she cuts us off: *Sit down. No, sit down.*

We stammer, sweat, blush in frustration. She flicks ashes, scowls. *No, no, terrible. Stop, sit down.*

What business do you have speaking lines, she asks ill-manneredly, *if you don't know what the words mean?*

She demonstrates. She stands like the actress she was in her youth and turns her gaze with startling tenderness to a piece of dirty floor. After a moment, language issues from her. The bottle is green and lying in the gutter and someone has half peeled a paper label from its bulbous middle . . . It has the translucence and hue of a lime sucker . . . Black rings of dirt cake the ridges at the lip . . . She is sculpting: her voice and fingers and eyes and thighs wrap round the bottle; it is inside her; she has swallowed it and is swollen with its many stories, its whole corpulent gourd of knowledge.

When she finishes, some of us have wet eyes, not because we are moved by her performance but because we are furious, shaken: how dare she demand from us this level of intimacy with every word?

She answers the unvoiced question with stern finality: *It is your obligation.*

We file, dismissed, out of the studio.

All week long I will be seeing bottles anew.

T w o

Secrets

Another border unrecognized by the sun is the temporal.

We regard our own selves as temporary; to us this border is absolute. It seems not only to exist outside us, circumscribing our transit through life as might a tunnel, but additionally to govern us from within: time as a condition we're born with, locked inextricably within the flow of our blood, within the ongoing microscopic regeneration of our littlest parts. And the central figure around which we've organized our idea of time is the sun; it is our chief marker for time's invisible presence. Extrapolating from the relationship of our movement to the sun's fixedness, we've imagined a whole system of slashes, meticulously spaced and composing by increments minutes, hours, days, weeks, months, years, centuries. According to the rules of our own dreaming, these units stack at uniform intervals into each next level, fitting with snugger precision than Russian dolls; they are standardized, identical. Yet each is also singular and unrepeatable. And each, for its point of reference, has the sun.

But does the solar body itself fall sway to any such boundaries? The sun—whose daily passage through the sky, whose monthly deviations in angle and duration of shining, whose stations, people long believed, were as shackled to time as was everything else—we cannot know. We only know *we* seem constrained to what we've conceived: an unimpeachable, unfurling, iron-clad skein of minutes.

Anyway, that's one view. Scientists, prophets, poets, saints, whole cultures, have long begged to differ. The Greek mathematician Pythagoras, who thought the ultimate nature of a thing boiled down not to a substance but to a number, believed that time is the soul, and the procreative element, of the universe. The Roman philosopher Plotinus proposed that the linear view of time, the familiar illusion of succession and change, is simply a result of humans' inability to grasp everything at once. The French philosopher René Descartes, demonstrating a breathtaking sweetness of faith, believed time is a series of ever-perishing instants, with the world's existence therefore dependent on continual divine creation. "To be conscious is not to be in time," wrote T. S. Eliot in *Four Quartets:*

> But only in time can the moment in the rose-garden,
> The moment in the arbour where the rain beat,
> The moment in the draughty church at smokefall
> Be remembered; involved with past and future.
> Only through time time is conquered.

Theologians from Origen to Aquinas have pondered relative and absolute models of time in the context of their respective implications for divine and human will. In Ancient Greek and some American Indian languages, words that mean "past" also mean "future." In all the myriad ways we have conceived of time, we learn less about time's intrinsic nature (if any such thing can be said to exist) than we do about our own.

We have been measuring time for thousands of years, in various ways and in various degrees of specificity, according to the concrete needs of different cultures. Australian aborigines didn't bother tracking hours throughout the day, but would signal the commencement of a particular event (an auction or a meeting, for example) by placing a rock in the crotch of a tree; when the sun struck the rock, it was "time." The Mayans developed an exceedingly precise astronomical calendar, with a correction built in for leap year that works out, over the course of a century, to be even more accurate than that which we use today. They built monuments and altars to mark explicit divisions of time; because they pictured time as a series of parcels carried on the backs of different deities, each parcel was itself a thing divine. Many early cultures divided time simply into periods of light and darkness; the daylight hours could be dissected further by sundials and water clocks if necessary; the nighttime hours hardly required cataloging. People of the Andaman Islands kept a kind of calendar based on the succession of different odors from various plants coming into bloom and dying; they clocked the time of year by smell. At some level, the compulsion to measure and create expressions of time seems embedded in human nature. Even the ancient temples and pyramids and stone configurations that have been found positioned on earth in apparent homage to the sun are, at their subtlest level, clocks.

In our society, evidence of the boundaries of time is hopelessly entwined with personal mortality; we can map its progress nowhere so well as within our ever-changing flesh, within all of our eventual deaths. Yet even this is uncertain. In city skyscrapers and basement rooms, in circus tents and suburban office parks, there are people who offer to help customers recall past lives or glimpse their futures. In railroad flats and ocean-front mansions, in old farmhouses and new condominiums, there are people who say they've heard ancestors bump into chandeliers, whistle big-band tunes, tip over soup cans in pantries at night. One day every year in March or April, rational businesspeople all across the land shutter their shops in observance of a resurrection of life.

In fact, businesspeople were at least as responsible for introducing our modern concept of linear time as were scientists. In feudal societies, people didn't think of time as a one-directional, unbroken line but, rather, as consisting of distinct, repeatable segments that came in cycles linked to the recurring seasons and the mystical signs of the zodiac. Time was measured and felt in relation to events, whether births, deaths, rains, full moons, or sunsets. Scientists and scholars, influenced by astronomy and astrology, supported this view, which happened to coincide neatly with a system where land was the basis of power: time and the soil then both shared cyclical, everlasting, unalterable natures. In this view lay the promise of eternal sameness; social station was as inevitable and fixed as the recurrent drift of constellations, the inevitable autumn harvest.

It was the development of mercantilism and the circulation of currency that loosened the roots of value and power from the abiding earth, made them transferable, ephemeral. The rise of a merchant class emphasized mobility, change, linear progress. Time itself grew to have a commodity value; it could be wasted, spent, and saved. The notion that time is money began to take hold, and the magical conception of the universe came to be replaced by the metaphor of a vast, mechanical clock with celestial bodies for cogs: stars and moon and sun.

And the economy continued to dictate our conceptions of time; hours had been subdivided into sixty units each, and these minutes further subdivided into seconds, since the mid-1300s, but it was when industry began to require greater synchronization of labor that the maintaining of a strict standard time became indispensable, and clocks and watches widespread. As dollars began to translate into wage-hours, so time-thrift came to equal money-thrift. A day worked, a dollar earned, *tempus fugit,* and all the rest: time became something that runs out and is forever lost, as sand through a glass with a hole in its bottom. It drags in its wake all that it touches: quicksand. Time may itself be infinite, but the parameters it casts around our lives are the most finite things we know.

As for the sun, then, what? Time's touchstone, its index, marching its yellow border across the earth's crust, relentlessly spelling out the confines of our every day on this planet—is the sun, too, subject to time's limits? Our current understanding tells us, queerly, that time has the power to diminish no thread of its rays. The sun may one day end, we are told, but its light cannot. Somewhere, at this very moment, light waves from the beginning of the earth are venturing yet deeper into space, burning still, telling their picture stories to distant galaxies—while on this planet we say we are nearing a new millennium, and tick off another day inexorably from our rations.

Riddle-ensconced, unknowable, time yet governs us; governs, also, the way we think of life and everything in it. In deference to those totems Calendar and Clock—forms of which we tack to our walls, bind to our limbs, carry with us in daytime and dream beside at night—we have organized an understanding of virtually every matter based on that expression of time we call history. Through history we attempt to comprehend war and art; through it we try to track the spread of beliefs and the spread of genes. We apply it to religious rituals, to dairy farming, to hemlines. We can apply it, too, to glass and paper and beans. History lets us progress backward along a line whose chimerical nature does nothing to lessen its stature: the cordage of history is as irrefutable, as imperiously wound, as the heavy ropes of velvet used to regulate flow in museums and banks.

Even when history is two parts fancy, it carries the patina of being something real, and fixed, and weighty, in the way that things having occurred in the past seem naturally to heft about extra bulk. History lends force of gravity, knots one event to another, ensures connection, explanation, rationale. The braided strands of history make up the core of any object. They contain its story, in a sense compose the principal back of its identity: slide a hand backward along time's bumpy spine and you are fumbling toward that object's essence.

Glass, paper, beans. What does history reveal about their essences? This: that they were each as gold—only rarer, more coveted, more deliriously elusive. It's true. Each one of these omnipresent three, which go about nowadays cloaked in drab, which have been worn thin and engrimed as coins conscripted to perpetual circulation, and which have been re-created in so many varied guises that each successive guise is borne up, is colored and informed by ghost images on an infinitely layered palimpsest—each of them, glass, paper, and bean, was once a thing of wonder possessed only by men of the cloth, men and women of the crown. The holy and the royal laid their exclusive claims; so long as these items were rare, they shimmered in the liquid heat of the singular and the sublime.

In fact, not one of these items is intrinsically rare, not in the way of gold. Each can be crafted or cultivated; with knowledge and care there is no reason they cannot be produced in abundance. Their rareness was a guise that had to be constructed, imposed. This was accomplished by restricting information, prohibiting understanding: by costuming the items in secrecy. So long as knowledge of how to make and grow these items remained clandestine, their value was assured. Eventually—it took centuries—the secrets all would be undone by love and war. (Then new costumes would have to be gotten up, new values imagined and assigned.)

But slide a hand farther down the velvet cord: not

glass, nor paper, nor coffee beans has its primordial root in secrecy. Each of the trio had an incarnation before human discovery made a commodity of it. Each, in the beginning, existed freely, at liberty from human usefulness and ken. Before they were secrets they were riddles: like time, locked fast within nature's fluid grid. In the beginning it was not humans at all who wrought or made use of these things. Their true discoverers, the story goes, were lightning, wasps, and goats.

Glass

The oldest, and coldest, of them all. Relying in its azoic form on nothing human, nothing creature, nothing that grows or lives or dies. Only minerals and heat and chance:

Lightning strikes, hits a beach. In the slimmest compartment of time it exists and vanishes. It leaves behind a jagged trace of seared sand. Within the trace lies a fulgurite, petrified lightning: a thin tube of glass, the instant progeny of this quicksilver union.

Or: a meteorite pierces the skin of earth's atmosphere and does not burn out but continues to fall flaming. In its collision with the mineral surface of the planet, small, glowing drops are spit back into the air. When these land they are already hardened into tektites, rounded bodies of greenish brown meteor glass.

Or: a volcano erupts. Lava writhes across the ground, and in its cooling wake are born pieces of obsidian glass, black and shiny, which fracture into hard, sharply curved planes.

These were the earliest glasses, created not for the

sake of use, nor desire, nor trade. Humans did find and begin using these natural glasses—particularly the obsidian, which they handily fashioned into knives and arrowheads—more than a million years ago. But it was probably only four or five thousand years ago that people began to make glass themselves. And when they did, having finally solved the riddle of its creation, their first impulse was not a practical one; they did not direct their energies into making a useful tool of glass. Instead, they began by crafting it in imitation of natural wonders—gems and precious stones—and for nothing but personal adornment, for no sake but loveliness'.

Already, even this much might be fable.

No one really knows how or when humans discovered the art of making glass. Neither is it a solid, nor does it obey the rules we have imagined for liquids: how did we ever get our hands around the secret of this improbable substance? Theories differ wildly. One says glass was invented by Tubal-cain, the great-great-great-great-great-grandson of Adam, mentioned in Genesis 4:22 as "the master of all coppersmiths and blacksmiths." Another chalks it up to an accidental discovery by ancient potters, who fired various concoctions at high temperatures in their experiments with new ceramic glazes. Flavius Josephus, a Jewish historian who lived just after the time of Christ, wrote that it was discovered by Israelites who set fire to a forest on a hill; the heat became so great that sand in the soil melted and flowed down the slope.

Pliny the Elder, a Roman who lived at the same time, wrote what has come to be the most widely retold account. He tells of a group of Phoenician merchant marines who'd beached for the night by the river of Belus, near Mount Carmel. The sailors, getting ready to cook their supper on the sand, looked about for some rocks upon which to rest their pots, but couldn't find any. So, from their cargo they borrowed cakes of niter (an alkali, used at the time for embalming the dead) and set these in their fires instead. But as the niter warmed, it melted, and acted as flux with the heated sand, which shifted shape and ran as liquid and pooled. Upon waking the next morning, the sailors saw that the strange pool had hardened into a shiny solid. Today experts doubt whether Pliny's sailors would have built fires hot enough to catalyze the chemical reaction, but the story appeals and so persists.

Some people look not to stories but to artifacts for the beginnings of glassmaking; they often point to Mesopotamia, 2500 B.C., from which period small glass objects resembling precious stones have been found. A thousand years later, according to this method of dating, artisans learned to pour molten glass into molds of metal, or shape it around dung-and-clay cores—for the earliest found pieces of more elaborately shaped jewelry, and statuettes of pharaohs and gods, as well as some cups and vases, date to around 1500 B.C.

The invention of the blowpipe came along thirty years before Christ, or fifty, or three hundred, or thirty-five hundred. Here again historians hotly disagree or else succumb altogether to the mystery, to the void of known facts. The earliest guess is based on paintings found in Egyptian tombs built about 2000 B.C.—but the paintings themselves are thought to have been made fifteen hundred years earlier, during the reign of Onsertasen I. They depict what appear to be ancient Thebans gathering molten glass from a furnace and blowing it into vessels on lengths of pipe; modern experiments with ceramic pipe prove that it can be used to blow glass. No evidence suggests that the art of casting or blowing glass was kept secret at this time. Conflicting evidence suggests that its uses were almost entirely ornamental, either as personal adornment or as tributes to human and immortal rulers; or that it was made into useful household vessels; or that it acted as a kind of currency, traded in the form of gemlike baubles; or that it acted as actual currency, cast in coin shapes with hieroglyphs pressed into their surfaces.

All of this, too, falls somewhere between fable and conjecture.

Then the Romans conquered Egypt in 31 B.C., and the history of glass acquires a new glint, particularly glinty to us perhaps because it is strangely familiar: the glint of commercial value. At first content to purchase the novel item from their new subjects, the Romans soon learned to make it and established glasshouses of their own. They deemphasized glass's mystical allure in favor of cultivating it as an industry. They created widespread demand for the product by blowing and casting it into useful objects: bottles, tumblers, vases, and toilet articles.

One reason the Romans wanted glass to be valued as a necessary, almost common, household item—not in its very essence exalted or sublime—was their fear that an inherently precious substance which could be mass-produced would rival gold and threaten the empire's gold standard, undermining its power. Another reason, quite simply: the greater volume of demand, the greater the profits. Glass's breakability was therefore an attribute in that it ensured recurrent demand. There's a story about a Roman architect who came up with a formula for malleable glass: if dropped, it would dent but never break. The architect brought a sample of this amazing glass to Emperor Tiberius, expecting to be rewarded for his discovery. Tiberius, after witnessing a demonstration of its special qualities, inquired anxiously whether anyone else knew the magic formula. The man proudly assured him no one else did. Tiberius, relieved, beheaded him on the spot.

That one even the history books label legend.

When the Huns—the barbarous Huns, as the history books are endlessly fond of saying—came to power, the Roman Empire split in two. Glassmaking survived, and thrived, in the East, throughout the Byzantine Empire, but it flickered out and became dormant, if not lost, in the West, not to resurface for nearly a thousand years. What glassware existed there until the Middle Ages was a rare luxury item, reserved for the nobility.

The renaissance of glass took place in the eleventh, or the thirteenth, or the fourteenth century in Venice. Different historians cite different dates; at any rate, by 1291 glasshouses had become so numerous in the city that they presented a serious fire hazard, prompting glass operations to relocate to the separate island of Murano. Or: authorities were so intent on maintaining the city's virtual monopoly of glass that they scurried all means of production off to the cloistered island of Murano. Whichever version is closer to the truth, it is the case that by the mid-1400s the noblemen who controlled the glass industry got the Venetian Council to issue a decree making it a crime punishable by death for a glassmaker to leave Murano or to impart the secrets of his trade to a foreigner. For their loyalty, the glassworkers had bestowed upon them the title of "gentlemen," and were the only manual laborers permitted to marry daughters of the nobility without those families sacrificing their status.

Murano, then. An island of glass in the Venetian Lagoon. Actually, a series of tiny islands, linked by bridges, that supported glasshouses and workmen's cottages as well as the mystique of the ethereal. For here in the light of the Adriatic, glass was recast again, this time as an alchemical marvel. Stories circulated about what went on at Murano: men were crushing and melting precious stones by a magical process and forming them into objects of all shapes, sizes, hues. Blue glass consisted of sapphire powder; red glass, of rubies; green, of emeralds; and so on. The only gemstone that defied transfiguration, it was said, was the hardest of them all, the diamond: no clear, colorless glass existed at that time. Far from Murano these rumors spread. In one popular tale, a robber was supposed to have stolen a stained-glass window from a church and placed it in a fire in order to melt it down to its concentrated jewel forms—only to be disgusted at the blackened, worthless mass it actually became. Marco Polo found a hungry market for Murano's false gems in India and China. The secret of this island shone fine and rare, and the filigreed vessels produced on Murano held the perfumes of countesses, the holy oils of priests.

The funny thing is that, in spite of the Venetians' tucking the glassworks away on an island, and in spite of their perfectly sincere promise to execute any worker who would not keep still, by the sixteenth century most of the rest of Europe was making glass, too. Regarding the question of how this leap was made, historians have surprisingly little to say. They treat this spread of glass almost with nonchalance, as though it were inevitable, an act of nature, as though glass's secret were a block of ice Murano had tried to contain by clutching in its hot fist. Perhaps. Perhaps if the natural tendency of humanity, or civilization, or civilization's rulers, is to horde and contain and conceal knowledge—perhaps an equally strong impulse is also at work, guiding oppositely, for secrets do leak, unstaunchably and consistently, throughout history.

Paper

Paper was invented first of all by the Vespidae family, whose members are known colloquially as yellow jackets, hornets, and wasps. Some of these build nests of mud, but the more advanced build nests of paper, and these are known as paper wasps. Paper wasps look for rotten or, at the very least, weathered wood, which they chew up in their tiny jaws, macerating it with saliva, and then deposit in little blobs on the site where they are building—possibly the very rotten log supplying them with their raw material, or a nearby bush, or your front porch. They work painstakingly and in concert, and construct remarkably strong and elegant nests, sometimes of several different kinds of paper: a sort of heavy cardboard for the outer walls, thin parchment to form the cells, and even translucent sheets like onionskin to act as windows.

The earliest human writing surfaces were clay tablets, bark, palm leaves, and, dating from at least the fourth millennium B.C., papyrus, a plant whose stalks were cut into thin strips and pasted together to form sheets. Bamboo and silk were used from the sixth and fifth centuries B.C., and parchment and vellum, made from scraped and dried animal skins, were used from the second. But not until A.D. 105 did a human being teach himself how to make paper in the way that wasps are born knowing. This was Ts'ai Lun, an official in the Chinese court of Emperor Yüan Hsing.

Ts'ai Lun's paper was made from mulberry bark, hemp, rags, and fishing nets, all mashed up in order to separate their filaments, then mixed into a pulp with water and spread on flat screens to drain. What remained was a thin, dry, relatively smooth sheet composed of tiny intertwined, or felted, fibers. In the nearly two thousand years since, papermakers have experimented with a staggering list of ingredients for their fiber sources, including pinecones, potatoes, thistles, frog spittle, swamp moss, sugarcane, algae, asparagus, corn husks, cabbage stumps, bananas, manure, ivory shavings, brewery refuse, fish, and dust—nevertheless, in all that time, the basic method used by Ts'ai Lun, and wasps, has gone virtually unaltered.

For the first five hundred years after Ts'ai Lun brought this method to the attention of his emperor, it also went unrevealed; the Chinese court kept a close secret of it. Papermaking was eventually introduced in Japan, by a Buddhist monk named Dokyo, who became a close advisor to the empress Shotoku. At the empress's behest the first mass publication was carried out: a million block-printed paper prayers. The dates generally given for all of this are confusing: papermaking supposedly began in Japan in A.D. 610 or 615, but the million prayers were printed in 770.

In any case, paper circulated ever more widely throughout the seventh and eighth centuries as China traded with Mecca and Turkistan, but the means of its production were still shrouded in mystery; except for possibly Japan, no other civilization learned how to make it until smack in the middle of the eighth century. The secret was finally prized open in 751, when Chinese soldiers attacking the city of Samarkand were taken prisoner. Among them were some skilled papermakers, whom their captors forced to build and operate a paper mill. From there, the knowledge slowly drizzled to Baghdad and Damascus, Egypt and Morocco, Spain and Italy, and so on. It took five hundred years to get from Samarkand to Europe, and was slow to catch on there when it did; more fragile and expensive than parchment, paper was also regarded with suspicion for having been introduced by Jews and Arabs.

After prayers, the next thing to be mass-printed on paper was money. The very oldest paper money, however, was neither mass-printed nor used as currency. Produced from the first year after Ts'ai Lun's discovery, and solely symbolic, it was called spirit money. Spirit money and spirit paper—which came also to be block-printed to represent all sorts of worldly goods: hats, shoes, horses, carts, treasure chests with little silver paper locks—were burned in effigy at Chinese funerals as a way of ensuring that the departing spirits would bring happiness and riches with them into the next world.

Printed paper money as we know it appeared in China at the turn of the ninth century. It was called flying money. Certainly it moved more freely than did metal coins, or pigs or rice or cloth; it hovered oddly free from any palpable tether to the goods it represented. In 1298 Marco Polo, trading in the Orient, wrote of this phenomenon, this feat of abstraction: money was the first printed paper ever seen by a European traveler. It was perhaps some time, however, before paper currency got quite wholly assimilated into the realm of the abstract. A story about Emperor Hung Wu, who ruled China from 1368 to 1398, tells that he wanted to create suitably ceremonious paper for the printing of money; he also wanted it to be difficult to counterfeit. One of his advisors came up with the suggestion of blending the hearts of great literary men into the standard mulberry bark pulp. Luckily, the empress declared that the heart of a true literary man could be found in his writings; therefore, only their manuscripts and not their organs were appropriated for the mixture.

Paper in the Orient, even as it entered daily life (and it quickly became useful for all sorts of things, from windowpanes to umbrellas to toilet paper, which existed in China from at least the ninth century), was not detached from a sense of reverence. From its first issuance, it was linked to the holy unknown. That upon the earliest sheets the sayings of Confucius were recorded; that the spirit papers, once turned to smoke, pass into the realm of the other world—these are fitting tributes to a craft that was undoubtedly a gift from heaven, and where the historical leaves no room for spiritual truth, it is gently edged aside or disregarded.

In Echizen, Japan, now an important papermaking

district, there is a story about a deity who appeared long ago on a river shore, dressed as a mortal woman. The woman wrapped a piece of her kimono around a bamboo stick, then dipped this simulated sieve into the river, where she shook it back and forth as if forming a sheet of paper. When the villagers asked what she was doing, she explained that she was teaching them to make paper so that they might live by this craft. When they asked her name, she replied, "Mizuha-Nome-no-Mikoto," and disappeared. Never mind Ts'ai Lun, or Dokyo, or Empress Shotoku: in Japan today there stands a Shinto shrine dedicated to the deity Mizuha-Nome-no-Mikoto, the founder of Echizen papermaking.

If a reverence for paper was never so pronounced in the West, people there did at least develop respect for the commodity when, in the seventeenth century, demand for it increased and it grew scarce. This occurred in connection with literacy and a hunger for the printed word, for after prayers and money, paper's next important role was as reading material. The first printed book, *The Diamond Sutra,* was made in China in 868. By the mid-fifteenth century, book printing began in Europe with the Gutenberg Bible, and relatively large-scale paper consumption was initiated. In the seventeenth century, regular newspapers appeared, and with them, a dearth of raw materials.

Notwithstanding that earlier, immoderate list of raw materials with which papermakers experimented, up until the latter part of the nineteenth century, the chief ingredients in most paper were cotton and linen rags. Newspapers and books, indeed all written communiqués, became increasingly dependent on people's willingness to recycle their old cloth. But as more matter got printed, printed matter became more popular. The spread of literacy and the proliferation of ever more periodicals meant that shortages would continue to plague manufacturers so long as they relied on rags to provide paper's fibers.

It was a French naturalist and physicist, René-Antoine Ferchault de Réaumur, who in 1719 suggested before the French Royal Academy the alternative that would eventually solve the problem of raw materials and lead to the modern production of paper. His idea, he explained before the Academy, came to him while he was looking at some wasps.

Beans

Coffee came to people late, in the fifth or the ninth or the eleventh century A.D., and until it came no one missed or dreamed of it, and when it did they kept thinking it was the fruit of the devil before tasting it and changing their minds.

It was introduced to humans by the angel Gabriel, or an exquisitely plumed bird, or an exiled dervish, or some goats.

The Gabriel story has two versions. In one, the angel teaches King Solomon to brew coffee in a town whose inhabitants are all suffering from a strange disease, and the beverage cures them. In the other, the angel delivers sips of coffee from heaven to Muhammad, who is either ill or having trouble staying awake to pray.

The bird story tells that a superbly feathered songbird appeared somewhere near the Red Sea. A holy man spotted it, and followed as the bird flew slowly toward a white-flowered tree. By the time the man reached the tree, the bird was gone, but the holy man found red fruits growing on the tree. From these he brewed a medicine that was able to heal sick pilgrims.

The dervish story is about a religious man of Yemen named Hadji Omer, who had been banished to the desert to die of starvation. But there he found some bright red cherries growing on a little tree, boiled and ate them, and began to whirl. Citizens of the nearby town of Mocha came out to watch, believed they were witnessing a religious event, and promptly canonized the dervish and the coffee cherries. Or Hadji Omer used the fruits to cure the townsfolk of a plague, and in their thankfulness they praised the plant as holy.

The last story is the most widely retold. It's about an Arabian or Ethiopian goatherd named Kaldi, out one day tending his goats not very closely when he heard them begin to bleat, a lot. He went to see what all the fuss was about and found his charges all prancing and dancing about on their hind legs, and taking nibbles from some bushes that were growing shiny deep red berries. Kaldi plucked a few and chewed them and soon he was dancing, too. Then, either a mullah found him in this state, or Kaldi himself brought some of the cherries to a monastery; in either case, a religious man initially scolded Kaldi for partaking of a devil's potion, then went ahead and sampled a little, and had the revelation that it in fact could help him stay awake for nighttime devotions.

Of course, there are more than four stories, four possible seeds. Numerous clues of coffee's origin have been sighted, and cited. Scholars have discerned what they say are references to coffee in various books of the Bible. Some suggest Esau traded his birthright to Jacob not for a plate of lentil broth but for something like coffee porridge. Others believe that manna itself, the bread of the angels, came not from the secretion of the tamarisk tree, as folk tradition has supposed, but from the coffee tree.

The first overt written reference to coffee is credited to either a tenth-century Persian physician named Rhazes or an eleventh-century Arabian physician and philosopher named Avicenna. Historians mostly agree that it was discovered and used in Ethiopia before then, that it grew wild there in the old kingdom of Kaffa, and that it was actually a kind of staple in the diet of the nomadic warriors of the Galla tribe, who thought to wrap roasted, pulverized coffee beans in balls of animal fat, and sustained themselves with these rations on hunting and raiding expeditions. They also mostly agree that cultivation of the coffee plant probably did not begin until Arabian traders brought it to Yemen around the beginning of the first millennium.

It was Arabs who gave coffee the name, *qahwa,* that would stick, in one derivation or another, all over the globe and across the centuries. Its etymology is slightly obscure. Some people say the word *qahwa* was used to talk about wine prior to the discovery of coffee. Its Arabic root means lessening one's desire for something; just as wine decreases the appetite for food, coffee decreases the need for sleep. Some people say it referred to coffee's bitterness. Some say *qahwa* is a phonetic spin-off of Kaffa. And some say it's related to the Arabic *quwwa,* which means "strength" or "power," because coffee is so invigorating.

It was also Arabs who thought to wrap coffee in

secret. While they would trade boiled or sun-dried (and therefore sterile) beans, they made it illegal to transport a viable plant beyond the borders of the Muslim world. For several hundred years, then, they managed to maintain a monopoly, both on the bean and how it was construed.

From the beginning, people regarded coffee as not just any kind of food. It was a spiritual aid; the Sufis used it as they did hashish, to help them achieve a trancelike state during their nighttime worship services, that they might come closer to the divine. It was medicinal; it cleared the skin, made the body smell good, suppressed coughs, warded off smallpox and measles, cured pellagra and gout and plague, was an aphrodisiac. It was a symbol of hospitality, a precursor to doing business, a condition of marriage (Turkish wives could divorce husbands who didn't provide the bean).

And to unleash all its special attributes, whether religious or restorative or otherwise, people tried out lots of different recipes. They mashed the beans to make a porridge. They crushed it into a paste with mutton fat. They beat the dried fruit into a flour, which they mixed with salted butter to make griddle cakes. They fermented the cherries to make wine. They soaked the skins to make a drink called *kisher*. They soaked the pits, or beans, to make a drink called *bounya*. They infused the whole fruit to make a kind of tisane. They accompanied it with dates dipped in butter, with chocolate, cold water, honey nougats, sunflower seeds, a dash of alcohol. And once they had settled on a favorite method—steeping the roasted, ground beans in hot water—each culture continued to refine and define its own distinctive brew. Arabs added saffron; Turks added clove, cardamom, cinnamon, and star anise; Moroccans added peppercorn, and Ethiopians a pinch of salt.

Also from the beginning, coffee had political implications, or anyway was perceived as having such by both civil and religious leaders. Coffee had a way of encouraging congregation. It was a symbol of welcome and warmth and hospitality; public houses serving the concoction acted as magical watering holes. People came to the *khave*s not only to drink coffee but to commune. They'd linger around the outdoor tables playing backgammon or mancala or chess, listening to music, ironing out business deals, talking. Talk was the activity the coffeehouses seemed to kindle most fervently: they provided brightly intoxicating centers around which to convene, teach, question, and debate lengthily and lucidly into the night.

It was this propensity of the *khave*s that eventually made the authorities so anxious. Although coffee was known as the Wine of Islam, they could hardly ban it on religious grounds, in the way that real alcohol was forbidden, when mullahs and dervishes and monks themselves imbibed it to help them pray. But alcohol, even if it intensified people's feelings, conveyed them in the end into sloppiness and sleep. Coffee was more dangerous; it only sharpened people's will and drive. As *khave*s grew more popular than mosques, the authorities fretted themselves into action. Shah Abas of Persia, to discourage political talk, stationed mullahs in the coffeehouses to discuss poetry, history, and religion. The grand vizier Kuprili of the Ottoman Empire simply shut the establishments down altogether. Khair

Beg, a Meccan governor, tried to outlaw the drink because of the free speech it fostered. Coffeehouses were banned in Mecca in 1511, wrecked in Cairo in 1534, forbidden by edict in Constantinople in 1554.

And then coffee spiraled out beyond the control of the Muslim world. About 1600 a holy man named Baba Budan smuggled seven fertile coffee seeds from Mecca back to India, to his home state of Karnataka. Dutch traders bought Karnatakian coffee trees, which they disseminated throughout their Asian colonies, most famously in Indonesia, where their plantations on Java grew, and in Ceylon. In Vienna, in 1683, Turkish soldiers retreating from a siege are said to have left behind in their haste five hundred sacks of a strange, dry black fodder. One man, who had spent time in Turkey, recognized their contents as coffee; he ground and brewed and sold the drink for the first time in Vienna. In one way and another, coffee's spread throughout Europe quickened. So long as the Arabs had cornered the market, coffee had remained rare in Europe, a luxury known almost exclusively to members of the court and nobility. Once commercially available, it tumbled into the ready embrace of common folk.

At first it was sold, particularly in Italy, France, and Austria, by roaming vendors, who clanked up and down the dirt or cobbled streets wearing elaborate copper armor composed of tray and cup and spoon. They went door to door peddling the drink, which they brewed on the spot over little spirit lamps, and sold with pickled cherries, strawberries, and nuts. But the real surge in coffee's popularity came with the proliferation of coffeehouses around the middle of the seventeenth century. They sprang up in Vienna, London, Venice, Marseilles, Amsterdam, Paris, and Hamburg, and worked the same curious magic here that they had in the Arab countries: they drew people together in secular establishments and induced free and open discourse.

European rulers were no more enchanted with this effect than their counterparts to the south had been, and during the next two centuries made repeated efforts to regulate coffee. In one story, the Roman Catholic Church initially condemned it as a Muslim beverage; Pope Clement VIII, however, upon having a sip, found it so delicious that he decided to baptize the drink instead. King Charles II of England issued a proclamation in 1675 that all coffeehouses were to be closed as "seminaries of sedition," but public outcry was so fierce he was forced to repeal the order before it went into effect. King Gustav III made the drink illegal in Sweden and conducted coffee raids on public houses. Frederick the Great tried to ban it in Prussia, where more money was being spent on imported coffee than domestic beer. He had crews of *Kaffeeschnüfflers* go around and literally try to sniff out any illicit brewing. None of these measures were any good; the public would have its coffee anyway. Smugglers crunched softly and bowleggedly through port towns wearing hip boots packed with beans.

In England, coffeehouses were dubbed penny-universities, because for the admission price of one cent, a person could sit and be edified all day long by scholars, merchants, travelers, community leaders, gossips, and poets. Many coffeehouses also had on hand, for their customers who could read, newspapers, which were as yet quite novel; the whole notion of an un-checked flow of information was a radical one then, at least as stimulating as the caffeine. Everywhere coffee went, unfettered thought and discussion seemed to follow. Everywhere coffee was prohibited, it seemed to stream regardless. But there was one place coffee had yet to reach.

The rulers of Europe, if they could not restrict coffee's consumption in their homelands, decided that at the very least they ought to be able to regulate it in their colonies. And so, as the Arabs had sought to keep the *coffea* plant from ever dipping roots into the soil of their European customers, the Europeans sought to keep it from growing in the New World. Two love affairs foiled their plans.

In 1723, or 1714, or 1717, Gabriel Mathieu de Clieu, a captain of the French infantry stationed in Martinique, was on home leave in Paris. He had a romantic relationship with a woman in the French court, and with her aid and the unlikely collaboration of the royal physician, de Clieu sneaked one night into the hothouse at the Jardin des Plantes and filched three seedlings from a coffee tree that had been a gift to King Louis XIV from the burgomaster of Amsterdam. At the end of his leave, he smuggled the stolen seedlings onto the ship that would carry him back to the Caribbean. The voyage overseas took longer than expected, however; two of the seedlings died of thirst en route; de Clieu shared his own freshwater rations with the third, which survived. In Martinique he hid it among thorn bushes in his garden. Four years later, he gathered from it two pounds of seeds. From this single plant came all the coffee that grows in Central America today.

The other story tells of the Brazilian lieutenant colonel Francisco de Melo Palheta. While traveling in 1722, or 1727, he met and became intimately involved with the wife of French Guiana's governor. At their public parting, in all her gracious diplomacy, she bestowed on him the gift of an immense and elaborate bouquet of flowers. Hidden among the bright petals and fronds were cuttings and seeds of the coffee plant. Back in Brazil, these eventually grew into the hundreds of millions of trees that today are the lion's share of all the coffee on earth.

Historians are ambiguous about whether either lover-robber was in what we call true love with the woman who gave him access to coffee. The versions of history are shaded each a little differently, some proposing a scene of cool-hearted seduction and conquest, others alluding to real tenderness of feeling and sorrow upon parting. In one version, the love affair is painted as being with France, and de Clieu the ultimate patriot in winning his country independence from the high-priced East Indian coffee market. None of the versions happen to let slip either woman's name; if only for want of attention, these must now remain secret. But what rare, imaginative valentines those two women proffered!—so laden with suggestion: the potent seeds yielding and being themselves renewed by creamy white blossoms, dark crimson cherries, which have cycled with the seasons ever since, marking every hour since the lovers parted, like living clocks.

Some of all this is quite possibly true.

· · ·

Roman conquerors, Chinese prisoners of war, Turks jettisoning provisions as they dashed in retreat. Sailors cooking on a beach, hearts mashed up with mulberry bark, a papal blessing issued to a hot, bitter brew. Missing names, conflicting etymologies. Bible stories that never made it into print. Details slosh blithely across the perforated margins of geography and time.

It is an uncommon pleasure when slippage appears in recorded history. Really it is not exasperating or confounding; it is just like clouds shredding apart in the sky, sun glimmering through. All those places where the timeline seems to loop back on itself, to fray or to knot; all those interlocking tesserae that bizarrely do not match, that halt the story, jam it up or leave hollows: they are small gifts, lucid whispers sounding against the deep framework of a larger understory, which is the story of guesses and riddles and yearning, the story of our imperfect groping.

History cancels out history. Fact supplants fiction, and in doing so calls its own certainty into question. Nevertheless: we want it.

The velvet cords get unraveled and replaited. We resume our grip, preferring to guide ourselves with apocrypha than to proceed storyless after all.

Glass

When we say "glass" today, we as often mean something from which to drink as we do the viscous liquid itself, and drinking glasses have a long and symbolic history of their own; they are hubs of social significance. As glass drinking vessels spread through Europe, gradually replacing wooden and ceramic cups and metal goblets, rituals evolved around their use that highlight their communal character. Glasses were things to be shared, passed around like peace pipes, and drinking from them was as much an act of touching lips to a common surface as it was an act of thirst-quenching.

Today we have drifted a step away from this practice; we only clink our glasses together before drinking, symbolically linking the separate cups. Also today the shape of tumblers is tamer than it once was. Ours have flat bottoms that allow them to be set down between sips; older glasses often constituted challenges in their very design. Frankish tumblers had bulb-shaped bottoms, designed literally to tumble over so that they couldn't be put down until drained. Sixteenth-century Venetian glasses were bell-shaped and, similarly, could be rested on a table only upside down. Yard glasses, named for their length, had rounded bottoms, and drinking horns ended in points: both also impossible to set down with liquid contents. Even flat-footed vessels were sometimes converted back to more teetery shapes: at particularly riotous parties of the British court, people snapped the stems right off the glasses in order to ensure that they were emptied in due haste.

Toasting gets its name from the chunk of grilled bread that used to float in the bowl of a drinking glass; after the glass had gone around the room and all guests had a sip, the host was expected to consume the wine-drenched remnant. Once people started to drink from individual cups, however, the toastmaster's burden was lessened. He would use a special glass, blown with slightly thicker sides and bottom, so that he could drain his glass satisfactorily after every toast without becoming too drunk to perform. Later, "firing glasses" became popular for toasts. These had thick, solid feet, meant to create a noise like a volley of musket shots when people banged them on the table in approbation.

All different kinds of glasses were designed, ostensibly for practical purposes, in order best to enhance varied drinks and occasions. Glasses got fashioned with bucket bowls and bell bowls, thistle and drawn-trumpet bowls, mushroom knops and acorn knops, and baluster knops, shaped like pomegranate blossoms. These developed into brandy inhalers and champagne tulips, pony glasses and squall glasses, coupettes and snifters, hocks and balloons, docks and flutes—all so preciously particular. We do love things.

Glass has been prized for its *clink!*, its clarity, its fragility, its faults. Its ring is its panache. A glass sounds not only when struck with another as in a toast, or with a spoon as in summoning attention, but also when its rim is stroked with a damp finger. Glasses filled with different amounts of liquid produce different pitches, which can be coaxed forth in sequence to spell a melody; this instrument is known as the glass harp.

Clarity is glass's ultimate fineness, and also the measure of humans' ability to outdo nature. People struggled for a long time to achieve brilliantly clear, colorless glass. The Bohemians tried adding various amounts of limestone to erase tints from glass, and the Venetians had a colorless glass they called *cristallo,* but a man named George Ravenscroft generally gets credited with alighting upon the proper recipe for truly clear, colorless "lead-crystal" glass, in 1675 in London. He patented it straightaway. Actually, color—amethyst, amber, ruby, cobalt, smoky-brown, milky-white, and green—as well as elaborate etching, continued to be popular in wineglasses throughout the Victorian era, largely because it did a splendid job of disguising the murkiness of inferior wines, and whatever else of a dubious nature might be swirling around in a person's drink. But aesthetes since then have agreed that the ideal glass features nothing more elaborate than simple lines and utter, aseptic, pristine clarity.

Fragility is glass's great asset. Because it is ephemeral, even the humblest factory-made tumbler retains in a way its singularity, its poignancy. Over the centuries, scientists have developed ways to make glass much more lasting, durable, even malleable. Today glass can be made to withstand a drop of several yards onto a concrete floor, drastic changes in temperature, even bullets. But we continue to favor drinking vessels molded of the more delicate stuff, the slender, tendrilly, light-bending stuff that goes to pieces if set down too hard in the kitchen sink. Since the 1700s this quality has been celebrated in the custom of smashing a glass against the floor or fireplace after a toast, so that the same glass may never be used again, to drink to another occasion, thereby diminishing the glory of the first. In its destruction its prestige is sealed.

Faults are glass's sweetest mystery, its most bewitching charm, whether serving to fix a piece of glass to a point in history or simply showing off its knack for disobeying what seem like rules of nature. Crizzling is a disease of glass that causes the lead oxide in it to become opaque over time. It occurred only in glass made during the five-year period between the invention of lead crystal and the time George Ravenscroft got his proportions quite right; crizzled glass is coveted among collectors today. A seed or a tear (pronounced to rhyme with pear) is what glassmakers call an air bubble locked into a finished piece of glass. This, too, is an imperfection, and makers have tried all sorts of things to get rid of tears, including, at one time, dropping a potato into the molten batch (the idea being that the potato, releasing steam as the heat consumed it, freed any gas trapped in the batch as well). But tears also pose a kind of visual paradox. The swirls of oxygen imprisoned in stiff liquid casing have a strange, magnetic beauty, and are frequently blown into glass on purpose. Glass's shiftiness is yet another flaw: old windowpanes go wavy and must be replaced—and this failing has its allure, too. Moving your head to and fro, watching the world beyond such a pane waffle and warp, you experience at once the effects of time's passage and evidence of glass's improbable feats.

Humans have keyed into glass's evocative powers at least as much as its practical ones. We've wondered at it in its spiritual forms: as stained-glass religious narratives, as protective amulets, as fortune-telling crystal balls, as the hollow, spotted, Nailsea witch balls that the people of western England once hung in their cottage windows to protect themselves from evil spells. Nor have humans been naïve about the prospect of harnessing this mysterious quality commercially, a notion the English were quick to exploit in their efforts to colonize the New World.

On the very first Jamestown venture, in 1607, the London Company sent along eight Dutch and Polish glassworkers. These men set up what is considered

America's first manufacturing concern—a glasshouse built about a mile outside the main settlement, in the woods. Some people say such a location was chosen so that if the glasshouse caught fire, it wouldn't destroy the settlers' quarters. Others say this is rubbish, that positioning a potential fire hazard smack in the middle of acres of fuel and far from any help was hardly a logical safety precaution. They say the glasshouse was tucked away like that for no sake but secrecy's.

It is true that what the glassmakers were making inside that house in the Virginia woods, besides some bottles and flasks and chunks of thick, turbid window glass, were beads. And it is true that those beads were used in trade with the people the settlers referred to as Indians, and that those Indians were willing to exchange warm, heavy animal skins and furs and beans and turkeys for those little glass beads, as if they were somehow useful, of inherent value; as if the beads were good solvent currency. And also it is true that the glassworkers had instructions not to let the Indians know where those beads came from or how they were made, and also to be careful not to produce too many of those beads lest, in their abundance, their value fade.

Glassmaking remained quite a rare and coveted skill; as late as the end of the nineteenth century, most of America's glassmakers still had to be wooed away from Germany, Italy, France, Belgium, and England with paid passage across the Atlantic and competitive wages once they arrived. Records from companies throughout the 1800s show as much as fifty percent of gross income going to wages, and glassmakers continued to be reluctant about imparting their skill to others, so that new workers had continually to be hired from abroad. Competition for labor was so fierce among the American glasshouses that sometimes, after one company had arranged and paid for a European worker to sail here, another company would step in at the docks and entice that worker elsewhere. Employers shamelessly recruited other workers directly from within the competition's glasshouses, causing their rivals to fume and overall pay scales to surge. Labor within the glasshouse was divided into specialized skills: blowers, finishers, flatteners, and pressers all made good money compared to that made by other skilled craftsmen of the day—painters, furniture carvers, blacksmiths, cabinetmakers, leather cutters, machinists, cutlery forgers—and their wages were as much as three times those of ordinary laborers. Gatherers and casters earned somewhat less than other glassworkers, but all profited by association with the glasshouse cachet.

Through the end of the century it worked this way, with fathers passing glasshouses to sons, keeping the chain of knowledge narrow and tight, the cherished secrets intact. Sameness prevailed over innovation. Few newcomers tried to enter the industry; glassworkers had done a good job of making their world inaccessible by cultivating the impression that only those with the right experience, if not actually the right genes, could manufacture glass successfully. Within the glasshouses, too, experimentation tended to be scant and superficial, for a radical innovation might pose a challenge to the old, guarded techniques, and in turn blow apart the notion that the secret of glass lay beyond the reach of outsiders.

Glass was used quite commonly by then, in kitchens and windows, for kerosene and then electric lights, for spectacles and medicine vials; and yet it had managed to keep its ability to enchant. Victorian ladies carried suitably ethereal glass eggs to cool their palms while dancing or being wooed. People collected such glass confections as millefiori paperweights and tiny, translucent, colored miniatures—animals, trumpets, umbrellas, bells, walking sticks and bowler hats, village pumps with little matching glass buckets. At the 1892 Chicago World's Fair, an exhibition factory set up by the Libbey Company drew crowds. Visitors watched demonstrations of glass being blown, and each received a little glass bow on the end of a stickpin. Also on display was a dress made entirely of spun glass, which so captivated one visitor, Eulalie, the Princess of Spain, that she asked for a copy to be made for herself. Much was made of the Spanish infanta's spun-glass gown; all around the country word spread of the glass pavilion at the World's Fair; sales soared. Glass seemed to be spanning and transcending the world of mass production and use, as well as the world of inimitable beauty and delight.

Then came the machines. They had already been around for some time, semiautomatic machines, hand-fed machines, machines that produced only the clunkiest, most basic wares, but even these relied on skilled workers guiding and tending the gathers of molten glass as they got pressed or blown into molds. So by the turn of the century, the blowpipe, which had been invented two or three or four or five millennia earlier, was still the indispensable tool, and the lungs and lips and inclinations of human workers still the means of plying that tool. But then came machines, bit by bit, and they were the nemesis of the skilled glassworker.

The workers, in sorry tribute to their once-privileged status, were being increasingly subjected to the advancing demands of industry and the difficult working conditions it imposed. During most of the nineteenth century, it was customary for glassworkers to put in ten-hour days, six days a week, in factories that had little ventilation and little light save the raging orange eyes of the furnaces. Employees often lived in company-owned, employer-dominated villages, and until the late 1800s were customarily paid in scrip, which could be redeemed only at a company store. Unions and brotherhoods of glassworkers came together, and subsequently dissolved, until 1878, when the American Flint Glass Workers' Union of North America formed. It has lasted to this day, but its present members bear not a lot of resemblance to their ancestors in terms of the actual chores they perform. By the time the AFGWU took hold, it was already too late to preserve or reinstate the old prestige of the glassworker, the intricate, intimate tasks of mixing and gathering, handling and blowing, the old rare art.

Machines were edging in, slowly but surely rendering the old expertise obsolete. The union members— skilled artisans, descendants of the only manual laborers who had once been allowed to marry daughters of the nobility, descendants of émigrés who had been courted and wooed across the sea by glasshouse owners, who had earned twice and thrice the wages of ordinary laborers, who had spun a glass dress for a Spanish infanta—resisted at first, refusing to use the new technology. But their secrets had been passed from human brains to machines, and these machines did not require their hands. They would chug on regardless of whose hands operated them, just as time would chug on and proceed methodically into the new century, where machines that conserved ever more time were invented, shaving man-hours off production and converting that time into more dollars. They came bearing names like the Three-man, Two-boy machine, which yielded to the Two-man, Two-boy machine, and after a while the One-man, One-boy and the One-man, No-boy. No one concerned could fail to guess where this was leading, and in 1917 a new machine for making bottles was introduced; it was called, with doleful simplicity, the No-boy.

Paper

When we say "paper" today, we as often mean newspaper as any other kind. Newspapers have existed in some fashion at least as far back as the first century A.D., when Romans posted public "news sheets," although the hunger for and tradition of circulating news certainly predates both paper and writing, if not language itself. Historically, trade appears to have acted as the sort of host-body for news, the vehicle through which it spread; and in this model, trade was clearly the primary goal, and the conveyance of news a mere by-product. The yams or shell necklaces or skins or guns or rum or tulip bulbs were the commodities, the items of value, the motive for the trip; any information that got passed along in the process was incidental to the endeavor. But the ritualistic customs of hospitality embedded in ancient cultures tell something else of news's value, the peculiar nature of which is that it exists only in exchange, only in the sharing, gratifying both giver and receiver in its transmission.

In fairy tales, again and again, the travel-weary stranger must be welcomed in, must be given bread and wine and a place by the hearth. Slowly, the stranger's hair dries; the ratty cloak is shed; color is restored to cheek and brow. The stranger is a deity, or a prince, or a sage. Reward then flows from the stranger's pockets or lips; kindness is returned with gold, silks, magic, news. The stranger sits up all night by the flickering fire and in verse requites the hospitality bestowed. In myths, parables, fables, folklore, this story recurs with the quiet fervency of a prayer.

The longing for news is the longing for true stories, for interlocking images that will connect up in huge, vivid portraiture, that will shed their cumulative light on our world so that we may more perfectly understand what it is to live in it. Or it is a longing for community, for solidarity, consensus on what we all agree to know, so that we may proceed with one another from a common conception, speak the same language, be less lonely. Or it is a longing for power—but this aspect of news can result only from its rationing, from the careful apportioning or guarding, the withholding or distorting of news; in this realm, news may be bought and sold and bargained with. But here it crosses the border into commodity; here it ceases to be news, exactly, and transforms itself into secrets. News itself has traditionally been free, not measurable according to units of price and property.

Before the development of paper and printing, news was passed orally. It was passed along at wells, coffeehouses, docks, markets, any place people came together. Societies created specific roles for their messengers: bards in India, griots in Africa, criers in

Vietnam, Gypsy musicians in Morocco, and royal her-
alds in Europe all carried word of happenings and
events. Whoever had control over messengers could
have a certain amount of power over the dissemination
of news, but unlike silver or rice or even water, news
was difficult to monitor and contain; its spread at some
level was virtually uncheckable. Which is not to say
that it was easy. Some Native American tribes had ceremonial runners who literally spent each spring and
fall running from community to community, circulating news of deaths and births, food supply and weather
conditions, tribal councils and treaties.

Why were they called ceremonial runners when the
purpose they filled was so plainly practical? It was
practical, but it also satisfied a more spiritual craving.
In the middle of the nineteenth century, the last sur-
viving ceremonial runner of the Fox nation in the Midwest is said to have warned his people about what life
would be like without him. "You will have no one,"
he cautioned, "who will go about telling anything that
happened to you." In this he made clear what we each
already know to be true: that the issuance of information about ourselves is at least as dear to us as is learning the news of others. News has always been a circle,
since the days it revolved around us as we gathered
water from the well, and we are drawn to that circle
still, in our longing to give as well as receive.

Lots of the early printed newspapers, which began
to appear on a regular basis in Europe at the beginning
of the seventeenth century, had names harking back to
earlier newsbearers: *Herald* and *Mercury* and *Messenger*.
Other newspapers would bear the names of celestial
time-markers, those fat cogs whose revolutions seemed

to pave the way for news to occur, for history to accrue: *Sun, Evening Star, Planet, Globe.* The early papers' spawning was chiefly the result of trade and economy, but they were perceived by rulers as symbols and vehicles of political agitation. Production and circulation were not as voluminous as they would later become; men would gather to read the news in the coffeehouses, many of which subscribed to all the available papers. So even after the principal method of communicating the news switched from spoken to written, the relating and ingesting of it still, for a time, occurred in public and communally. Women were as a rule not allowed in these venues, these "penny-universities," or "seminaries of sedition," depending on your point of view and what you had to gain or lose. But if they were barred from the process of directly consuming the news, they played an instrumental role in its dissemination.

All the early newspapers were printed on sheets of cloth fiber; they were called rags not derogatorily, but descriptively. It was typically the women upon whom the manufacturers relied to supply them with old clothes, moth-eaten sheets, and threadbare curtains, which they then rent and beat into papermaking pulp. Publishers sent bell carts through cities to collect rags; paper mills paid a few pence or shillings or cents for every pound of rags donated; newspapers printed pleas for rags. In 1666, England issued a decree that forbade burying the dead in garments of linen and cotton; in this manner the country was able to save two hundred thousand pounds of good papermaking rags annually. In America at that time, regular newspapers did not yet exist (the first, a weekly called the *Boston News-*

Letter, appeared in 1704), but within the century the shortage would be felt keenly here as well. In what may have been the primogenitor of subliminal advertising, one Massachusetts paper mill in 1799 watermarked every sheet it produced with the shadowy exhortation "SAVE RAGS."

Publishers crammed as much news as they possibly could onto each page, squeezing printed matter into the margins, and going up sideways, and upside down. They pasted torn sheets back together. They threw straw into the mix, and water lilies and turnips. The pages they produced came out brown or gray, and mottled; no methods of bleaching were yet known. In wartime, shortages got even worse. Generals were hard put to find even scratch paper on which to send their dispatches; they ripped blank sheets from old ledgers, flyleaves from books. Soldiers tore up Bibles and hymnals for cartridge paper; they wrapped their shot in parable and prayer. All the while, all around them in hot summer air, wasps buzzed ripely, dancing out a rebus, as they built their ancient, conical gray paper nests.

People didn't see them, though. Perhaps they saw, but no connection was made, nothing clicked or was apprehended—not, however, for want of industry or imagination; throughout this period, experiments grew ever more far-reaching and bizarre. During the Civil War, at least one papermaker, a man named I. Augustus Stanwood, grew so desperate for raw materials that he was inspired to ship mummies from Egypt to his mill in Gardiner, Maine. These he stripped and pulped in order to make a rather coarse brown wrapping paper, which was used by grocers and butchers to package their goods. Besides their wrappings, the mummies brought with them aromatic gums and residues left over from their embalming—among them olibanum, labdanum, issoponax, and ambergris—materials that were used in preparing incense for the Catholic Church. They also brought cholera; an epidemic broke out among the mill workers in the mid-1850s. Besides his workers' health, the only cost to Stanwood for purchasing and transporting the mummies was three cents a pound. If his materialism was depraved, it was not without precedent; mummies had been turned into paper in twelfth-century Baghdad. As for Stanwood's peers, not only does history allude to other American manufacturers dabbling in mummy paper about the same time, but the national Egyptian railroad itself had, for a decade, been using its nation's mummified ancestors as fuel for its steam-powered locomotives.

It was 1840, more than a hundred years after Réaumur had pitched his notion to the French Royal Academy, when a German named Friedrich Gottlob Keller invented a machine that defibered blocks of wood against a wet, revolving grindstone, and turned the resulting sodden mass into paper. Another twenty-eight years passed before the United States produced its first wood-pulp newspaper: a single issue of New York's German-language paper *Staats-Zeitung*. And not until the 1880s did groundwood paper become the standard stuff upon which to print the news.

Wood changed the nature of paper, not only compositionally but in terms of how people would regard it evermore. The groundwood process evolved right at the moment when people in Europe and the New World were enjoying a sort of lover's crush on the material; paper had finally come into its own in the Occident the way it had centuries earlier in the Orient—only here, people's appreciation had a giddy, sprawling largeness about it. It was as though the same impulse that had moved the Chinese to make their spirit paper effigies had at last hit people in the West, but with the blunt force of a mallet: this time the impulse got translated with literal fervor. The middle and late nineteenth century, then, saw paper collars, cuffs, and dickeys; paper waistcoats, bonnets, aprons, and hats; paper curtains, carpets, boxes, buckets, cuspidors, barrels, and roofs. During this period people were busy developing and securing patents for transparent paper, square-bottomed paper bags, lace-embossed paper, corrugated paper, paper twine, and manila paper. Young ladies learned to make curled "paper work" decorations; this involved rolling thin strips of paper, gluing them end-on in pattern to the piece being worked, almost like embroidery, then gilding or painting the edges and covering the whole work with glass. And a London music hall in 1870 featured a number entitled "The Age of Paper," sung by a man in a paper suit.

Wood made paper at once more available and less refined. Wood-pulp paper is literally less fine; it's less durable, yellows, and grows brittle more hurriedly than cloth-fiber paper, so that even today the preferred medium for important documents and fancy correspondence is paper with some, if not total, rag content. News, on the other hand, is the ideal commodity to make use of that humblest of wood-pulp papers—its namesake, newsprint. Durability is a moot point in regard to news, which has by definition a dizzyingly short shelf life. In the case of a daily paper with several editions, an individual newspaper may be worth the price printed on its cover for six hours—or three, or two. But during that time, during its brief window of relevance, that paper is a best-seller linking together an entire community, uniting it in knowledge and deed. It will be the only thing in common, besides perhaps the sky, that all members of that daylong paper-reading community will rest their eyes upon, the only common thing they will all pass between their fingertips; and when the day is finished and the sky is pitch, all those papers will be discarded—lying along curbs, stacked in piles by back doors, left spread out and mangled on couches and under coffee tables: expired.

With the advent of wood pulp, newspapers quit imploring their customers to "SAVE RAGS." Their materials would no longer be supplied by women sorting out their family closets, their baskets of mending and scraps. The raw ingredients were never again to include people's tattered old bedsheets and petticoats and mobcaps and antimacassars and diapers and bandages and handkerchiefs, the refuse of ordinary human society. The papers turned their needs over, instead, to the lumberjacks: those crews of thick-muscled, unshaven, half-mysterious men who spent so much of their lives apart from civilization, holed up in rough-hewn, kerosene-lit bunks in the woods, who spit tobacco juice and cussed and danced, and who spun legends of a giant with a blue ox when they weren't out felling and dodging the massive, mighty columns of trees. From now on, newspapers' raw ingredients would comprise only spruce, only fir, only pine: the soft conifer woods that grew so tall and abundant in forests across the land.

Beans

Coffee, coffee bars, coffeehouses, coffee breaks, coffee consciousness, coffee prices, coffee carts, coffee seminars, coffee grinders, coffee klatches, coffee chains, coffee journals, coffee 'zines—it is, in ludicrous understatement, ubiquitous today, this little bean, this little bitter, jolting, wrinkled brown heart of the cherry, gonad of the plant that grows within the fat belt of earth stretching twenty degrees north and twenty degrees south of the equator. Over the past several years a spate of books and articles about the beverage has cascaded into print; in cities and villages across the nation, cafés replicate themselves like frenzied strands of DNA; corner stores vend macadamia nut cappuccinos and Creamsicle lattes; coffee gets roasted in the service of new blends with such fancy handles as Intermezzo, Dancing Goats, The Kid from Brooklyn; ordinary citizens stock espresso machines, milk steamers, French presses, and electric mini-grinders in their kitchens. The bean is in the grip of a new guise.

People have, of course, gone pie-eyed in the past over various incarnations of coffee—fearful as well as fond. It has been called the devil's drink, the liquor of infidels, puddle water, a poison that God made black. Women, prohibited from participation in coffeehouse society (except as the occasional serving wench), petitioned in England for coffee's prohibition, and in France they argued that coffee made men sterile. For a long time men and women in many different cultures felt pretty sure that mixing milk with coffee would lead to leprosy.

More often, though, coffee has been favored, adored. In eighteenth-century France, in celebration of the drink and its "feminine charms," members of the royal court drank coffee out of cups that were modeled after Marie Antoinette's breasts; so accurately were they sculpted that each one required a tripod of little porcelain legs to hold the nipple up off the tabletop. People have used it as currency in many lands, from Africa to Arabia to America, with a particular number of beans equal to one birr, or asper, or dollar; and the gerah, an ancient coin and unit of measure, gets its name from the Hebrew word for bean. People have offered coffee to gods and to the dead, by trickling some of the brew over a fire so that its vapor may ascend. People have used it for divination; in England and Greece and Germany women have read coffee grounds, as tea leaves, left in the bottom of a cup.

As for those coffee valentines via which the plant got smuggled to the New World, they multiplied quickly, and coffee's adoration spread. Within fifty years of de Clieu's introduction of a single plant into Martinique, more than eighteen million coffee trees were growing in that country alone. The bean scattered from there to Haiti, Tahiti, Cuba, Jamaica, Puerto Rico, Venezuela, and from these places continued on into nearly every South and Central American country. Today this region—where the plant is really just a baby, in the vast scope of earth's time still so relatively new and foreign to the soil—produces by far the largest part of the world's coffee crop. At the northernmost tip of this great coffee territory lies Mexico. The plant first arrived here between 1740 and 1744, but organized production and cultivation didn't commence until the turn of the next century, and coffee didn't become a significant commercial export until 1870. Mexico is today the world's fourth-largest coffee-producing nation. Its entire harvest's lineage can be traced all the way back to the Jardin des Plantes, and therefore to the Dutch plantations on Java, and the pilgrim from Karnataka, and Yemen and Ethiopia and the goatherd or plumed bird or angel Gabriel.

Coffee was introduced to North America in the early days of its colonization. It might possibly have reached these shores as early as the first Jamestown venture; Captain John Smith would anyway have known of coffee from his Turkish travels. Some have suggested it came over on the *Mayflower* a few years later; that ship's cargo list includes a wooden mortar and pestle of the sort used for pulverizing roasted beans into what people then referred to as coffee powder. It was most definitely present by 1664, when the British got hold of New Amsterdam from the Dutch; an account written a few years later mentions that coffee had replaced beer as New York's favorite breakfast drink.

The coffeehouse tradition soon caught on in this country as well; the first, called The London, opened for business in Boston in 1689. But coffeehouses here acquired a different, distinctively American flavor, which is to say more hodgepodge, if not necessarily more egalitarian. The establishments tended to specialize less; different coffeehouses didn't cater so much to particular crowds of artists and intelligentsia. They functioned in a more motley fashion. They served tea, chocolate, wine, ale, and applejack as well as coffee. Their functions included letting rooms to travelers, conducting votes by ballot, collecting and giving out mail, acting as lost-and-found offices, serving as assembly rooms for court trials and council meetings, even granting marriage licenses. And they drew noblemen, dissidents, loyalists, governors, redcoats, conspirators, merchants, and rogues all. Women still were not allowed as patrons, but many of the coffeehouses had female proprietors, the whole hostelry side of the business coinciding appropriately, in people's minds, with images of domesticity and nurturance.

In addition to all of this, coffeehouses make the bold claim of having played a direct role in the creation of the United States. The Green Dragon, in Boston, was the site of so many important planning meetings that Daniel Webster dubbed it the headquarters of the American Revolution, and the idea for the Boston Tea Party is supposed to have been cooked up in that venue. After which event, coffee became the beverage of patriots, and both the French and Dutch capitalized on that new image—and loaded their political eggs into one basket—by arranging to ship beans to the colonies at bargain prices. Another Boston coffeehouse, The Bunch of Grapes, was the site of the first public reading of the Declaration of Independence. In New York the Merchants Coffeehouse became the de facto headquarters of the new government immediately after the Revolution began, and President Washington met with the governor and mayor there in 1789. As its name suggests, the Merchants served also as a center of commerce. The Bank of New York was planned there in 1784, and in 1790 brokers first sold stocks there. Its rival, the Tontine Coffee House, built in 1793 at the northwest corner of Wall and William streets, was really something of a private club, in that it sold shares to members; in addition to sponsoring grand banquets and balls, the Tontine served as the original abode of the New York Stock Exchange.

As America bullied and bought and sneaked its borders south and west and north, swallowing up land and people through annexation and immigration, coffee spread runner roots through the country's history. When Florida joined the Union, it was already a state of coffee drinkers that had been importing the bean from Cuba. Similarly, the Louisiana Purchase brought to the nation whole towns of dedicated French coffee drinkers, scattered along the banks of the Mississippi. European immigrants brought with them their own deeply embedded coffee-drinking traditions. Soldiers in the Mexican and Civil wars carried coffee as part of their military rations, receiving, by one account, ten pounds of coffee for every hundred pounds of food. Pioneers frontier-bound in wagon trains and prospectors seeking gold all brought coffee beans west with them, both to brew and to trade with Indians. And everybody knows the cowboys liked their coffee strong: six-shooter strong, they liked to say, belly wash, brown gargle. They drank it black or with "lick" (molasses), after boiling grounds in water over an open fire for a good thirty minutes or so.

The industrial revolution shook loose any remaining vestiges of coffee's exclusivity. For the sake of productivity, the mantel of luxury was removed, the spell undone. Now, much as it had once let Sufis and dervishes pray and whirl through the night that they might move closer to God, coffee helped enable men and women and children to work ten- and twelve- and eighteen-hour shifts in factories and foundries and sweatshops. The demand for cheap, abundant coffee grew, and led to creative adulteration. Preroasted coffee was coated with a sugar-and-egg-white preservative for nationwide distribution. Coffee had for ages been blended with cheaper additives or replaced altogether when it was scarce (blends and proxies have included chicory, dried figs and peas, dandelion root, brown bread crusts, acorns, plum pits, sawdust, mill sweepings, dried ox blood and horse liver)—but early-twentieth-century America probably takes the cake for lack of epicurean regard for the drink, not so much because we stumbled upon new, more appalling additives, but simply because the specialness with which everyone since ancient times had apparently viewed the bean was now trampled, spent. Not until just recently has this regard been shrewdly lacquered, like a flavoring oil, back over the bean, with the specialty coffee industry quite unblushingly reeducating consumers as to what we ought to think of when we say coffee.

For most of the twentieth century in the United States, we remained preoccupied with mass consumption and mass production; we learned to freeze-dry and vacuum-pack, decaffeinate, and produce coffee in soluble, "instant" flakes. We bought robusta beans (cheaper and harsher than the higher-grown arabica) and overbrewed them in fashionable new percolators, so the liquid turned bitter and turbid. By extraordinary coincidence, we all began to receive our coffee from a single smiling, avuncular, mustachioed man, forever strolling complaisantly among coffee trees with his trusty donkey, at the same time that the large plantation system was in fact crushing many of the old family farms a continent to the south.

The potable that had been blessed by a Pope and sipped from porcelain replicas of a French queen's breasts became the lowly cuppa joe, imbibed by ho-boes at back doors and by paper-pushing suits; taken, as aspirin, for function rather than fulfillment; swilled from Styrofoam cups, stirred with plastic rods, light-ened with powdered, perfunctory approximations of cream, sweetened with similarly simulated sugar. It be-came the beverage of the cross-examination room; of the trucker, the junkie, the insomniac, the homeless; of the stakeout, the hangover, the vending machine, the queue. It was not that the rituals had gone from coffee but that they had shifted once more.

Here is Father Time, beard to his knees, pate pink as a baby's, carrying like a lantern a curvaceous glass of sand. His names are Cronus, Geras, Saturn, and Kalpa. Sometimes he dangles a pendulum. Sometimes he leans on a staff, which is a reaping hook, which is a scythe. Sometimes he becomes a huge beast with the head of a lion and a black, gaping mouth: he is the devourer of all things. Sometimes he stoops to help Truth out of a cave: in time all things come to light. Here are his granddaughters, sisters of the seasons, the impassive Fates—Clotho, who spins; Lachesis, who measures; and Atropos, who snips the thread of destiny: in time all things come to an end.

The great lesson of history, people say, is that it repeats. Look to the almanac, study the past, recognize the cycle when it comes round again.

No: the great lesson of history, others say, is how not to repeat it. Learn well the past, consume the apple, move forward altered.

Whatever its lesson, it has molded all we know, as surely as rivers lick rocks into eggs. What we think of as a line of time has rubbed and nudged and polished glass, shaped paper, contoured beans. Stories have given way to stories, secrets cracked open to hatch new secrets. The secrets, especially, we have been careful to maintain; when one comes undone, we replace it. This is as true today as it was in the beginning. The early secrets of glass and paper and beans are potent no longer; any inquisitive child may uncover the fact that glass is made of the very stuff of sandbox or seashore; that real paper may be fashioned at home with various chopped-up plants and a kit bought at a crafts store; that coffee comes of course from beans and is good to smell and to feel through the walls of a mug on a chilly morning. But there are other details, other passages within the story, which the child may not learn, and which we may not learn: which are kept hidden and forbidden, still. For secrets have power. History has shown that this knowledge has always been there in us, shored up in our canny human hearts, braided into the story of everything.

*Pl*ace

In the library I discover the atlas. I am eight, waiting for my mother, who is wandering somewhere in the grown-up section, among the tall, hushed stacks. This is the dull part of the library. The stories in this room, dense as a forest, are unintelligible, uninviting, and I am on my way to becoming irritable when I notice it there for the first time: the atlas perched on a wooden stand, giant, spread open.

Edible-looking colors draw me in. On tiptoe I press close to the page and travel my eyes across it, sipping at the vast blue, which grows lacy and pale at the fringe of landmasses. These, veined with rivers, crusted with mountains, are pink-orange, watery grape, green, sienna. I pretend to taste that one and that one and that one; furtively, I bend and touch my tongue for a second to the page.

There are tiny circles and dots with words by them; my eyes are so close to the page the letters blur; I skim over them; I am an airplane buzzing the towns and villages that these dots are. They are real, not imaginary. I find my own. I cover this dot with my finger. Now I am contained under my own finger; my finger is making a shadow over the town.

I look out the window: clouds. I lift my finger from the page: sun. Not really, this is what I pretend. But maybe. Light and shadow are alternating against the windowpane. Maybe in the Outer Hebrides or in Nova Zembla somebody else's finger is passing over my town's dot.

I turn more pages of the atlas: more colors, veins, and crusts. Someone has inked all these outlines, colored in all these shapes. Someone knows about all these places; now I do, too. It's the places very high that draw me, and the ones very low, the tiny ones scattered at the periphery, and the wonder of them all having names and being remembered, included, assigned their own hues.

The names make me marvel. Eriskay. Færøerne. Dogger Bank. Knyszyn. Zalaegerszeg. Sikaripara. Qala-i-Jadid. Flin Flon. They are like the names I made up for my very earliest dolls.

There are people at this moment living in each dot, washing hands, falling asleep, eating soup, waiting for mothers. They don't know me but I am thinking of them now, of a child my own age in Silchar (peach) and one in Medicine Hat (magenta), and I greet them each with a silent, brief message: *Hi,* which I transmit by touching my finger to the spots where they are. It seems to me that later we will all be meeting up.

T h r e e

W_{ork}

Brent

He reaches his stumpage ground this morning before sunup, pulls onto the shoulder of the main road just past Four Corners, and shuts the engine. The road, the soil, the snow, the door of the half-ton as he slams it, his own fingers, even—all feel brittle, unyielding, in the frosty air. Grampy Boyd, in recalling his "old-time lumberjack" days, when the men would build camps in the forest and live there all winter, likes to tell how every morning before washing up they'd have to punch through the rind of ice that had formed a seal overnight on the pail of wash water. The earth itself sort of feels like that this morning, its viscera locked away under a skin of cold. Brent's boots punch through crusts of icy snow as he heads toward the black spruce swale.

Stars still glitter overhead, and a smidgen of moon helps light his walk, carves a silver path down the short, tire-gouged slope that connects the highway to the swale. The tire gouges are chiefly from Howard Boyd's rig, a purple-cabbed twenty-two-wheel logging truck. Howard, Brent's father, collects Brent's cut logs and delivers them to mill, whichever mill Brent has contracted with for a given piece of stumpage, sometimes Irving's operation up in Chipman, or Juniper Lumber, or Trevor Macmillan's little local mill, which he likes to support, right over in Belleisle. Brent prefers not to send his lumber south of the border, because it takes jobs out of the province, but sometimes price differences compel him to sell it down in Maine, to Georgia Pacific outside of Calais, or to the spoolwood mill by Moosehead Lake. Depending on how far away the mill, Howard delivers two or three loads a day. Right now, with March thaw threatening to turn the roads to mush any minute, Howard's jaunts are quite piddling, just a skip down the road to Irving's Sussex operation. Year round, Howard hauls loads for other loggers, too, as many as can keep him busy; he gets famously bored whenever he's not trucking. Even during the imposed hiatus when logging operations are halted, he'll get out his smaller rig and haul road salt, gravel, anything someone wants moved from one place to another.

Entering the swale, Brent threads among the rushes and low, tangly bushes he calls hardhacks, aiming for the spot where he left the harvester last night. Right now, walking is easy, the frozen ground supporting his substantial mass securely, and he is well accustomed to navigating the bushy knots of felled boughs and tree stumps the harvester leaves in its wake. He passes first the dormant hulk of the porter, the larger and heavier of the two woods machines, its boom arm and clam grip all folded and tucked in upon itself now, like the wings and beak of a sleeping bird. Dave, his employee—or, as Brent would put it, the guy who runs the porter for him—works six-thirty to three-thirty; he won't arrive for a half hour yet.

A touch farther back, parked where the tree line meets the clear-cut, the harvester rests on its six giant tires. The front two on either side are linked together with metal track and come up to Brent's chest. He scales them, using the metal treads as steps, in order to climb up into the cab. First thing he does each morning, after he's started the engine idling, is to go over the entire drive wheel and boom with a grease gun, pumping grease into each of two or three dozen metal nipples. Brent has ample light to see what he's doing: the harvester, equipped with twenty-four halogen work lights, is designed, as the marketing material says, to give about the same amount of illumination in the dark forest as would light a typical office. Where once Grampy Boyd might've offered water and oats to his team of horses, then hitched them up for a day of forest work, Brent now perches out on a tire, grooming, as it were, this metal creature.

He's careful not to get more of the black hydraulic oil on his bare hands than he can avoid, for somehow that's the worst, the most biting cold he knows. He'd rather stick his hand in a snowbank, in icy water, than get it coated with that oil in the wintertime: the slick stuff seems to clamp on his skin, bite in with mean, icicle-sharp teeth. And it spreads. Of course, a morning like this one is mild to Brent; only a month ago temperatures were dipping regularly to twenty and thirty and forty below. Only a month ago this swale would've been frozen solid, a piece of cake to maneuver around, a cinch to harvest. Now it's loosening, with every day a new pool of liquid gazing limpidly up through the snowy marsh, and an ever-frequent dripping sound, quiet and dainty and all through the trees and grasses, like hundreds of tiny tongues steadily lapping at the edges of winter.

Back in the cab, then, with both the heater and radio broadcasting, Brent gets right to work. The way he operates the harvester is so subtle and smooth it seems impossible that the snapping off and processing of trees, occurring on such a grand rhythmic scale just beyond the glass, could be a result of the barely perceptible manipulations of joystick and push button at the end of Brent's arms. Sweat would be seemly, and panting, and great exertions of muscle commensurate with the wreckage of such tall and thriving organisms. But there is only a low, steady jostling inside the cab as the body of the harvester responds to the actions of its extremities, accompanied by the coziness of the heater warming up the glass bubble, and the calm, erudite voices of Canadian Broadcasting Company reporters talking thoughtfully about people and stories from all over the world.

Sealed there high in his bubble, his hands linked to the trees they fell by clean, efficient buttons and levers, Brent is not unmindful of the controversies and paradoxes attached to his occupation. Indeed, he understands them better than most. He knows that some of the feeling against what he does is based on ignorance about the distinctions among different types of forestry work; that, for example, logging on the West Coast, where many trees have the genetic capacity to grow for hundreds of years, calls into question different issues than logging on the East Coast, where the natural life span of the forest is only sixty, maybe seventy, years. For the most part, the types of tree that grow out here fall susceptible to disease, or insect, or wind, or forest fire by then; even in the absence of a single ax, the East Coast forests would be continually dying and regenerating themselves at a fairly steady clip. East Coast logging therefore does not involve the same emotional stake as does West Coast logging, where trees are literally chopped down in their prime, where something "natural" is routinely interrupted, suppressed. Also, the West has forestry-related slope and erosion problems, unlike the terrain out here. But a lot of people, Brent knows, are quick to paint all logging operations with a single, tarry brush.

On the other hand, he's equally aware of all kinds of flaws and failings that do exist in his own work. Even given the most optimal conditions—a landowner who lets him harvest selectively, thereby improving the genetic stock of the forest while leaving most of the trees still standing; and his state-of-the-art machine, which does less damage to the forest than the massive old feller-bunchers—even then he's doing damage. Lithesome as it is, the harvester is incapable of actually floating through the forest, or threading past trees and bushes without leaving a mark. Even in a selective harvest, some clear-cutting goes on: everything within the path of the machine must come down, with the soil beneath getting compacted to some degree. And even if Brent were to wave a wand and render the harvester weightless, or if he were to jettison the harvester altogether, revert to the old ways and trod on the forest floor with his own boots only, no more than an ax and saw by his side, still he would not counter all the negative effects of his work, simply because when a tree dies of its own accord, it does not generally vanish from the forest floor, magically transported to mill, but remains, to rot and reenter the soil, and in the interim to provide nesting grounds and nourishment to all manner of wildlife, from lichens to insects to rodents to moose.

The nostalgic image of old-time lumberjacks working in perfect concordance with nature is a bit of romantic folly, in any case. When people from England and France and Ireland and Scotland first settled this land, less than three centuries ago, the forests appeared as abundant as the oceans they had just crossed, and equally fearsome and untamed. They harbored all manner of wild animal—caribou, wolf, bear, sable, mink, lynx, cougar—and grew so thick people referred to them as the poor man's overcoat, for in a winter storm you could huddle deep in a thicket and find respite there from slashing winds. So no one gave any thought to such notions as stewardship, silviculture, or sustainability. No one fussed over things like the watershed, or particular species of songbird or fungus, or the ratio of softwood to deciduous trees. Everything wild was plentiful: land, berries, game, fish— people liked to say the salmon were so copious you could cross the Kennebecasis River on their backs.

In those early days, consumption, not conservation, was the task at hand. People toiled and sweated to prod the earth into more orderly shapes and divisions. They turned the trails of the Maliseet and Micmac Indians into regular roads, and moved rocks into piles and plowed furrows in the soil. They found that people in England would pay handsomely for Canada's fine lumber, so they began to chop down not only what they could use but also what they could sell—all the while continuing to carve out for themselves great blocks of farm and field. Whatever trees encroached on what they saw as crop and pastureland, they trimmed back. They raised cattle and made butter and cheese and ice cream. What had once been mostly wooded became the dairy center of the province. And all this was an act of goodness, of virtue; the cutting of trees was not destructive but, rather, an improvement upon the land. As the New Brunswick Historical Society phrased it in an early-nineteenth-century document, "As the pine disappears, houses and barns will raise in its place, and the country, instead of a barren waste, will exhibit flourishing settlements."

In the history of woodswork, then, concern about the ecology is still very recent, the new philosophy still very raw—even to relatively modern old-time lumberjacks. In Everett Boyd's day, selective harvesting meant taking the tallest, strongest trees, leaving space for the scrawny ones to grow bigger. Much as he delights in his grandson's wonderful prowess in manipulating that modern machine, Grampy Boyd cannot help but think Brent's version of selective harvesting is all backward. Never mind what the scientists are saying now, and the university students and wildlife people and television crews and politicians, with all their talk of genetics and biodiversity, aesthetics and global warming, computer programs and integrated resource management—it just goes against his grain the way Brent takes the poorer specimens and leaves the really promising ones untouched.

To other woodsworkers—those who still rely on older, more labor-intensive methods of harvesting to earn their living—Brent and his machine are veritable blights on the industry. For Brent and Dave, working the harvester and porter on a piece of stumpage together, each isolated in the cabs of their separate machines, do the work of eight or ten men out on the ground with chainsaws and skidders. And such modernization is hitting the industry relatively abruptly; trucks and tracked vehicles began to replace the old logging camps, with their teams of horses, only in the 1950s. The more that people like Brent come around with their selective harvesters, and the more that government task forces publish reports endorsing new forestry techniques like selective harvesting, the fewer jobs there'll be for chainsaw operators.

Brent understands all of this. And it bothers him; how could it not? He's grown up among people who've always counted on the woods for work, people without university educations, some without high school, people with no more job credentials than their muscles and their heritage—for New Brunswickers have looked to the forest for their livelihood ever since the settlers arrived. Even today, timberland covers nearly ninety percent of the province's twenty-eight thousand square miles, and one in seven jobs is directly related to the woods industry, which generates fully half of the province's economy. Meanwhile, New Brunswick's unemployment rate hovers constantly around twenty percent; young people grow up and gravitate toward jobs in the richer interior provinces; and traditional woodsworkers look likely to drown in the irreversible wave of the future.

All in all, it's a tense frontier Brent inhabits. In his snug bubble smelling of fake pine air freshener, humming with public radio and the heater fan, he pushes slowly across the forest floor amid the felt clamor of controversy, righteousness, disappointment. He could think himself into paralysis if he tried to solve all the moral dilemmas inherent in his work. No answer, he has found, no truth, is bedrock: each one peels away to reveal a new layer of fact.

The very language used to discuss and debate silviculture is vague and subject to interpretation. Biodiversity, sustainable development, integrated resource management—all are as yet terms undefined. Even the whole notion of the "virgin forest," that chimerical ideal of environmentalists, is not absolute. Before Brent, his grandfather harvested these lands. Before his grandfather, there were others, nineteenth- and eighteenth-century lumberjacks, all the way back to the first European settlers, who initiated major commercial logging here around 1760. None of the land Brent harvests has not been harvested before. It has alternated over the centuries in persistent layers: woods over farm over woods over farm over woods. The saddest thing about Brent's work is when he comes across evidence of old homesteads, right there amid the trees he is taking down: a square cellar filled in with bushes and moss; a pile of stones where someone once cleared a field; or the shell of an old church, even, long since abandoned by its congregation, its weary, buckled frame half kneeling into the grass—all evidence of families that tried to make a living from the earth and gave up, defeated.

Before the European settlers, Maliseet and Micmac Indians had long been using the wood from these forests for canoes and kindling, snowshoes and spoons—and *their* ancestors had crossed over the ancient land bridge from Asia thousands of years earlier. And before them, before the first human presence here—was the forest then virgin? No one seems to agree on what degree of intrusion—by what force of nature or sort of creature—constitutes loss of that virginity. After all, the surface of the earth had been altered, sometimes violently, time and again before humans ever lived. The rain forests in Brazil were in an earlier incarnation grasslands; deserts were once oceans; and oceans, deserts. The layers peel away to reveal new layers, and the mystery continues, unsolved.

Brent is not one to think himself into paralysis, however. The facts he knows sift through his mind but gently, like dust motes, or the fine clouds of sawdust the harvester blade sends up when he saws through a trunk. Early, milky sunshine illuminates these pollen-like sprays now on the other side of the bubble. Frost coats every pine needle, every tendril of marsh grass, like white feathers. He shuts off the halogen work lights. Dave has come; the red porter has been ambling along through the brush behind him for a good hour now, and suddenly Brent realizes with a cringe that he forgot to give Joy the six-forty-five wake-up call he'd promised. He finishes slicing up the tree he's working on, lowers the boom head to rest its closed mandibles on the snowy ground, and dials the harvester's cellular phone. The machine is nothing if not well-equipped.

Brent quits for dinner at ten to noon. The morning has flown, disappeared somewhere in the steady lurching movements inside the cab, the regular progression of trees sawed off, delimbed, and cut to length outside the window. Brent shuts off the motor and steps out onto the harvester's big tire. The sun is filtering through the tall black spruce trees to one side of him, and glazed like syrup over the clear-cut to the other. Twice this morning Brent rolled the machine forward only to have its tires pierce through ice; he'd been able to maneuver then around those soft spots and carry on, but truly he is working on borrowed time.

Joy, when he'd finally called her, had been in a mad rush to get Ellen dressed and fed and off to her baby-sitter's (another mother who lives right in Fennel Sub-division, two streets over), and herself off to work (Joy runs Tara House, a group home for troubled children in Sussex), but they had quickly made plans to meet for lunch in town, which is a novelty and slightly amusing to them both. Given Brent's usual commute, they often count themselves lucky to manage supper together, by the time he gets home. There's an almost frivolous feeling about working in the woods yet meeting your wife for the noon meal in town, as though you were a businessman or something. It's a far cry anyway from Grampy Boyd's day, when the men stayed in the woods all winter long, or even from Brent's preharvester, premarried days, when he'd stay in the woods a few days at a stretch, sleeping in a little

camper, eating from tins. That was before the government decided such practices were unsanitary and put
the kibosh on logging camps on Crown lands.

Brent sees the porter parked and vacant across the
snowy swale, and figures Dave's helping himself to a
real dinner break, too, as long they're living in the lap
of luxury here just a quick hop from town. For both
men, dinner break usually consists of stepping out on
the wide ledge of a tire, removing a meat sandwich
from its plastic wrap, and chewing it, standing up, *en
plein air*. Actually, half the time Brent eats his sandwich
between the Irving station where he purchases it and
the stumpage he's headed for, all before the sun comes
up. Then he'll work right through the noon hour without noticing it pass; contrary to the old image of the
ravenous lumberjack eating all the camp cookie could
set before him, Brent can work all day long without
wanting for sustenance. Grampy Boyd still reminisces
about the best cookie he ever knew, a man by the
name of Jim Sleep, and the hash and stew and baked
beans (dubbed "echo plums" by old-time lumberjacks), the doughnuts, pies, and puddings he could
whip up. In those days, the men might have taken as
many as four dinner breaks throughout the day, constantly restocking their stomachs for the hard physical
labor they did. Of course, as Brent is the first to point
out, it was hard *physical* labor they did. Sometimes the
most exercise he gets in a day is climbing up the tires
to get in his cab.

Brent could head out to the road either by winding
through the woods or by tramping straight back over
his brush-strewn path. From the vantage point of his
tire, he surveys the high, green, sunlit path. Melty

spots wink wetly up at him. He opts for the shaded woods route, where the snow will be crustier, and drops from the tire to the ground.

The smell of Brent's workplace is incomparable. The manufacturers of his harvester tout, in their marketing literature, the superior ergonomics of the machine, but all the interior comforts and amenities cannot rival the dazzling smell of the fresh-cut forest. Walking to and from the harvester is like sticking your head into a vat of wintergreen oil; it's like tripping over a field of candy canes while chewing a whole pack of spearmint gum. Brent walks briskly through the wooded patch he has yet to cut, stepping around wiry bushes and young trees, avoiding the wettest spots, where ice floats on spreading beds of water. The air is hushed and still beneath the canopy of branches; the tiny lapping, trickling sound is amplified within this copse, and some of the low bushes are studded with hard kernels, the tight beginnings of buds. He won't get to this patch before the thaw. Spring will come here: the buds will open; the palest green leaves will unfurl their tiny ovals; birds will begin piecing nests together. Then the sun will harden things up again, and Brent will finish the job, cut down the rest of this block.

He emerges with a splash onto the muddy road that leads up to the highway where he left the half-ton, his high boots plunging into water among the thin rushes. His father is just now backing his rig down the steep slope from the highway, going slowly, churning up lots of mud as his tires sink halfway into it. The mud is aerated, almost fluffy. What happens this time of year is that water freezes and swells each night in the dirt, then thaws the next day, leaving tiny pockets of air throughout the mud, so that it's really almost the consistency of a very thick milkshake. Actually, it kind of looks like that chocolate mousse Brent made last winter (he and Joy had given a "triple-moose" dinner party to shake up the winter doldrums; they'd served moosemeat filets and Moosehead beer in addition to the dessert). Anyway, the road is nearly impassable.

His father continues to back up the truck; it strains and inches and its tires sink deeper into the mud, but he succeeds in getting it to level ground. He swings down from his purple cab, on which his name has been custom-painted in orange and white shadow-writing. He steps forward and eyes the steep portion of the strip, now deeply and muckily scored by his tires. He's a large man, larger even than Brent, with hands like catcher's mitts. He wears his usual work clothes, matching shirt and pants of a heavy ranger-green cloth. Whitish tufts of hair poke out from under his baseball cap. Like Brent, he has the exuberant grin of a ten-year-old, only he keeps his a little more under wraps.

"Hi, Dad," says Brent, in his light, springy way.

"Hi." A tiny, rather sweet smile. One front tooth edged in gold.

From here they continue the conversation in silence a minute, both with their hands in their pockets, looking at the mud and thinking the same things without speaking, so that when one of them does speak, the conversation is already in progress.

"Thinking do we want to gravel it?" utters Howard.

"I don't know how many more times you're going to get down."

"Two or three days of sun would dry it out to a nice crust."

"Yeh," says Brent, on a little in-sip of breath. "Right before that happens would be a good time to smooth out your ruts, eh?"

Howard spits neatly between his teeth and nods once at his muddy tracks.

Father and son toss off casual good-byes and Brent climbs through the soft, chocolaty stuff up to the main road, where Dave is leaning on the hood of a car parked on the shoulder. A middle-aged couple sits up front with the windows rolled down: Dave's parents. All three are eating nuggets from cardboard takeout boxes marked "Dixie Lee *Poulet Frit.*"

Brent laughs. "We're getting real slick, getting to go out for dinner."

Dave, a little older and girthier than Brent, wears a mustache like a giant frown over his lip, which makes him look gruffer than he is. He smiles at Brent's comment and goes on eating his chicken there on the hood of the car.

Down the slope, Howard's getting ready to load his rig with the logs Dave has been retrieving all morning and stacking by the mud road. To do this, he climbs a built-in ladder to a special little seat, like a metal lifeguard chair, mounted in the center of the extralong flatbed. From here he operates an articulated boom arm with a clam grip at the end. This seizes as many as ten logs at a time and lifts them as easily as sticks of dry pasta onto the bed. The truck holds about twenty cords, and can take close to an hour to load. Howard manipulates the boom and grip as easily as most people manipulate a fork and knife. The huge metal parts splay and dip, fold and lift, with the precision and finesse of Russian dancers. In theory, Howard could pick up a bottle of pop with the mighty grip.

When he's done loading, Howard uses the boom head to tap in the butts of logs so nothing pokes out. Just last week he got fined a hundred fifty dollars for driving an untidy load, which, Brent reports with a fair helping of amusement, had Howard hopping mad, particularly since on that day, like this one, he was carrying it only half a mile down the road. It takes him all of about a minute to reach the mill by Four Corners, then another hour, nearly, to get weighed in and unload.

Brent has a good idea, when he's cutting, where the wood will end up, which is to say he knows by the species and size and quality of a tree whether he's harvesting studwood, firewood, spoolwood (which is tasteless and therefore frequently used for things like tongue depressors and Popsicle sticks), or pulpwood (most of which becomes paper). He cruises a piece of stumpage and assesses the stock even before he begins to cut. This largely determines which mill he'll contract with to buy the wood, since different mills specialize in different types of forestry products.

Irving's paper mill is located down in the city of Saint John, on the Bay of Fundy. Depending on which way the tide is flowing, you get wind of the plant's stench before you catch sight of the buildings. The smell—a great nose-wrinkling, sulfurous halitosis permeating the air—is related to the paper's bleaching process. Some of the pulp gets turned into novels, teabags, surgical gowns, tissues, diapers, catalogs. Some of it gets turned into newsprint, which is then transported by truck and rail and ship to customers: Irving-owned newspapers right here in the province, as well as other newspaper companies located far across national borders, to the south and overseas.

But Brent doesn't mostly think about this step—he doesn't, for example, buy his weekly *Kings County Record* and mull over the fact that the ads and articles he holds in his hands may be printed upon a tree that he cut down. In spite of the fact that about fifty percent of the wood he harvests ultimately winds up going into the vats of porridgy fiber that becomes paper, his mental relationship with the wood does not extend that far. He remembers being taught as a schoolkid about the heartland and the hinterland. The role of the former was to be the shining center of industry, commerce, and culture; the role of the latter was to quietly supply the raw materials.

From the time he was old enough to grasp the concept, it was plain that New Brunswick was indisputably hinter. Nothing of import actually got produced here, not your sneakers or your schoolbooks or your hockey pucks or your hit songs. Those things all came from cities to the west, magnificent heartlandy places like Toronto and Montréal, or, of course, from cities to the south, in the United States. New Brunswick might contribute some plain, humble offering of fish and wood and cheese, but the real, proud creations of humanity came from elsewhere. And that hinterland feeling, that old sense of belonging to the backcountry, the nether zones, lingers with Brent still, makes up a definite part of his New Brunswicker identity, so that no, he does not think of the end products of the trees he harvests as being directly traceable back to himself.

. . .

They meet for dinner at Rory's Pub, behind the Irving station—not the Four Corners Irving but the one on the other side of the railroad tracks, past the LoFood and the Eighth Hussars Sports Center, over the little hump of a bridge, right in town. Sussex proper, home to about four thousand Canadians as well as a few pockets of expatriate Americans (or draft dodgers, as Howard persists in calling them), appears on the surface a kind of sleepy place. Downtown features a fair smattering of shops (including two farm-supply stores and a fishing-and-hunting store), a weekly livestock auction, and a special local attraction known as the Egg Fountain, which is an old stone fountain and ever-dripping spigot built over a natural spring. An old practical joke is to direct an unsuspecting visitor here to partake of the much-exalted water, which, the visitor discovers once he has filled his mouth, tastes exactly like incredibly briny rotten eggs. Another local pastime used to be bowling in the single-lane alley in the basement of the church right across the street from the fetid fountain; the space has since been given over to a nursery school.

Town today is studded with weary crusts of snow, like tough scabs lingering long after cuts have stopped hurting. Signs of spring are perceptible only in the mud on people's boots and in the storefront displays: Easter books in the No Other Name Christian Book Store, sales on snow-removal equipment at Moffett's Hardware. Even though the softening ground is beginning to impinge on woods operations, true spring won't poke through for a while yet. In Hatfield Point, where Brent grew up, spring used to take near forever to arrive. Sometimes Belleisle Bay would stay a block of ice 'til June; Brent could stand out in front of his childhood house and in one breath inhale the fragrance of flowers in the fields and the bracing coolness of breezes still coming off the ice.

Brent parks his half-ton and crosses the lot to Rory's Pub, which looks like nothing much from the outside: just a long, windowless, slightly forbidding shed. The moment he steps inside the door, smells of hot grease and cigarette smoke swarm over him like a couple of ecstatically welcoming dogs. The whole place is cozily bustling with the noontime crowd. Pool balls click; darts thud into cork bull's-eyes; laughter and silverware and country-western music mingle in a homely tapestry of sound.

Brent and Joy first met each other here, back when it was a dance hall. Joy had been living alone in a little brick building on Main Street; she'd had the apartment over a luncheonette called The Anthill. Brent had been living more or less in a camper in the woods, going home to his parents' house every few days for a shower and a good sleep. When they started dating, some people had thought it a bit of an odd match: Joy living in town with her degree in social work, Brent living in the woods with his degree in nothing. They had over-lapped unknowingly during their years at the University of New Brunswick, where Brent goofed off more than he now wishes, and eventually left two courses shy of a degree. In those early dating days, Joy used to get funny reactions whenever she'd answer people's questions about what Brent did for a living.

"He works in the woods," she'd tell them, using his phrase, or even better, perfectly ingenuously,

"He's a slasher"—referring to the piece of woods equipment he operated before the harvester.

And they'd say "Oh! . . ." and do a little thing with their eyebrows, mentally relegating this piece of information to certain lowly spot in their minds, trying to keep their faces politely neutral.

To which unspoken judgment Joy could hardly launch into a retort about how Brent possessed, contrary to what some of her friends might assume, a witty and philosophical mind; or how he read Alice Munro and Michael Ondaatje, and made her home-made pickles and fruitcake, and followed the stock market; or the way he liked to linger on, really studying each exhibit at the aviation and science and war museums in Ottawa, long after Joy would grow bored. The sad fact is that even within the province, where woodswork is supposedly familiar to everyone, negative stereotypes persist. In 1987 a Ministerial Task Force found that "the image evoked by the term woodsworker (or 'logger') today is one of a subsistence job or of a career of last resort." Fortunately, neither Brent nor Joy cares overly much what others might think of woodswork. The flip side of a certain national trait, what Brent refers to as being "Canadianly apologetic," is an easy lack of self-importance, a freedom from fretting too much about your reputation.

Anyway, Rory's is an unabashedly hinterland kind of pub, from the brawny clientele in boots and work shirts to the shiny new all-terrain vehicle up on crates in one corner (a raffle prize: winner gets the wheels as well as the case of Alpine beer perched coyly on the jump seat) to the waitresses who know everyone's name. Joy orders Caesar salad and *poutine* (French for cholesterol, Brent likes to say), an Acadian dish involving sliced potatoes, gravy, and cheese. Brent orders fish and chips. And onion rings. When they come he ketchups each one individually, dangling a fried loop from one finger and applying blobs of condiment from the plastic squeeze bottle.

Their banter as they eat is laced with playful bonhomie. It's as if they've pulled off a caper by managing to see each other in the middle of the day; the rendezvous has a hint of something scrumptious and stolen. Brent's got jobs lined up already through next fall, none of them remotely as close to home as his current one; it'll be a long time before they can meet for dinner at Rory's again. Still, even when Brent does commute an hour and a half into the woods, these days are a far cry from the first year of their marriage.

Brent had just invested more than half a million dollars (of mostly the bank's money) in the harvester and porter. In order to pay back the loan on time, Brent decided the machines had better operate around the clock; he hired two other men to work them through the night. But the harvester, the first of its kind owned by anyone in the entire province, was far more technologically advanced than other types of woods equipment, and all sorts of glitches and breakdowns kept occurring. That whole year Brent was forever arriving home from work at seven or eight in the evening clutching a handful of wires and the harvester manual. He would spread these out all over the rug and be up past midnight trying to smooth out a malfunction, then drive back to the woods the next morning not knowing whether he'd solved the problem or not. Or else he'd arrive home, only to have Joy tell him the night-shift guys had called saying the harvester had broken down, and he'd have to turn right around and drive back to where he'd just been—all the while fretting over time lost while the harvester and men sat idle.

In the end, cutting back to one shift proved more productive. And although he was sorry to have to let the men go, it was also a relief. Brent is, by his own estimation, a lousy boss, it being against his nature to manage other people. Technically, however, he remains not only a boss but also in fact the director of a company—for he is not in strict terms a freelancer but an employee of the business he officially began in university, when he found himself doing woodswork to help pay his way.

At that time Brent had no inkling he'd end up working in the woods for his actual living. He'd had a strong but unfocused interest in political science and social studies, no concrete career aspirations or academic ambition, and an underlying, persistent drift toward the woods. Still, when he set up the company, he imagined it would be only a temporary endeavor, and so he went ahead and named it, with all the jokey bravado of a young man having too good a time in university, after one of the more famous crown jewels of England. Then before he knew it, woodswork had become his livelihood, and the company's officially registered name, to Brent's not immoderate embarrassment, had followed him into adult life. All of which explains why today he's the director of a company called Koh-I-Noor.

Brent sends an exploratory fork into the remains of Joy's *poutine*.

"Did you get mousetraps?" she remembers to remind him, dropping her voice a little, as if to avoid appalling people at the surrounding tables.

"I will." Joy reported a deer mouse sighting yesterday, and Brent, after first trying unsuccessfully to reassure her that "mice aren't in the biting-people business; they're in the avoiding-people business," has promised he'll go hunting for a trap today. He has noticed, not without amusement, that any vermin that makes its way into their house, from ant to deer mouse to, presumably, wild boar, automatically becomes his personal responsibility, as though he had issued it an invitation.

Joy says she has to stop at LoFood this afternoon to pick up supplies for the group home, and asks Brent if there's anything he can think of that they need for the house.

"Mousetraps." He is being funny.

She wrinkles her nose at him: *Ha ha.*

They play off their differences right and left, teasing and sparring, poking fun at each other's local expressions (Joy says "plum loaf" for "raisin bread," and "sloppy joe" for "sweatshirt"; Brent says "a puckle" for "a little" and "a whack" for "a lot"). Brent dwells also in the language of numbers: that woodlot is so many hectares; that load is so many cords; the mill is so many kilometers away; the rate is so many dollars. He knows his hand span is nine inches, his wingspan six feet, and that a dollar bill measures two by six inches; more than coming in handy, such measurements are the kind of thing that delights his mind. On car trips he is fond of shielding the odometer with one hand and making Joy guess how many kilometers they've gone. Joy, who likely as not hasn't the faintest idea, finds it amusing that Brent finds this amusing, and she'll play along indulgently. For her part, she knows he's squeamish about things like holding hands in public; naturally, this acts as powerful incentive for her to seize his hand whenever they are walking down Main Street. In any situation that might position them at odds, they seem to find humor. When Ellen's diaper needs changing, they shoot a round of paper, rock, scissors to determine who'll do the honors.

Now the waitress puts down their bill and they each fish out some bills, inspect what they have.

"Oh yeah, I got a call from Norm," Brent mentions. Norm is the district engineer for the Department of Highways. He works just down the road from Brent's stumpage, over by the road-salt shed. He's also a neighbor of the Boyd's; it's his wife who baby-sits Ellen each day. "He's got some visitors, wanted to know if he could bring them round this afternoon."

"Going to put on a show?" says Joy. "Who are they?"

Brent shrugs. "Government guys." He's used to this, people coming out to watch him work: forestry students, people from Irving, rangers, whoever. He knows it's not he himself exactly, attracting such attention, but his harvester. The machine is Finnish-made, and used around the world, from Australia to Russia to Chile to Zimbabwe, but it is still so novel and rare in the province—indeed, in North America—that when people come watch they end up gaping as though Brent were operating a spacecraft or time machine. In their expressions resides a truth, something easy to lose sight of when you sit behind the controls day after day—that there *is* something awesome, even shattering, about the speed and ease with which the harvester transforms living trees into mill-ready logs.

Joy herself has never tried working the harvester, although she has operated the porter—once, for about fifteen minutes, a few years ago. But something occurred while she was doing it that made her first time her last. In spite of the fact that she was handling the machine really remarkably well for a novice, managing all the controls and getting the wood loaded smoothly, she all of a sudden burst into tears, and had to radio Brent, in the harvester, and tell him sobbingly to come get her. She still can't name the feeling that overcame her that day; it was perhaps something to do with the vastness—of the woods or the machine or the solitude—some weighty, infinite vastness that impressed her terribly.

They laugh about it now, Brent and Joy, both with a palpable fondness for the incident. It's rendered all the more comical by the fact that what brought Joy to tears is, after all, Brent's chosen occupation, his sole activity for eight or ten or twelve hours a day, the rhythm in which he flourishes. In myriad ways they are unalike. This fact seems to please them, as if somehow in the territory where their differences lie they realize a marvelous common frontier; as if everything contrary and foreign in each other only enhances their bond.

Ruth

Her first shift back at the plant after four days burrowed deep inside the teacup of her farm, Ruth always feels kind of lost. It's light out, in a noncommittal sort of way, when she pulls into Anchor Hocking's lot this raw afternoon. Traffic outside the factory itself is relatively sparse, the three-to-eleven-o'clock shift having started about an hour ago. But general signs of closure have been evident throughout her drive to work, as if the whole town were gearing up for its daily denouement, marked by the graying of the air, the first musky threads of woodsmoke, the late buses dropping off kids who had after-school club meetings or detention, the thickening traffic along the commercial strip, where everyone seems to be converging in a tangled rush to buy ground beef and baked beans and jars of tomato sauce: basic, heavy foods, easy to cook on a cold evening. There's a feeling of everyone heading home, in body or in spirit, with an eye on the clock and the darkening sky, everyone aiming toward living rooms and slippers, supper and TV.

Ruth idles her truck at the gatehouse, where a broad-backed man with a gray crew cut and a windbreaker that reads ''Tri-Angle Security'' drawls, ''Heeeer's Ruth,'' and hands her a wad of pink and yellow call-off slips, each one representing a line worker who's called in absent for the approaching shift. Ruth pinches the wad, frowns slightly at its density, and plunks it on the dashboard as she drives on past the gatehouse to park. It'll take her some time to reconfigure work assignments based on the new numbers before the next shift starts, but what irks her more is that she'll have to say no to most of the people who sign up on the Go-Home sheet tonight. Invariably, some of them just plain won't feel like working, but others will have real medical or personal reasons for wanting the evening off—Ruth knows most of the workers well enough that she nearly always can tell the difference—and it's hard to turn that latter bunch down. But there are orders to be filled and ware to be selected, loads to be packed and shipped before the night is through. She hasn't even entered the building yet and already her thoughts are migrating from the farm, curving toward glass.

Slips and yellow plastic dinner bag in hand, brown-and-navy pocketbook over her shoulder, Ruth heads across the lot toward the ramp, a slight stiffness in her gait (she gets what she calls clubbiness in her joints), and passes from the cold blue Ohio evening into the constant air of the plant. Inside is the steady, faintly orange light of perpetual sleeplessness, and perpetual noise from the machinery—the great, fiery revolutions of the furnace room's complex apparatus, which release molten glass down chutes twenty-four hours a day, like mechanical laying hens, and then press and pat and pinch each cooling glob into a given shape with metal arms and fingers. There are also the chattering vibrations of ware riding down the lehrs, those long, conveyor-like slow-cooling ovens; the periodic tinkling smash of defective ware being culleted; the persistent, baby-bird bleating of tow motors backing up; and, somewhat futilely through the rest of the din, the marginally intelligible pages sounding at intervals over the public address system. Ruth waves and calls greetings to a half-dozen people as she follows the painted path to the sluer office. By the time she arrives there, on this as on every evening, a pencil stub has seemingly materialized behind her right ear.

The sluer office is a humble affair; it resembles a

long, light blue shed tucked against a rear wall of the plant, next to the machine shop and in front of the annealing room. Through its two meager windows— more like portholes, really—one can survey the shops, or work stations, set up at the end of each lehr. To-night fourteen shops are in operation, each represent-ing a different sort of ware. Beyond the shops one can also glimpse, at the distant end of the floor, the fur-nace room, which manages to communicate a glow that is qualitatively different from the rather jaundiced light of Select and Pack. The furnace room broadcasts an entrancingly mobile white-orange light, something like a hot, flickering Creamsicle, and Ruth likes that she can see it from her office.

The sluer office door actually reads, in black letters that have been partially rubbed off, "SELECT PACK OFFICE." "Select and Pack" and "sluer" are used interchangeably at Anchor Hocking, although no one is quite sure where the word "sluer" comes from. Some early American glass factories used the term "sloar" for their logbooks, which recorded how many of which items were made each day by whom. Ruth has heard that the word comes from French. Many of Lancaster's early settlers were not French, but German glassmak-ers who'd moved west from Pennsylvania. And a Dutch dictionary defines the word *sleur* as something routine, repetitive, humdrum. Whatever its actual der-ivation, the word is embedded in plant lingo, and it's how Ruth most often refers to the office where she works.

Inside, the door shut, the din muffled, she greets Pam, her day-shift counterpart, and hangs her cardigan in the skinny black locker next to the desk they share.

Ruth is wearing a beet-colored turtleneck, denim jumpsuit, and black sneakers. Simple gold hoops are threaded through her earlobes, and around her neck a small gold Mickey Mouse charm hangs from a short chain. Pam is younger than Ruth, with baby-fine blondish hair, cropped at the jawline, and large eyes made to appear larger by owlish glasses. Between the women flows an easy, somewhat wry affability, unencumbered by social graces or formalities. They have the laconic intimacy of war buddies, born in their case of sharing the same job, the same hassles, and the same gender in the workplace. With little pause for pleasantries, they launch into the business at hand: Ruth leans on the metal desk, her gray head bent to read over Pam's shoulder, while Pam, in the black swivel chair, begins her annotated narration of all the pertinent job information she has recorded during her shift on various loose sheets and in the rumple-edged logbook.

This all occurs in glass-factory lingo, Pam's rubber-band drawl bending extra syllables out of the words: "Now, two-four, that's been running like gangbusters all day . . . Two-five? I'd give it seventy and it's getting better all the time. There's one mold got a patch on it or something—looks like a chip but it isn't . . . I culleted three quarters of the first load . . . Three-three, I'd hate to say this too loud, can you believe this came out fifty on start-up?"

"Gee," says Ruth, in her deep, throaty voice, as pleasantly textured as the skin on her face and hands.

"You're gonna have a good night. Three-four, you need seventy-five loads and they're on fifty-four right now. That'll be a job change for the morning . . .

Okay, pillar-pack here, if you can get your new kids to keep up. This one they went to do up in Carton Assembly at eleven . . . Oh, and I found the fiber partitions . . .''

And on and on like this, all numbers and codes in deft, rapid succession. Some of the numbers refer to specific shops; three-four, for example, means the shop handling ware coming down the fourth lehr affiliated with tank three. Some of the numbers refer to different types of ware; a fourteen-ounce margarita glass, for example, may be distinguished from a fifteen-and-a-quarter-ounce margarita glass by its different job number. Some of the numbers refer to the rates of acceptable ware coming off a lehr; each job has a standard assigned to it, which is the percent of product expected to be favorably selected—for sturdier ware the standard may be set as high as eighty-five percent; for more fragile things, like stemware, it may be set as low as fifty. Whenever the actual rate of favorably selected ware exceeds the standard, the men back in the furnace room get a bonus.

Pam flips a page and skims one finger with a whispery rasp down the log, chomping gum with a little more energy than a person ought to have at the end of a twelve-hour shift; it's second-wind energy, a bit antsy and haggard. Ruth listens, frowning in concentration, picking up on all the implications, translating the numbers Pam rattles off into their practical application to her own night's work. She absently molds a pair of yellow foam plugs into her ears. A box of these, individually wrapped, sits atop the filing cabinet; everyone's supposed to wear them out on the floor, and goggles, too, unless you happen to wear eyeglasses, in which case those suffice.

"Oh yeah." Pam spies something relevant among the notes she's written herself on a yellow legal pad; she swivels her chair a quarter-turn to pluck a sample off the desk behind her. It's a batter bowl on which a quality control technician has drawn a circle in blue felt-tip pen. The circle is there to mark what is a virtually imperceptible streak in the glass. Ruth takes the dish, tilts it in the light, nods. "I wouldn't throw that one out," says Pam, "but it's something to keep an eye on." Next she fills Ruth in on the ailments of a few workers: this one shot himself in the foot and needs to be put on a "set-down" job; that one's hoping to get sent home tonight because her kid has a blood clot; another's being suspended for leaving repeatedly without clocking out. Down at the other end of the tight office, the other two Select and Pack supervisors, Andy and Floyd, have come in and are going quietly through their own changing of the guard.

Pam, finally finished imparting all the notes on her list, takes a moment now purely to vent, relating an incident from earlier in the day. She had taken some faulty ware back to the furnace room to let the men there know that what was coming down the lehr wasn't passing muster. It's part of their job in Select and Pack to notify the furnace room of any recurrent imperfections cropping up on the line, not least because the furnace room workers, unlike those in Select and Pack, have a vested financial interest in exceeding the standards, so a person might think they'd be glad for the information and the chance to correct the mistake. Pam and Ruth both know, however, that delivering these communiqués can be a delicate business, depending on who's working down in the furnace room on a given shift. Some of the men take the news of defective ware as a personal rebuke. Their hackles go up; they won't allow as there's any imperfection, and won't do spit to fix it.

"Well," says Pam, slouching back heavily in the chair and leveling on Ruth one of her magnified wry looks, "he did one of those 'Good-*bye* honey,' like he ain't going to talk about it with me anymore, and I about flipped a gasket. I was fine 'til they got smart."

Ruth presses her mouth tight, deepening the crease above her lip, and gives a knowing grunt, as much to sympathize with her colleague as to steel herself. Ruth Lamp does not take flak if she can help it. It's like she used to tell the twins when they were growing up: *You don't have to love me, but you had darn well better respect me.* She's spent too much of her life undernourished in respect, all those years in Columbus, too many memories of herself on her hands and knees, both literally and figuratively—always cleaning, she was, as a young wife and mother, scrubbing the floors, washing the windows, tending to every surface, trying to please her husband and mother-in-law, trying to erase any complaints before they could voice them. She let herself be diminished, spent decades apologizing for other people's miserableness. Now, after nearly threescore years on this earth, respect is something she can't afford to do without.

Done passing the torch for the day, Pam rises, revealing a long, lean, Olive Oyl frame interrupted by a neat bulge in the middle: she's expecting her first child. "All right, and you should have a nice night," she sums up. Her face is drawn and ashy with fatigue, but her voice twangs chipperly now at the prospect of leaving. She retrieves a quilted navy jacket from the locker, grabs her purse from the desk, notices the yellow sticky note she's stuck to it reminding herself to "GET GAS," transplants the note rather punchily to her jacket front, which makes Ruth chuckle, and issues her final blessing before she heads out the door: "Hopefully, it should be boring as all hell!"

The clock's hands lug themselves indifferently into the four-thirty position, a full half hour before Ruth's shift technically starts, but it's her and Pam's custom to pass the baton a little early; Pam will reciprocate by coming in before five the next morning. Ruth prefers her lock shift to the line workers' rotation; with that schedule, her body never could quite catch up with what it was supposed to be doing. And although she's not wild about the twelve-hour duration, she doesn't mind taking the night shift; it lets her gets things done around the farm in daylight. Besides, even though machinery and workers alike operate around the clock, or "twenty-four/seven," the plant floor tends to be somewhat less populated, and therefore less stressful, at night. She'll have sixty-eight in Select and Pack tonight, barring any more call-offs.

Ruth takes up position in the prewarmed swivel chair, bends over a calculator, and begins punching in figures. Eight feet away, Andy and Floyd confer in their sober, low-key way. The only other noise comes from the asthmatic air conditioner mounted over Ruth's desk, which no one can quite figure out how to turn off. It chugs sporadically on and off at will, doing little to freshen the sluer office air, but keeping it generally on the chilly side of hospitable.

Nothing about the office contributes to its being what could be called a warm place. The floor, a cracked linoleum of no particular color, is neither brightened nor softened by the couple of reddish black rubber-bottomed mats strewn on it. The drop ceiling has the look of an unhealthy set of teeth: the musty gray punctuated here by the too-white gleam of a block of fluorescent lights, there by a gaping void where one of the panels is missing. Between floor and ceiling is contained a room whose sole purpose is continual productivity. Personal effects are scant: a one-page calendar bearing the legend "Greetings of the Season" from the Colonial Inn Restaurant in Logan, Ohio; a tiny American flag sticking out of a pencil jar; a doll-sized Pittsburgh Steelers jersey suction-cupped to the window.

Mostly the office is black metal and gray plastic, and paperwork: endless forms with headings like "Record of Discipline," "New Hire Evals," "Run Down Sheet," "Gate Sheet," "Return Stock Sheet," "Job Change Slate," "Labor Control." Amid the dull clutter sit random pieces of ware, like the batter bowl, a lone whiskey glass, a defective cake set, and a round amber ashtray—all of them looking somehow forlorn, and cheap, beneath the sterile glare. In this environment it does seem more fitting to think of these items as "ware" rather than "glass," as if the room were imparting its utilitarian dreariness to the objects in it, coating them with its own want of loveliness and light.

Neither, however, could the sluer office be called a cold place. What warmth graces it is generated by the people who habituate it; by this measure the warmth is not effusive, but kindles effortlessly and unassumingly in a way that is more familial than anything. Ruth scoots the adding machine aside now and looks up: the clock hands have dragged themselves nearer to five, near enough that she might as well start the first pot of coffee. Andy has already donned his jacket and baseball cap and left for the night; Floyd is going over paperwork at his own desk, and Ruth has to sidle behind him to fill up the pot at the shoebox-sized sink. "If I wanted to put out some oats," she says, with no preamble, over the running water, "when would I plant 'em?"

Floyd lifts his gaze two inches from his desk, purses his lips. "Oats're spring, wheat's fall." He has the air of a shy, solemn man, lean and unfussy in his navy trousers and blue button-down shirt and pocket protector that reads, "Safety is a part of every job at Anchor Hocking." His belt is so old the leather's split and furry in places. He whistles through his teeth a fair amount, a soft and surprisingly joyful sound.

"So I'd have to put them in pretty soon." Ruth shuts off the tap and carries the pot with her stiffish gait to the table where the copier and coffeemaker sit. "Got the rototiller up and running this morning," she announces, with the kind of animation usually associated with announcements of birth and love and such rites of passage.

Floyd nods slowly, his prominent lower jaw digging a groove in the air. He himself has a cattle rack on the back of his truck for transporting the beef cattle he buys each spring to fatten up and slaughter in the winter, and he and Ruth, on their twelve-hour shifts in the stale factory office, often discuss farmwork. Ruth tells him now about the garden she's fixing to raise this spring, the first full-fledged garden she'll have at the farm, since last spring she was kept busy just patching the roof and mending windows and things. It's too cold yet to plant the sweet potatoes, though she could maybe start peas. String beans, she's planning, too, and a couple hills of cucumbers. The daffodils have already been poking up shoots, nonchalantly jumping the gun. "I had some snow this morning, Floyd," Ruth tells him, measuring grounds into a filter. "A little bitty dusting."

He nods again, although her back's to him. "Some wind," he supplies after a moment, as an affirmation or maybe an addendum. "You probably didn't even feel the wind back in the holla' there."

"Nope. Didn't feel it back in m'little teacup." In fact, the dusting of snow had melted away in the frail morning sun, and it had felt nice then out on the front porch, breathing in that bracing convergence of cold and warmth: the one season old, almost stale, nearing the end of its tether; the other young and tender and welcome as the first crop of new potatoes she'll fry up this spring with smoked sausages. Ruth had stood there, cupping chilly fingers around her coffee mug, barefoot and without even her robe (she can do that, go robeless, back in the privacy of the hollow), looking out over the shallow dips and rolls of the lawn and into the deep, brambly gully beyond.

One fat tongue of the gully laps up boldly between the house and barn, and in this crevice enough garbage has been piled so that it lies nearly flush with the lawn—a reminder that Ruth has not lived here long enough to attend to all that needs mending, and that before her the farm belonged to other folks, such as saw fit to use their own lawn as a dump. By now, most of what stocks this mini-landfill is rusted metal: tin cans and old appliance parts, springs and nails; and plastic: some jugs and caps, a flap of tarpaulin; and the occasional scrap of rubber: a portion, possibly, of inner tube, a piece of old sneaker. Most anything else has long since gone back into the earth, been released from its contrived form, been reunited with other elemental molecules in the soil and sky.

Another of these dumps lies in the woods behind the house, smack on the way to the power line, where Ruth often roams with Shenna among the wood columbine and black raspberry and touch-me-nots. There's something curious and insistent, benignly meddlesome, almost, about the enduring presence of this other family's garbage. Shen'll sniff at it some, but no more than she'd investigate a tree stump or wild mushroom or mossy rock: in her wolfish impartiality, these remnants of human life hold no especial allure. But to the human eye, these discarded skeletons, now largely unidentifiable—no more than ciphers, really, for the things they once were, once meant, once did— remain evocative, alive with the certain histories of people lost and never known.

Standing robeless on her front porch, Ruth is untouched by any neighbor's gaze, but she is not exactly alone out here. There's Shen, of course, and the wild turkeys and deer and the songbirds in the walnut tree. And there are the cherished objects she keeps at the farm: the remains of her old dogs Cheyenne and Princess, buried beneath the apple tree; the folded-up accordion that reminds her of church revival meetings; the framed pictures of her family; the few pieces of hand-me-down china and crystal from a dear old friend in Columbus. But Ruth is kept company as well by the presence of the foreign junk, by those clear vestiges of other people, strangers to her, who nonetheless performed the same acts, in this same house, as she does today: cooking, eating, washing, gardening, romping, sleeping, waking. And although she plans to clear out the dump between the house and barn one of these days, she doubts if she'll ever get around to disturbing the refuse on the woods path. That pile, those totems whose significance is unknown to her, she will most likely let remain.

The dingy white telephone on her desk rings once and she answers automatically, as if these words could not be uttered one without the others: "Select-and-Pack-Ruth." A short silence and then it's more of the factory talk, succinct and numeral-studded, ending with a friendly "Thank you much." The pencil stub comes from behind her ear; she writes; the stub gets replaced. A sip of coffee and the mug goes down. Still practically brimful now, it will likely have cooled by the time she gets back to it, the powdered creamer congealed around the rim of liquid. One more sip. She rises.

Ruth walks the plant floor as much as she sits in the sluer office—to the supply room for more bar code labels for the packers; to the annealing room, where samples get put through a battery of tests; to the box shop, where cartons are printed; to the decorating room, where special-order glassware gets sprayed with the logos of companies like Chi-Chi's, Pizza Hut, Red Lobster. Sometimes she's gathering or disseminating specific information; other times she's on more general reconnaissance, just keeping abreast of a hundred things, from the ware itself to the teams of workers stationed at each shop, from the Go-Home sheet to the tray partitions. Her stride is long and swift, if somewhat jerky due to her clubbiness (she sometimes appears to swing her legs forward nearly without bending at the hip), and as she traverses the floor she wears her work face, which is to say keen and concentrated: her denim-blue, rather opaque eyes click from one focal point to another at sharp intervals, like a bird's; the breve mark wrought by time and endurance is sharply scored above her lip.

But she sheds her work face easily and a dozen times on a single tour of the floor: when a burly young man in green safety goggles and a plaid work shirt pinches her waist in impish greeting; when she leans over to ask an older woman in a yolk-yellow sweatshirt how her skin rash is getting on. She walks right up and rubs her fingers against the back of another man's skull. "Just checking for lumps," she tells him, not quite deadpan, and he turns pink and guffaws—she's making reference to a well-known incident involving him, a barstool, and gravity.

In the environment of the plant floor, nearly everyone appears oddly fragile or exposed—lessened, almost. There's something relentless about the quality of the light and the nature of the work. Skin appears waxen, or pasty, or doughy, and everything shows: spidery veins, flaky dryness, pimples, wrinkles, blotches, sags. Most of the workers dress for comfort: sweats, sneaks, untucked T-shirts; there's no call to go to any more trouble than that. The cumbersome OSHA-mandated safety goggles and bright-colored earplugs are the finishing touches; depersonalizing,

clownish, they are like small humiliations to which everyone is subject. In this atmosphere the infrequent
outbreaks of jesting and flirting and bawdiness—a man
on his way to the break room catches a pal's eye and
jovially flips him the bird; a woman pretends to boob-
flash her fellow line worker—become acts of valor, of
life-affirming irreverence.

The combined blare of the fans and scramblers and
lehrs and tow motors makes it necessary to speak lips-
to-ear, as in a child's game, and in Ruth's case a hand
on the back or shoulder complements such interaction
not infrequently. She calls everyone, subordinates and
superiors alike, by their first names, many of which
have an old-fashioned feel; they reek of the American
prairie, of gingham and Model T's and hoarhound
candy: Dottie, Erna, Myrtle, Rex, Smokey, Eldon,
Homer. And at the close of speaking, she always pulls
back to make eye contact for a moment, her gaze not a
bird's now, not the impassive chronicler of data, but a
point of human contact, a promise of something familiar. It's as if the one face were for the glass and the
other for the people, and she slips from one to the
other without thought or fuss, responding to each in
the mode it requires.

When she examines glass, her manner suggests that
of a veterinarian. She moves among the ware coming
off the lehrs with a mixture of clinical detachment and
infinite care, pausing to handle the whiskeys and the
juice glasses almost as if they were kittens or chicks she
was checking for sex. She picks them up as if by their
scruffs, two to a hand, four at a time, and turns them
upside down, scanning their bottoms for infinitesimal
markings, then replaces them on the moving belt.

Sometimes she checks for more subtle defects, holding the glass to the light, or twirling it slowly against the flat of her palm, feeling its base and walls for unevenness. Once out on the floor, it's as if her old line worker duties reenter her blood; even on her way to answer a page or give a message, she cannot keep her hands from interacting with the glass, from culleting, for example, when she sees a substandard piece tootling by, a candy dish with too many tears, perhaps, or a juice glass with a sharp flange that the fire polishers failed to smooth. She'll pluck it then, the offending ware, from the belt and chunk it unceremoniously down one of the chutes that convey cullet on an opposing belt toward the furnace room, where it'll eventually get melted back down into some future batch: a magnificently terse and simplified life cycle.

Sometimes when people cullet a piece of ware, it hits the lower belt in such a way that it shatters crashingly, spraying bits of glass on the floor. Sometimes it falls like a feather and completes its journey virtually intact. No one seems to care either way. The naughty pleasure that a layperson might associate with deliberately smashing glass has no meaning here, no bearing on the monotony of Select and Pack; even culleting is carried out with a surgical neutrality. The clink and crash fail to register; the workers are past flinching; they are past relishing the tiny explosions, past noticing the play of light on the sharp, transparent crumbs that litter the plant floor, which can sometimes resemble a crazily starry sky.

Ruth lifts a couple of rim-tempered Pilsners fresh off the lehr and winds up sliding her thumb straight down an invisible crack. A fat bead of blood wells up on the fleshy pad, trembles there a moment, and begins to descend. She regards it the way a driver might regard a large crate lying in the middle of the road, and then skirts it with about the same level of interest, simply tipping her hand the other way to avoid dripping. She scrutinizes the other glass, replaces it on the belt, cullets the cracked one, inspects a few more, being careful not to smear any blood, and only then, unhurriedly, makes her way to the infirmary. The infirmary lies just yards beyond the factory floor, and is marvelously quiet and pristine in comparison, everything washed and orderly, the green linoleum floor impossibly smooth, like the mirror surface of a lake on a calm day: free of broken glass. The nurse, Sally, is busy on a phone call behind her office door; Ruth washes and bandages the cut herself and heads back onto the floor.

Cartons, printed up in the box shop, identify the different sorts of ware that sit packed and ready for distribution. They're stacked on pallets, waiting to get tow-motored over to the lift, which will lower them into the basement for direct rail transport over to the twenty-three-acre distribution center, three miles west of the plant. The cartons say things like Fully Tempered Excellency Wines, Sweetbriar Beverage Set, Canfield Footed Cake Set; other product lines are Beacon Hill, Essex, Regency, New Orleans, Alexandria, Hoosier, Hampton, Rhapsody—the names evoking images and settings that have little to do with the ware's origins in Lancaster, Ohio. Ruth threads among them, registering their appellations not as incongruities but simply as work orders; Beacon Hill triggers for her not the aura or cachet of Boston Brahmins but, rather, pebbly-bottomed highball tumblers.

"Hiya, Ruthie!" hails a determinedly cheerful young man who has been given the job of steering a push broom along the factory floor, endlessly sweeping broken glass. "Say, if it snows tomorra', you've gotta help me throw snowballs at the bosses!"

Ruth laughs her deep, dry chortle.

"Oh," remembers the man, "I'm supposed to say, they're short a table for the party."

A retirement party is being set up just now in one of the break rooms, where line workers are allowed to relax for ten minutes every hour, and where they may take a half-hour dinner break once a shift. (All three shifts call it dinner break, whether the meal in question goes down the gullet at six P.M. or six A.M. or any other time.) Ruth manages to locate a small wooden table not currently in use for any packing operation. She lifts and maneuvers it across the floor, keeping to the painted pedestrian track, pants past the vending machines, above which a huge banner advises everyone, "Lifting's A Breeze When You Bend Your Knees!" and arrives finally at the break room in the corner, where it becomes apparent that "short a table" is putting it modestly.

Food covers every visible surface in the windowless, cinder-block room, where two women are arranging Rice Krispie squares on a tray and blowing up colored balloons. It could be a church social, a school picnic, a town fair, for all the food people have brought in: pans of fried chicken, pots of potato salad and egg salad, casseroles teeming with macaroni and spaghetti sauce, bowls of baked beans and jelly beans and three-bean salad, pretzels and potato chips, deviled eggs, pickles, Jello salad, a sheet cake the size of a small bedsheet. "Heard you could use a table." Ruth relieves herself of this item and surveys the room. "My golly," she says, impressed.

"Thanks, Ruthie," says the woman without the balloon in her mouth. "Help yourself. We got a acre of food in here."

"I may come back," she promises, passing a last admiring gaze over the spread before she heads out again. Next door is the smokers' break room: where most of the action is. Through the glass pane in the door, she can see there is indeed a sizable crowd in there, some of them with loaded paper plates already installed in laps. One man notices her peering in and lifts a plastic fork in greeting. Ruth grins and waves back. She stopped smoking last summer, after first getting into a car accident with a drunk driver and then contracting pneumonia—she, who never gets sick. She didn't make any grand plans or pacts with herself, but something moved her each day not to smoke, until now it's been seven months without a cigarette. It just felt like someone was trying to tell her something.

There was only one other time, back on one of the tenant farms where she lived as a child, when Ruth can remember being seriously ill. She supposes she was about six. She'd been feeling poorly for a few days, but her family didn't believe in doctors, and this one morning she'd been left to rest in the house alone while her mother went to the barn to do the milking. The little girl's symptoms were aches and chills and labored breathing, and while she lay on the sofa there alone, the act of breathing grew more and more difficult, as if million-gallon jugs of water were pressing down on her lungs. It was as though the idea of Ruth were slipping out of her fevered child's body that morning, as though something were edging her out of her own flesh, and when her mother finally returned, Ruth told her, "Call Reverend, please," in a sick voice but very clear and certain, as though the person speaking were much older than six.

The Apostolic minister came right out to the farm where they were staying and prayed over Ruth for three solid hours, until she felt better—which she did, miraculously better, from no more remedy than his prayers and faith going into her like a golden broth, so that the chills subsided and the pain in her chest abated, and in a matter of a few weeks, she was entirely cured. No medical doctor ever examined her or named her illness, but Ruth suspects, from what she knows about the symptoms, that it was pleurisy, and the experience of that faith healing more than fifty years ago is imprinted on her now as if it had happened yesterday.

Just as strong are her childhood memories of church itself, at least the early memories, before Ruth hit junior high school and began to balk at how the teachings of the Apostolic church set her apart from her classmates. Around that time she began to mind missing out on things: band practice and Girl Scouts, if they fell during a prayer meeting, and going to the movies and listening to worldly music. And she began to mind all the rules about no makeup, no jewelry (not even her class ring), no hems above the knee, no sleeves above the elbow, no shoes that exposed toes or heels, and, worst of all, no cutting her hair into a swingy, stylish bob. That was when she began to break her mother's heart, bit by bit. Ruth began to snip her hair in increments, only an inch or two a week, so that she thought (hoped) her mother wouldn't notice. And then she started playing her accordion in the weekly jamboree down at the radio station in town. She drifted more and more into what was worldly, until almost before she knew it she'd left her mother, and her high school, and Lancaster altogether, to get married and move to Columbus at age seventeen.

No, the memories of her churchgoing all come from early on, from when she was still a young girl attending the New Life Christian Center with her mother several days a week. There she got steeped in a tradition of faith as potent as moonshine. She remembers falling asleep in church with her head in her mother's lap, only to be awakened by the strange, familiar sounds of the minister speaking—hollering—in tongues, or by the gasps and garbling cries of members of the congregation who had personally felt the Holy Spirit enter them. Ruth herself was saved, or received the gift of tongues, as they called it, when she was nine or ten, and, like the memory of her earlier faith healing, the rhapsodic ecstasy of that experience remains clear, unmistakable, and unmatched in her mind.

Whenever Ruth drives past the sleek new quarters of the New Life Christian Center today, out on Route 22, with its curving spaceship architecture and its mammoth blacktopped parking lot and that thing like a movie marquee out front, advertising to commuters, "HEAVEN BOUND! FREE FLIGHT LESSONS IN-SIDE," she can't help but feeling a little skeptical—not of faith, or of the gift of tongues, or of the power and mystery of the presence called God, but of the trappings her church has acquired. A scandal a few years back about a minister having an affair with one of the women in the congregation didn't help matters, not that Ruth was in regular attendance even then; she's only set foot inside the current quarters a handful of times. By now, two more ministers have come and gone without ever having laid eyes on Ruth, but they have received her money twice a month all the same, ten percent of every paycheck. Oh, sometimes she'll mail her tithe to the Salvation Army, or to Project Concern, the relief fund set up at Anchor Hocking for employees in emergency need, but mostly she still sends it to the New Life Christian Center.

Maybe she does this partly out of loyalty to her mother. Maybe it's partly in gratitude for her own faith healing so long ago. But mostly she's just following through on a commitment she made in her heart thirteen years back, when she'd hit rock bottom and had no material lifeline at all, nothing she could grab on to excepting faith. She had looked to her own mother then, considered the story of this woman so small and steady and serene, who had weathered pain and desertion and poverty, and always—this is the part of the story that chimes, that sends a real physical, silvery peal—and always, for ninety earthly years, been provided for.

In spite of Ruth's own disassociation from, and even disaffection for, this particular church, she sees nothing compromising in sending her tithe there. As far as she's concerned, the exchange she's worked out in her heart takes place directly between herself and God, never mind the actual addressee. As for keeping track of the ultimate whereabouts of her tithe, this does not concern her. The money itself is only worldly. Just as she believes herself to be an instrument in God's hands, so it must be with her tithe; it assuredly ends up with the One she intends. Here again is where her mother's faith spills over. It comes to Ruth as natural as breathing, believing in what she does not know for sure.

Basilio

Nearly every morning as he passes along the road below the cemetery, Basilio sees fresh-picked flowers at some of the graves: creamy calla lilies, sprays of dainty bridal veil blossoms, pale jasmines, and other sprigs of peacock blue and scarlet and fuschia—unfaded bundles laid down the day or evening before—and in this way the cemetery in Pluma Hidalgo is no less lively a place than *el centro,* really, or the secondary school at recess, or the red-dirt soccer field at the entrance to town, where the burro market is held on weekends. In Pluma the dead are no less a part of life than the living, and life no more finite than the rainfall. All those candy-bright patches that assail Basilio's vision each morning are like scenes from a mute carnival, like actors signaling to him from an otherworldly pantomime. It is comfortable, almost cozy, to live on the border of all those spirits; they, too, are woven into Basilio's family.

Today he passes by the cemetery on his way to the nursery—not the *kinder,* the school for three- to six-year-olds where his older two go, but the coffee nursery, down the mountain from the basketball court at La Palma. Today is a strange day because when he walks the sun is already touching things—those chickens cavorting in the dirt road, the rust-streaked tin of that house's roof, his own bare arms and head. Basilio never wears a hat. His hair is as dark and thick as *café natural* (native coffee, which is what the people of Pluma call the brew made from the inferior beans they do not sell but keep for their own use), and because he lets it grow rather long in front, he is forever raking it back from his eyes with the artless grace of a young boy. Today, already, his hand comes away from his forehead moist.

He has set out later today than usual. Usually, he and his family rise by five-thirty or so, but today Basilio slept in. That's because yesterday he spent down on the coast, in Pochutla, at a meeting at Rincón Alegre, UCI's main headquarters. Ever since Basilio volunteered to become the UCI *técnico* for Pluma Hidalgo two months ago, he has been taking increasingly many trips to the coast for planning meetings, where he can talk with the seven other *técnicos* from nearby regions and attend seminars given by agricultural engineers. A few times a month now, he may ride down in the morning with a handful of men in the back of Hipólito Pérez's truck—Señor Pérez is president of the local UCI branch—and return to Pluma late the same night, his body stiff from bracing itself for so long on the swaying truck bed, his mind nimble and hopping with thoughts of organic fertilizer and shade cover and pruning and collective ownership. Each time he makes the trip down to the coast, Basilio apprehends a little more of the big picture: that Aztec Harvests is not simply the brainchild of a gringo but has UCI for one of its parents. And if what the directors say comes true, it will one day be the shared fruit of all the farmers' labor.

The coffee compound down at Rincón Alegre (which translates into Happy Corner) is an almost absurdly cheery-looking place. To reach it, you drive several kilometers beyond Pochutla proper and turn left off the main road at what is apparently nothing more than a wide dirt shoulder with a few stick-and-tin houses huddled on it. Then you point your truck off diagonally into a thicket of trees and jounce a few hundred yards over rocky earth until you see, deeply ensconced behind the brush, the two large cinder-block buildings that are UCI's newish headquarters—built after the previous ones burned down in 1989. The buildings are painted the most improbable shades of hot pink and lavender and midnight blue, and are fringed by lovingly landscaped palms and ferns and crimson-flowering bushes. A drying patio between the two buildings doubles as a full-sized basketball court, with all the appropriate circles and lines painted in, and real nets dangling, intact, from the hoops. This is where the beans that grow on the mountain get trucked, processed, sorted, and bagged, and then the highest grades sent out again, either to the port of Salina Cruz for shipments to San Francisco, or to Vera Cruz for shipments east: to New Orleans, New York, Europe.

If the place seems tucked rather deliberately out of sight, so much the better; the old headquarters, situated unshyly in Pochutla proper, had been filled to the eaves with sacks of coffee ready for shipping when they went up in smoke that night, under circumstances that remain suspicious. If the aesthetic seems rather overwrought for a coffee-processing plant—again, so much the better. UCI is still very young, and Aztec Harvests

barely out of its infancy, and as yet the entire operation is fueled as much by faith and pride as by labor
and profit. In a culture where things spiritual are routinely made manifest in material tokens, the unabashed
flamboyance of UCI's new digs is like a living omen, a
promise, something concrete for the farmers to bring
back to their villages, talk about, see behind closed
eyelids.

Last night Basilio returned to Pluma close to eleven,
a good three or four hours past the time that he and
his family usually unroll their sleeping mats. Down at
Rincón Alegre he and the other *técnicos* had played basketball for a while after their meeting broke up, and
then there had been supper to eat and hands to shake
and still more words to exchange before the slow
crawl back up the mountain. Señor Pérez's truck
stopped in *el centro* to let the men disembark, and from
the quiet town square they scattered then, down roads
and paths familiar and pitch-black and fog-laden,
toward their homes.

This morning Basilio's brother Lucío went to rake
out the beans at La Palma, and Basilio slept in, letting
the women get breakfast and usher Silvestre and Yolanda off to the *kinder* before he himself rose. So that
by the time he heads off to the coffee nursery, it is
later than usual—but not so very much later that the
sun should be already this robust. It is a bully today,
the sun, fairly banging its rays against the tin roofs and
cement road. It will make the coffee sad.

This is how Basilio thinks of the wispy tails of mist,
which ordinarily at this hour would be bobbing like
filmy sea horses among the trees and across the road:
that they keep the coffee from becoming too sad when

the sun is hot. Everyone knows that the mist nourishes the coffee plants, caresses them like handmaidens with damp, cool fingers, cradles them in a moist pellicle all through the dry months, of which this is one. In May and June, and then again in September, the water falls daily from the sky, and everyone's rain barrel is always full, and the earthen floor of everyone's home loosens, a little, and the palm *petates* for sleeping smell constantly of damp. But this is winter, the dry season, and now especially the coffee relies on the mist to keep it happy. Basilio rounds the corner by the *kinder*, where the road becomes paved and forked: one tine rising toward *el centro*, the other sinking drastically, leading past the secondary school toward La Palma. There where the land dips he does spy some mist, milling in the light like chalk dust from clapped erasers.

He sees, too, Genoveva, his wife, climbing the hill with her strong, unhurried strides, a smile tweaking at her lips now as she sees him, but she says nothing, does not even wave, only smiles as if she's got a pleasurable secret, which is how she always smiles. Her clothes are a loose, sleeveless blouse and a faded cotton print skirt, black with blue roses, and brown plastic sandals, and she has a way of wearing them that suggests the pieces of fabric have no bearing on her body. She climbs, solid-calved, up the road beside the *kinder*, and Basilio waits for her, his own lips a cipher beneath the thick mustache, and rakes a heavy shock of hair out of his eyes.

"Have you seen the kids?" Genoveva asks, rather casually, when she is standing beside her husband. She is slightly out of breath and gleaming along her collarbones and brow.

"No. The kids?"

"Yes. The *kinder* is closed." She gestures loosely behind her toward the two-room cement building, which sits in an ample, weedy yard behind a high fence. It was built only in 1988; before that, children stayed home until they were seven, when they could enter the primary school in *el centro*. The secondary school, just down the hill, was built only in 1985, and before that, the few children who went beyond elementary education had to attend school near or at the coast, in Candelaria or Pochutla. Most, like Basilio, simply ended their schooling at age twelve. Now, about half of Pluma's children attend the secondary school, whose student population this year is a hundred and twenty. Of these, perhaps four or five will continue their studies beyond secondary school, going away for this purpose to the city of Oaxaca or the coast. Virtually all the students come from families that depend on coffee for their livelihood. Even the schools themselves seem derived from coffee- -the buildings loom up out of fields of the plants, and the parents all donate time during the harvest to pick and pulp the ripe cherries, proceeds from which subsidize supplies and teacher salaries.

Today, as Genoveva has said, the door to the *kinder* stands shut. The windows are dark, and no squeaky children's chatter or singing carries into the street. "The teacher's not there, or anyone." Genoveva wipes her palms on her skirt and squints, unperturbed, down the dirt road Basilio has just traveled.

He assures her that when he left the house, he left only Isidra, looking after Juan Diego and the baby, Enriquetta, and he met no one on the road just now.

"Maybe they're at my mother's," he suggests; but no: Genoveva has just come from Los Naranjales, cutting through the woods path behind La Palma, and nobody was home. Their Spanish is as fleet and delicate as rustling leaves; in their mouths, the language is like a soft-shoe.

"Entonces . . ." With her air of mild amusement, Genoveva shrugs, and sets forth at a relaxed pace along the tine of the road that leads to *el centro.* Basilio falls in beside her. It is a quiet day in Pluma, hot dogs skulking around with their tongues out to here, cooking fires lacing the air with their musky fragrance, the knowledge of unseen bodies at work in the wooded slopes above and below town, picking coffee, gathering the cherries.

Up ahead, on the left, built in somewhat precarious fashion on a wedge of flat land before a steep drop, stands a house made of sheets of corrugated tin. One wall says in English, over and over, "Nature's Best Whipped Light Cream." Another wall is made from tin tattooed with the logo for Eagle Peanuts. At one end of the house, a large paneless window has been cut out. On the other side of this window is a booth-sized room filled with shelves, and from the road one can see that these shelves are stocked with goods in bright, printed wrappers: soap and batteries, toilet paper and Alka-Seltzer, factory-made cookies and chewing gum and iced sponge cakes, all kinds of things that come from outside Pluma, that have made the journey from the city of Oaxaca, and maybe even beyond. After school, the front of this booth is always crowded with lucky children who have been given some centavos to spend, calling for, *"¡Chicle!"* and *"¡Chocolate!"* and lingering over the visions of factory-made sweets in their bright paper and plastic jackets, preferable, naturally, to the homemade desserts: the sweet *atoles* and tamales, guava pastes, and flan.

Standing before the booth this morning are a few familiar figures: those of the children, Silvestre and Yolanda, and Basilio's mother, Señora Salinas. The three renegades turn at the sound of footsteps in the street, and grin, the children with lips dyed a novel shade of green, the grandmother not without a touch of sheepishness. Señora Salinas, a small round-faced woman with beautiful posture, is indulging her grandchildren in treats of lime Jello, which the makeshift shop sells in little glass cups; you eat the snack there on the street, with metal spoons, then return the dirty dishes to the woman in the booth.

Genoveva laughs to see her green-mouthed children. They laugh back, delighted with themselves, and rattle their spoons against the glasses. Señora Salinas says she heard the *kinder* teacher will be in Oaxaca for the rest of the week, attending some course. *"Sí, es verdad,"* confirms the woman inside the booth, nodding slowly with her arms crossed over her chest. That makes the children giggle some more. Genoveva clucks her tongue as if cross with them, but she is only pretending. No one actually seems the least ruffled by the mix-up, the lapse in communication. No one even seems particularly surprised by it. In Pluma Hidalgo, plans shift like the weather; the unexpected is part of the day's natural rhythm.

Basilio takes his leave now, with a nod to his mother and his wife, who will stay behind to wait out the Jello, perhaps even accompany them all on a walk to *el centro,* for Señora Salinas appears on her way to do some shopping; she has knotted around her back and across one shoulder a woven shawl, lying flat against her dress just now, but which can be stuffed like a knapsack to transport home her corn or rice or sweet buns, whatever she is buying; young women use this same sort of sling to carry their babies. Silvestre darts a few steps after his father, shouting *"¡Adiós!"* and Basilio looks back and nods once more, almost shyly, barely smiling, remaining cool, *tranquilo,* in the fashion of men of his village.

The men here like to say that the women and children are shy, that that is why the men are so deeply protective of their home lives and their nuclear families. But the women laugh and claim that just the opposite is true: it is the men who are shy, the men who are guarded.

When Basilio arrives at the basketball court at La Palma, he must step around a great blanket of pale yellow beans drying on the cracked cement. His brother Lucío has been and gone. Later, when the sun wanes, Basilio will rake the beans back up. On the huge *fincas* there are men who do nothing but rake beans all day long, turning them over and over so that they will dry evenly. Sometimes, when you are walking along the mountain and looking down through the trees, you can spot them, these *patieros,* far away and looking like tiny mechanical dolls walking endlessly back and forth, up and down the perimeters of the drying patios with their long wooden paddles and straw hats. It kills you more, to work on a big *finca* for a rich *patrón;* this is how Basilio thinks of it: simply, it kills you that much more.

Along one side of the patio, at a right angle to the newly finished UCI bunkhouse, sprawls an older dwelling. This one's boards are weather-darkened, warped, and crooked, its corrugated metal roof streaked with rust. It is a caretaker's house. It had already been standing when UCI bought the *parcela,* and already inhabited, by a landless Zapotec family. UCI let the family stay on; the family now thinks of UCI as its new *patrón.*

A little girl with blue-black hair to her tailbone stands outside the house. She is Gudelia Surita, the youngest member of the caretaker family. With no *kinder* today, she leans against the table propped against the outside wall of the house and practices making the letters of the alphabet on a lined tablet with a very short piece of pencil.

"Gudelia," salutes Basilio, with a brief nod, as he passes the seven-year-old, and she ducks her chin and beams.

Her mother, Sabina, reaches a thin hand out the open doorway of the kitchen half of the two-room house and catches the hem of Gudelia's skirt. A tiny, retiring woman with a cautious smile and a back that is already beginning to hunch, Sabina keeps often to this dim, smoky kitchen room. As far as she is concerned, Basilio is himself a kind of *patrón,* an important man on this *parcela* where the Suritas have been allowed to stay in return for service. Everyone in Pluma may be poor, but it is one thing to be poor yet have a *parcela* you call your own, and quite another to be poor and landless. When the land where you lay your head every night is not your own land, you become weary in your heart, and Sabina is this, weary of the act of shrinking apologetically into her own small bones, and weary of tending other people's coffee year after year after year—but what else is there to do? In the meantime, you have your children to feed and keep safe. She whispers something now to Gudelia, and the little girl disappears into the dimness of the kitchen as silently as smoke around a corner.

Basilio crosses the basketball court, cuts behind UCI's new palm bunkhouse, and heads down the mountain. Even where the trees grow thickest, they are spaced along the steep slopes such that supple tides of light swim among them, and the woods are dappled many hues of green and yellow, with warm, humid breezes pinwheeling through branches. The descent to the nursery is so steep that a person must carve a lightning-bolt path, cutting back and forth jaggedly through the trees. Basilio's work shoes are an old pair of rubber thongs. Some of the workers wear leather sandals and some go barefoot; few wear anything sturdier. Basilio passes near some pickers working quietly down the slope, machetes and baskets slung over their shoulders. There is Juan Surita, Sabina's short, silent husband, and a few associates who have come down from La Pasionaria, the small colony above the village, to put in some time working UCI's *parcela*. For this they earn fifteen pesos a day. On the mountain floor, mixed in with dry leaves and fallen lemons and limes, lies the occasional candy or gum wrapper, evidence that this pathless, hushed spot is also a daily thoroughfare for schoolchildren taking shortcuts home through the *parcela*.

Farther down the slope, Basilio arrives at a deeply tranquil, greener place, where the earth temporarily resolves itself into a wide cupped palm before plummeting again toward sea level. This is land UCI cleared and terraced for the building of a tree nursery last summer, shortly after acquiring the *parcela* from the previous owner.

The nursery actually consists of two parts, the *semillero,* where the seedlings begin, and the *vivero,* where the larger shoots continue to be nourished until ready to plant. All the tenderness Basilio does not publicly demonstrate toward his own children, he allows himself here, on this quiescent plot of land, with its well-ordered rows, its well-tended sprouts, as clean and pacific as a mountainside chapel. Here lives the soul of his work as *técnico.*

The nursery presently houses ten thousand three hundred trees. The *semillero* plants, each swaddled in its own clump of *abono orgánico* (organic fertilizer) mixed with soil and wrapped in plastic, are protected from too much sun by a handwoven arbor of leaves and string, held up by a tidy bamboo frame. To cultivate a new seedling, Basilio soaks a bean overnight in water. In the morning he plants and covers it with bits of palm frond, then waters it two or three times a day until "the heart of the bean leaps"—until it sprouts. Then he clears away the palm frond coverlet and waits for it to grow. A coffee plant initially puts forth only two leaves, which look like wings, and Basilio refers to them at this stage as "little butterflies." He cares for these individually, picking out dead leaves and twigs that might have fallen on them, rethreading parts of the shade cover that have come loose.

After sixty days in the *semillero,* the little butterflies are ready to be moved down to the *vivero.* Basilio rewraps them in larger bags of *abono*-and-soil mix, taking care to plant each one just so many centimeters deep, just so many centimeters wide, and arranges these bundles in trim, regularly spaced rows, each bordered by a long strip of bamboo. The larger plants don't need the painstakingly customized sunscreen of the *semillero;* for them, the same shade cover that shelters mature coffee plants suffices. In Pluma the shade tree of choice is the *cuile chalu,* which grows quickly and unfurls lush foliage over the more sun-sensitive plants. The first thing UCI did, when starting the nursery here last summer, was to plant lots of *cuile chalu* down in the *vivero,* and plenty of these young trees now stand tall among the pews of baby coffee; they arch slender, leafy branches high above them, filtering the light like a dome of emerald stained glass.

After eight months in the *vivero,* the young coffee plants will be ready to move to the mountainside, where they will be planted just so: spaced two and a half meters apart, with a half-moon dug out around the elevated side of each thin trunk and a kilo of *abono* packed in around it, and leaves heaped on top of this to keep the *abono* from running off downhill. Basilio and others will come by at intervals during the ensuing years, pay repeated visits to each growing plant, redig the half-moons and add more kilos of *abono* as they grow. And each year in March and April, the men will look at the *hijos,* the ''sons,'' growing out from the main trunk, and the spindliest of these they will slash off with machetes, so as not to sap strength wastefully from the tree; the most promising *hijos* they will allow to grow. Careful pruning can extend the life of a coffee tree to one hundred years. Three years after being planted, when the trees have reached a man's height, they will be harvested for the first time. First the trees will frill up and bloom with sweet white flowers, and then each flower will "throw forth its cherry," which turns from hard and green to red and ripe, and then the men will come with their baskets, and with their fingers claim the fruit.

The *abono* with which the plants are nourished is a homemade concoction of ash, fermented cherry pulp, chopped-up foliage, lime, and manure. All but the last come from Pluma's own land. The manure is the one expensive ingredient; it must be trucked up from the coast, as too few people in Pluma own animals to supply enough manure for all the coffee. The *abono* marinates for two or three months before it is spread. Here at the nursery a large cement tub, one cubed meter, is used for that purpose. Basilio rotates this smelly porridge every two weeks with a bamboo pole, then extracts the pole and feels it for warmth, an indication that the desired chemical process is taking place; this he learned about from the agricultural engineer. The recipe for this *abono orgánico* is something Basilio allows himself a certain measure of pride in. It is altogether more complex and labor-intensive than the chemical fertilizers that the government subsidized and most local farmers used during the eighties, but for Basilio there is pleasure—contentment, he would say—in making it from scratch with all familiar ingredients. "Everything we use here is from here," he says, as if offering a definition of happiness.

Today Basilio moves among the nursery aisles with infinite patience and attention, removing bits of forest debris, plucking dead leaves from the growing plants.

He is methodical, observant as a monk—but free from reverence, from devotion. He does not daydream while he works, never hums or sings or lets his mind make up stories to amuse itself. The work alone fills up his mind, like something full and round, seeking every crack and corner; it leaves no room for other thoughts, for ideas. The nursery itself is like an idea. It is the largest idea of all, with its bed of little butterflies, and its thousands of young plants in pristine columns, and its canopy of *cuile chalu,* whispering now with breeze, bowing now to let pass a veil of mist. Basilio moves within the living body of the nursery and the idea of it dwarfs him.

He neither enjoys nor dislikes his work. These are not questions he ever forms for himself. In that sense, too, the nursery is like a church: he comes not so much deliberately as inevitably, moved by tradition and the demands of human life. It is as if the notion of choice cannot hold up here; meaning slips from the word, leaves it dumb, inert. Basilio threads and bends among the plants with the same familiar ease that he stands and sits and kneels throughout the priest's service. Except that among the coffee he can remove his T-shirt, feel the weather on his back, soil his hands and knees, hear birds jabber and old dry trees moan as they sway on the slopes. Still, he would not say he enjoys his work, any more than he would think to say he enjoys his liver or lungs. It is more of an absolute.

Basilio brings this same lack of introspection to his new role as the *técnico* of UCI's Pluma branch. He wears the extra responsibility seriously and humbly, seems reluctant to perceive it as a change, as a choice. As to why he supposes he was selected for such an important position at the age of twenty-six, Basilio will only blink softly, rake his hair aside a couple of times, and from beneath his heavy, humorless mustache offer simply, "I volunteered."

Basilio traverses the side of the mountain in the afternoon, the fog having reasserted its dominance over the sun, and also real clouds, up high, having moved in, so that the sky is putty-colored and the mountain flora more poignantly green somehow against its dullness, as if lit from within the earth. Basilio alternates between steep, pathless shortcuts and wide, well-worn dirt roads that undulate with the side of the mountain. The earth changes color at least every kilometer; there is *tierra roja,* the color of barely ripe tomatoes; *tierra negra,* like moist chocolate cake; and *tierra blanca,* which is mostly clay. Very high overhead he sees a vulture circle: so ugly on earth and so lovely in the sky.

Basilio passes people occasionally: two women and a man gathering firewood; a group of young women and children hurrying rather gaily past him with wet hair and laundry; a man holding a child in one arm and a chicken under the other. They all greet one another in a polite, subdued manner. Even when he comes upon his brother, not Lucío but another brother, Guillermo, hacking fat bunches of green plantains from a tree and tying them across the back of his burro, they greet each other decorously, quietly, as though the forest were someone's parlor. Guillermo, taller and clean-shaven, with long hair and a leather sheath for his machete slung over one shoulder, continues to secure his load as the brothers chat briefly. The machete itself sticks out of a mound of dark chocolate earth.

"Soon the water will fall," predicts Guillermo,

with an eye to the sky. This is how people in Pluma speak of rain.

"Yes," agrees Basilio, a little dolefully. *"Now* it decides to fall."

"What can you do?" says Guillermo, with a gentle shrug. It has been a disappointingly dry season. World coffee prices are up this year, but local yields are down; it seems that no matter what, the people of Pluma must find themselves scraping to get by. Guillermo shrugs again, plucks his machete from the ground, and slices loose a few plantains from the bunches he has collected—a *plátano macho,* the size of a man's femur, and a stubby green banana the size of his index finger. He hands these to his brother.

"Okay. See you."

"See you."

Basilio continues down the varicolored dirt road, tucking the larger fruit under one arm and peeling the smaller to eat as he walks. Many days he visits one or two UCI associates before heading back to his own *parcela.* Another part of his job as *técnico* is to check on how the associate farmers are doing, see if they need help mixing their *abono* or digging their half-moons properly, or find out how far along they are with bringing in their crops. Although the people have been growing coffee here for generations, some of the technology is new, and each time UCI holds a lecture or seminar with a guest agricultural engineer, Basilio has more expertise to bring back to the region. Also, familiarity with each associate's farm lets him keep the people at headquarters apprised of the larger picture in Pluma—not just how many kilos of beans come down the mountain each week, but how the families are doing, what their concerns are. Perhaps the very fact of how unimposing Basilio is, his very lack of swagger and ambition and even charisma, makes him particularly well suited to this aspect of the job.

As he cuts along the mountain, he passes from *parcela* to *parcela,* always knowing whose land he is on, although no low stone walls mark dividing lines, nor are lengths of wire strung between trees, nor even blazes painted or notched on any of the trunks. The Zapotec way of indicating borders is to plant living things along them, certain trees, which everyone recognizes and respects. The most commonly used is the *tzompantle,* or "machete tree." Its nickname comes from the silky carmine blossoms, shaped like curved, tapered blades, that dangle from its branches and speckle the ground beneath it like festive toy machetes. Basilio crosses these borders easily; here in Pluma there is no such thing as trespassing, except on the *fincas* and haciendas, the ones where families do not harvest the coffee themselves but hire poorer people to do it. Those large ranches and plantations may be guarded or fenced; at any rate, everyone knows they are restricted, inaccessible, private property. Among the UCI associates and other small farmers, however, land may be entered onto and crossed freely, with nothing but petal knives for loose suggestions of territory.

On a pale clay stretch of road, Basilio stops and calls into the trees. No one, not even a rustle, answers him. He waits, expressionless, arms slack, the *plátano macho* hanging from one hand, looking up the steep grade that rises above the road. Nothing. Then a whistle. Then a figure in a pale green dress appears through the trees, zigzagging swiftly, surely, down the mountain. She has a basket slung over each arm, a sheathed machete in one hand. This is Guadalupe Salinas, harvesting cherries on her *parcela,* Predio Escondido (Hidden Estate).

"*Tía* Lupe," greets Basilio. She is his father's sister.

Lupe smiles and descends the rest of the way limberly through the brush. She is a tall, agile woman who from a distance looks much younger than her age. Up close, her face is more noticeably worn. Like Basilio, she has a couple of silver-framed teeth. She is barefoot and wears blue jeans under her dress. Black braids fall down her back like ropes; at the ends a piece of string ties them together.

"How goes it?" asks Basilio.

"Okay, okay." Lupe peers into her baskets and shrugs. She tells Basilio she has done two cuts on this land already, and is now just taking a last sweep. Harvests generally include two or three cuts. Her baskets contain mostly hard, green cherries, those that won't ripen any further on the tree. The soft, red cherries have been all harvested by now. She offers to show him, and the two amble down the road. Lupe's *parcela* comprises two and a half hectares, which she works alone for most of the year; one teenaged daughter helps out during the harvest. Her house and drying yard lie down the embankment on the other side of the road. Lupe and Basilio climb and skid down a pebbly path, spilling out by a chest-high mound of decomposing cherry pulp. The pulp, which encases the coffee beans as they grow, is removed in one of the earliest stages of processing, then saved carefully to be mixed into future batches of *abono orgánico*. Fruit flies swarm around the sticky, stinky stuff, and over Lupe and Basilio as they tread near. Neither bothers to swat. They move out among the palm mats that checkerboard the yard.

Predio Escondido indeed has a desolate feel, secreted as it is in one of the mountain's low, gray hollows, nearly two kilometers from the village. Today the yard is sunless and damp. A sketchy twist of smoke writhes from a hole cut in the tin roof. Lupe lives here alone except for the teenaged daughter, Sirenia, and a black-and-white pig tied to a stake in the yard; she is a widow whose other children are grown. But she does not consider this a lonely spot; there are neighboring *parcelas* off in the trees, and the walk to *el centro* is not so long when you know the shortcuts through the forest. There is too much work anyway for her ever to feel lonely; instead, Lupe calls her life peaceful—a struggle, of course, but a peaceful one.

Here on her hidden pocket of land the sun emerges for little more than a teasing wink each day. Now the mist is rolling visibly back in, nuzzling the beans and pig and sagging wooden house. Like virtually all of the smaller associate farmers, including Basilio, Lupe has no cement patio on which to rake out her beans. She dries them instead on the palm mats, which retain moisture and are therefore less effective than the cement. (Some people dry their beans on their corrugated metal roofs.) The same wetness people wished for earlier in the season, when the coffee cherries were just beginning to grow, arrives as a nuisance now that the drying process is under way.

"No sun, no sun," murmurs Lupe, philosophically. "You have to have a lot of patience for this work, eh?"

And she begins folding up the mats with the beans still in them; they tumble stickily to the middle. Now, bundled into shrouds, the mats will keep the beans from absorbing quite so much of the afternoon's moisture. If the sun cooperates, Lupe tells Basilio, she might have three bags ready to send to the coast by the end of the week. In unison they glance at the sky, then nod gently at the beans as if to say what is plain, *It is not up to us.*

Coffee prices have been good this week: five hundred sixty pesos a bag. Each bag holds forty-seven kilos, each kilo about two thousand hand-picked beans. Basilio is hoping to reap between fifteen and seventeen bags this year from his *parcela,* to earn perhaps nine thousand pesos (about fifteen hundred U.S. dollars). UCI determines what it will pay its associates based on the spot price for coffee as reported by the New York Coffee, Sugar and Cocoa Exchange; this information gets relayed daily by computer to Oaxaca, faxed to UCI headquarters in Pochutla, and transmitted by radiophone to UCI's Pluma branch. Pluma farmers benefit from an additional premium tacked on to the price, which they look upon as a reward for the extra labor involved in growing organic coffee.

Coffee has been growing in this region for little more than a century—since only about 1870—but for most of that brief history, all of it was farmed organically. It was only around the time Basilio was born that chemical fertilizers and pesticides were introduced and encouraged in Pluma, subsidized by the government's Mexican Coffee Institute, or INMECAFÉ. INMECAFÉ advised the farmers to chop down their shade trees to make room for more coffee plants, and to pour chemicals into the soil. But within two decades, INMECAFÉ collapsed, as did the international coffee market, which bottomed out in 1989. With government subsidies yanked away, the farmers could no longer afford to buy chemical fertilizer; meanwhile, their shade trees were gone and their soil was dried out and drained of natural nutrients. This was when many owners of large and medium-sized farms (such as La Palma's previous owner) abandoned their *parcelas* altogether and took off to try to make their fortunes in the city. The small peasant farmers, however, had no means to flee, to choose something different for themselves. They had no alternative but to try to salvage what they could from their depleted land.

These factors led to the resurrection of organic coffee. UCI trained its associates to return to the old methods, to replant shade trees and replenish the soil with natural ingredients. Since 1992 all UCI associates in the Pluma region have been officially certified as organic farmers. Not incidentally, this was the same year that Aztec Harvests began to sell (the premium tacked on to the price of organic coffee is not so much a reflection of extra labor-hours as it is of the simple fact that customers in the United States and Europe are willing to pay more for this "specialty coffee"). In constructing its niche, its identity within the world coffee market, the company does promote the fact that it is a worker-owned, profit-sharing co-op, comprised of indigenous peoples—but more commercially salient, and more directly lucrative, is the simple fact that it can label its product organic.

All of this is far from Lupe's mind as she works alone, mixing her *abono,* digging half-moons, trimming weak *hijos* from the trees, picking cherries, pulping them, laying them out to dry. It is far from Basilio's mind as well, although his trips to the coast have given him more exposure to the large scheme of Aztec Harvests and its relationship to himself. Still, he cannot yet fathom the idea of being in any way a member-owner of the company; in his world this has nowhere manifested itself as a reality. He practices and passes on the new methods of farming because he has been told that they are better for the crops, not because he thinks they will please the gringo customers, whom he does not anyway consider *his* customers; whom, in fact, he does not consider.

The world beyond Pluma remains in many respects obscure to Basilio, not wholly conceivable. The picture of the world that wends its way into the village is by turns so fragmented or peculiar as to seem often doubtful. When a huge earthquake rocks Tokyo, the story that filters down to the farmers is that the event occurred in Mexico City (or in some versions, Oaxaca), and all day long then workers debate whether they felt the motion in the night. When the value of the peso plummets on the world market, it takes weeks for the knowledge to register on the residents of Pluma, and even then speculation ranges widely on how just poor the peso has become and whether the trend might even have reversed by now. Yet on his trips to the coast, in his increasing interactions with people who own televisions, who have access to newspapers and to travel, Basilio is garnering larger and clearer fragments of the outside world; and he is piecing these sometimes dubious items together against the background of what he knows for sure.

Basilio takes leave of his aunt as casually as he greeted her. He climbs up toward the clay road, but just before he reaches it, Lupe's disembodied voice calls "Wait!" and he turns, obediently, gazing into the misty scrim of greenery until a figure appears—not *Tía* Lupe's but that of his young cousin Sirenia, half running up the incline with a shy smile and two bunches of plantains, one reddish, the other green. She hands them to Basilio without a word, only the sound of soft panting, and he adds them to the *plátano macho* already under his arm.

"Ah, gracias, Sirenia."

"Sí, sí," she responds like two notes on a piccolo, and then she is tripping deftly back home.

At La Palma in the afternoon, two of the dogs are sleeping on the beans. Basilio shoos one with a mimed kick, and both leap up and shrink over behind the bunkhouse. Basilio takes up the wooden paddle and begins to rake the beans into a heap. The fickle sun has wafted out of the clouds again, but the hottest part of the day has certainly past; it is time he put the drying coffee beans back in the burlap sacks where they slumber each night, safe from dew.

At home it is the women who do this, Genoveva and Isidra. They spread four palm mats in the dirt yard every morning, spill their *parcela*'s beans out evenly on them, rotate them with wooden rakes and paddles in the sun's heat, and scoop them back into burlap sacks again when the air grows more moist than dry. Silvestre and Yolanda help, squatting beside the mats and smoothing out the coffee with their little hands in the morning, scrambling after mischievous roll-away beans when they are bagging them again in the afternoon. The women and children take care of this job; the men tend to everything else: harvesting, pulping, mixing *abono,* spreading it, pruning, tending to the nursery— for Basilio has started his own coffee nursery at El Corozo, a smaller-scale version of UCI's nursery at La Palma. Even with Lucío to help him, it is a lot of work, and Lucío has responsibilities elsewhere, too: he tends the coffee on the local doctor's *parcela.* And Basilio now divides his own time exactly in half: one day at La Palma, one day at El Corozo. Already he is teaching six-year-old Silvestre the other facets of coffee growing. He sometimes brings his son among the trees with him; already they are beginning to work side by side on the *parcela* that Silvestre will one day tend.

Sabina and Gudelia Surita appear now from out of the woods, both with wet hair hanging in loose strings down their backs, the mother hefting a yellow plastic bucket in both hands. They cross the basketball court, skirting the beans, smiling silently in Basilio's general direction as they head toward their house. He nods at them, continues to rake.

The Surita women are returning from the birthplace of water, which is the way everyone refers to the various springs and brooks that dot the mountainside. Nearly every *parcela* has at least one such place where the people bathe themselves and wash their clothes and dishes. In addition to bathing, Gudelia and her mother have been catching crabs. This is the time of year when the mountain streams run full of tender baby crabs; they will make a good dinner. Standing in front of the house in her white cotton dress, Gudelia reaches into the yellow bucket and, squealing a little, fishes out one tiny wriggling crab. Her mother watches, amused, with one of her rare unsquelchable smiles, all high, protruding cheekbones and lips knit tightly over poor teeth. Gudelia grapples with the crab, gets nipped by a pincer, and drops it hastily back into the bucket. She emits a shuddery laugh, hops, and appeals to her mother, who reaches for another crab, delicately tears off a leg, and hands it to the girl. Gudelia crunches it like a stick of candy.

Basilio leans the paddle against the side of their house and takes up a couple of empty sacks and a large metal can for scooping. A rooster crows from some invisible neighbor's yard, signifying nothing in particular, and a burro brays its melancholy response. They might be chiming the hour on a clock of vague calibrations, a Pluma clock, keeping time according to unseen rhythms, fancy and whim. Here, when people say "right now," what they mean is "in an hour, or if not, then tomorrow"; when they say "soon," they mean "sometime, maybe." They mean "when it becomes necessary or possible." And the hours elongate and drift like the mist through the trees, and there is no hurry, no point in rushing. Basilio bends and scoops the drying beans. Sabina combs and combs her daughter's drying hair.

Now the men, the day workers, trickle out of the woods with their baskets of cherries. Those from La Pasionaria cross the court, headed for the secondary school, where the paved road ends. UCI sends a truck at the end of most days to carry them back up the mountain; some days the truck does not come, and they wait awhile and then trudge the hour or so uphill to their homes. Among them is Juan Surita. Without acknowledging his wife and daughter, he carries his baskets to the front of his house and kneels. Sabina sets down the comb and comes to crouch quickly beside him. Juan, the landless caretaker, has a heavy brow, which gives him a perpetually glowering, bruised look. His very posture seems mute, submissive, as if in accordance with his station in life. He and Sabina sort the cherries, red from green, into two piles. Gudelia stands against the wall, watching. Basilio, finished tying up the sacks, drags them over to the bunkhouse, where he drapes a plastic tarp over them. No one speaks.

Some of the older boys from the secondary school appear with a rubber ball too flaccid to dribble but all right for shooting, and they begin a sloppy game on the newly bean-free court. Basilio joins in, and some of the day workers from La Pasionaria who have drifted back down, their ride not having yet shown. Juan does not join the others. In his slow, silent way, he travels around the court to its outer perimeter, and with a machete trims several leaves off a cactus growing there. These he delivers to Sabina, who stands in the kitchen doorway and with a smaller knife slices out each spiny needle in preparation for roasting. With a sprinkle of salt, these will make a fine accompaniment to the crabs at dinner. Juan retires to the sleeping room of the little house. Gudelia and her mother slip into the kitchen, from whose roof smoke begins to curl pungently.

The air is turning ashy, dusk-textured. On the court the day workers are saying they will wait extralong tonight for their ride back to La Pasionaria, because there is a rumor that Señor Pérez will be bringing their money. They work six days a week and officially get paid each Saturday, but this schedule is adhered to no more rigidly than any other in Pluma, and they are more often paid on whatever day Señor Pérez has been able to deliver the week's coffee and get the workers' money from UCI headquarters; this may be contingent on whether the truck is running and has gas. (There are no gas stations here in the mountains, and people commonly resort to siphoning from one tank into another to get by; every vehicle has a couple of rubber tubes in the back for this purpose, which entails sucking gas from one tank until just before your mouth gets flooded, then transferring the tube into the other tank.)

At any rate, the workers don't complain about the slightly sporadic schedule on which they are paid. "At least we get paid by the day and not the basket," says one, and takes a free throw with the saggy ball. He departs the court then for the low cement wall in front of the bunkhouse, and the other workers join him, leaving the teenaged boys to play on. The *finca* bosses, everyone knows, pay by the basket, five or six pesos for each one filled, which is all very well during a lush harvest but doesn't address the workers' needs when pickings are slim. After the harvest the *fincas* pay no better, forty pesos for each thousand coffee plants pruned, fifty centavos for each half-moon dug. UCI, at least, pays a guaranteed wage for a day's work, so you move along at a human pace and fill your baskets as best you can. It would be nice, though, one worker adds, if UCI could pay a little *more* each day. Couldn't they manage eighteen or twenty pesos, say, now that the price of coffee is going up?

Basilio listens and nods, commiserating; he earns no

more than his comrades here, chatting on the wall as the sun begins to wane. They all work hard in order only to scrape by, and the workers have been gearing up for some time to ask for a raise, next month at the associates' meeting, perhaps. Whatever the answer, though, at least they have the right to ask, and as associates—as co-owners, if what Basilio is learning at his meetings in Pochutla really is true—rather than as peons. At the very least they will be heard; their voices count at UCI; UCI consists of them. And they can sit here, as the air turns blue and grainy with the onset of a long dusk, and do as they please, go home or play ball, their freedom intact.

The church bells ring lazily in *el centro,* and a chorus of dogs bark at one another through the trees. One of the boys on the court takes a slingshot from his pocket and begins to aim pebbles at the hoop. Gudelia emerges from the house, yawning, fetches the bucket of crabs, and half drags it into the kitchen. Cooking fires are unleashing their familiar, faintly bitter aroma all around the village, and now the boys are heading home, the day workers rising to check again whether the truck has come to deliver them back to La Pasionaria.

Basilio, too, rises. As he crosses the court, he finds himself thinking of the men who work on the big *fincas,* laboring and eating and sleeping there all week long, away from their families and homes, and he feels a sadness pull softly at his chest. How strange to think that the *finca* bosses were once Zapotec, too, like the workers themselves. As Basilio understands it, when all the land was being divided up and given out around the turn of the century, certain families were simply smart, simply prepared. They somehow had the fore-sight to quickly claim great portions of land for them-selves—as many as three thousand hectares apiece. In doing so they became *finca* bosses, and, in Basilio's mind, simultaneously ceased to be Zapotec. All the residents of the village, all the small farmers with *parcelas* scattered about the mountain, he calls family, but the *finca* bosses he cannot think of as kin. "Before they were indigenous, but now they're civilized" is how he phrases it. They may have dwelt in this region for generations, but they are strangers to him.

*T*ime

In the cramped shop I move slowly. The sign above the door says "Antiques," but this establishment always strikes me as having rather more the air of a junk shop, what with the merchandise all jumbled together on dusty tables and shelves. The items themselves—a plastic bin of tarnished forks; a row of lunchboxes dating no further back than my own childhood; an assortment of glass souvenir ashtrays purporting to be from, variously, Niagara Falls; Shiprock, N.M.; Havana, Cuba; and The Mint Julep Lounge—appear not so much antique as used. They seem to me intangibly and not unpleasantly engrimed, patinaed with unseen fingerprints. The prices, written directly on most of the items in green marker, are low.

I am not, strictly speaking, a customer. The truth is, I am waiting for a bus and have come in to avoid the rain. But I might buy something. The shop's owner sits up front in a ratty gray cardigan, her left cheek lumpy with a hard candy. She is always rude to everyone. The rain beats furiously against the sidewalk and awning outside. It makes the sound of something frying in hot oil.

The single other browser, a man in a dripping slicker, fingers a wooden metronome. He frees the pendulum bar and slides the weight up near the top. It begins to tock out widely spaced beats, a luscious slow motion of sound. The shop's owner looks up and glares, switches her candy to the other cheek.

I turn sideways and make myself thin in order to sidle past the man without contacting his body. My coat brushes against the table behind me; a toy sleigh falls off, and a wooden darning egg. The sleigh, I see, bending to retrieve it, has been handpainted with snowflakes and the name *Cora M.* Different handwriting, in green pen, on the underside, reads *$2——.* The darning egg, when I pick it up, feels mysteriously pleasant in my hand. I turn it over: *80¢.* I decide, for no reason, that I will have it. The man with the metronome edges the weight down the bar; the beats tock through the shop a little faster.

A stack of books lies by the sleigh. I lift the top

volume: a history of aviation. On the flyleaf is an in-
scription: *Fred, This is a damn good book. You better like it.
—Ralph, Christmas 1937.* The second volume, a cook-
book, looks as though its binding has been chewed by
mice. Almost as soon as I pick it up, it flips open to a
page on which a four-leaf clover has been pressed. I
stare at the clover, forty-odd years out of the ground,
then at the recipe, for Cocoa Chiffon Loaf Cake, then
at the aged chocolate thumbprint in the corner of the
page. On impulse I hover my own thumb above it.

The metronome quickens its pace again. I fantasize,
briefly, that its pulse is actually emanating from each of
the musty items in the shop, and for that short moment it unnerves me. I replace the book on the table,
check my watch. A minute 'til the bus. I pay for the
darning egg, and am already at the door when I realize: it is exactly like one I have seen in my grandmother's house. As I step out into dampness, the tock-
ing speeds up once more, fast as the heartbeat of an
unborn baby, a little softer than the rain.

F o u r

The Fetish

*F*eitiço: "a thing made." That's the word Portuguese sailors used in the eighteenth century when they went floating and docking in scallop patterns down the humpy coastline of West Africa. That's the word the sailors used to describe those bits of carved wood that the people they encountered, their trading partners, wore on strings around their necks or hung in their doorways. The little figures had scowly faces, some of them. Some were adorned with cowrie shells. Some consisted of nothing but a bit of stiff, oddly stained rag tied to a stick. Some were good and some were bad; all had great and mysterious powers.

These fetishes were concocted, and consecrated in special ceremonies, by *ogangas,* or "magic doctors," or "spiritual leaders." The fetishes could be made not only of wood but also of snail shells, nut husks, gazelle horns, clay beads, leopard whiskers, koka-bird feathers, lion teeth, turtle jaws, serpent spines. They might be anointed or stuffed with the ashes of certain medicinal plants; gums, spices, and resins; the entrails or eyeballs of animal or human remains. If a fetish was to have power over a specific human being, it might also include crumbs from that person's food, her bathwater, her fingernail or hair clippings, a drop of her blood. A newborn infant would have a health-knot fetish tied to its wrist. Fetishes hung from the bows of fishers' canoes to provide a safe voyage; got tied to hunters' arms to ensure good aim; were draped over plants in a garden to prevent blight and theft.

The Portuguese sailors' name for such a complicated device was deceptively simple. Their word, from the Latin *facere* (to make), indicated something manufactured, something crafted by human hands; pushing that definition a step further, it could also mean something artificial, a fabrication. But a second definition of the Portuguese term doubles over on itself in peculiar fashion, hinting at something more complex: "that which is made in order to make." And *feitiço* indeed contains a more sinuous meaning, folded into itself like eggs into batter. That is, the meaning of a thing enchanted, bewitched, a thing invested with a charmed and potent spirit—as were the fetishes: they had the power to make your stomach ache, make the rains come, make you fall in love with your neighbor. This is what the people who kept them believed, and from no more than that faith sprang the objects' power.

Fetishism, then, in this earliest sense, was the religious veneration of material objects. It was, in a way, the act of recognizing God everywhere you looked.

Africans weren't the only ones who had fetishes; all over the world people had them, made them, saw them. And the range of fetish objects, the materials that could serve as vehicles for the spirits, was unlimited. Anything on earth and in the heavens might hum with a fetish, a mighty inner nature that could act on other things; that, through human manipulation, could bring about results beyond the power of ordinary individuals. We have, over time, fetishized and worshipped tree bark and wind, stars and bones. We have apprehended the divine in sunshine, egg shells, a bolt of silk, a face in the moon.

Even stones, even the dullest, dun-colored pebble, so grossly inanimate, so apparently inert and soulless—even in them we have found the presence of spirits. Ancient Lapps believed that stones moved about at night, and they thought of certain rocks as having familial identities such as mother, father, and child. In churches of the Middle Ages, stones were anointed with oil, blood, and wine as offerings to the spirits within. Meteoric stones, especially, were sacred, being perceived as "incarnate rays of the sun." But stones of this world were sacred, too, being the children of Gaea, our Mother Earth; in their most awesome form, stones rise up into mountains, and these have been fetishized by peoples from North America to Africa to Siberia.

Water is alive with spirits, and since antiquity people have paid it worship with prayers and sacrifice. In Acra a pitcher would be cast into a river, which was to act as messenger then, conducting that pitcher out to all other rivers and streams, where it might gather their waters and return home with enough to irrigate all the fields. The Kamchatkales appeased dangerous whirlpools by flinging offerings of carved wood and tobacco into their roiling depths as they sailed by, reassuring the waters that they had not forgotten their reverence for them. Before the time of the Incas, Peruvians regarded the sea as the supreme deity. People have made offerings to this great salty body, before setting sail, of animal entrails, millet, blood, and gold.

Winds have been worshipped and hurricanes pacified by throwing coins and meal into the air. The Payaguás of South America, when the winds blew so hard they threatened to whisk apart thatched houses, would take a burning poker from the fire and run with it thrust against the wind in an effort to frighten and subdue the storm. Or they would simply pummel the churning air overhead. The worship of fire and thunder and lightning all have been practiced as well. Rain has been revered by some as the Giver of All Things, and by others as a direct ancestor. The rainbow, too, has been fetishized among many peoples, usually as a bringer of wealth or fortune, or as a passageway between mortal and divine realms.

Flora and fauna, being what we call alive to begin with, are not surprisingly held to be rife with magical and sacred spirits. Druids spread boughs of holly at winter solstice as protection against evil fairies. The Greeks of Dodona heard in rustling oak leaves a sacred language; the written words of their human oracles were thought to be no more than cabalistic transcriptions of the messages of these trees. Germans also worshipped oaks; long after the introduction of Christianity it remained a punishable crime to violate such a tree. Mandrake plants and jack-in-the-pulpits were both thought to house magic; if someone should be so foolhardy as to pick one, a terrible dark scream would rip from the earth and the picker would die on the spot. But if you managed gently to remove a mandrake from the soil without causing it pain, and then washed it in red wine and wrapped it in red and white pieces of silk, and bathed it again every Friday and gave it new vestments at the new moon—then it would reveal your fortune.

As for animals, people have registered behind the blandest elephant's eye the presence of a deity and have called this animal sacred; similarly designated have been cows, bears, snakes, tigers, sharks, moose, oxen, wolves, monkeys, crocodiles, and butterflies. We have fetishized members of our own species as well, perceiving special links to the divine in albinos, dwarves, hunchbacks, fools, twins, the blind, the deaf, the mad. If such a one were a slave, she might be given her freedom; or else locks of her hair might be sold as holy relics. All over medieval Europe, peddlers passed off little sacks of unrecognizable material as remnants of some dead saint's or martyr's body, a bit of bone from the pinky finger, perhaps, or a tooth, or some ashes from the burned corpse. Today, in our own country, some of us dangle crosses and figurines from rearview mirrors, meant to bless us with safety while driving; some of us tote silky rabbits' feet for luck; some of us are careful about how we dispose of our fingernail clippings, just in case.

Fetishism, the most ancient and universal form of worship, the seed from which all world religions are said to have blossomed, has been classified by scholars as "primitive" and a behavior of "savages." In 1760 a

Frenchman named Charles de Brosses brought the term into use to describe the type of religion practiced by "the lowest races." But fetishism is at bottom directly opposed to ignorance, naïveté, or crude ways of thinking. It implies instead nothing more than a heightened kind of recognition; it betrays an awareness of the incomprehensible, and an effort to commune with it. What could be more sophisticated, more advanced, than to admit a sense of wonder into daily life? And if fetish worship really is a behavior of savages, then we are every one of us a savage still, for we all engage in fetishism on some level.

"That which renders it a fetish is nothing intrinsic to the thing itself," wrote Fritz Schultze, a nineteenth-century German philosopher, "but the view the fetishist takes of it." This holds perfectly true for the items we fetishize today. The extent to which one pair of blue jeans is favored over a virtually identical pair is the extent to which the cotton label stitched on the first pair's back pocket functions as a kind of totem, imbued with, and conferring on the wearer, its spirit of status and desirability. (And should that label become passé, status and desirability will instantly be exorcised from the jeans.) The extent to which the uncle's homemade corn relish and the granddaughter's hand-built coffee table are favored over equally fine store-bought goods is the extent to which the uncle's and the granddaughter's spirits dwell in the products of their labor. (And should someone with no connection to the uncle or the granddaughter come into possession of the relish or table, those special qualities will immediately vacate the objects.) The extent to which almost anything appeals may be the extent to which it *signifies,* to which it evokes and resonates with associations and meanings in our own minds. The more powerfully an object signifies, the more fetish-like it is.

And we don't require *ogangas* to turn things into fetishes—or perhaps we all have *ogangas* dwelling within, mitochondrial witch doctors as part and parcel of our human nature, an inevitability, a birthright. Because everyone knows things are more than what they seem: the designer jeans, the uncle's relish, the rabbit's foot, the good luck charm. A world devoid of fetishes would be like a world without memory, without language or meaning, uninhabitable by human beings; a world lacking atmosphere.

And so we kick and curse at the chair we bump our shins against, and we pick up and stroke the seashell once presented to us by one we miss, and we throw away in the *outside* trash the hateful letter we cannot bear to have sitting in the kitchen garbage all week. And none of this is rational and none of it is savage. It is simply us, living here in the pale last crack of the twentieth century, where everything comes bar-coded and shrink-wrapped and smelling like the factory, where everything is comparable, exchangeable, reducible to price. It is simply us, as yet incapable of being blind to the presence of the spirit in things.

The idea of the fetish got appropriated, and recast, twice during the past hundred years: once in terms of economics and once in terms of psychoanalysis. The latter sense is probably the better known, and its use attributed most famously to Sigmund Freud, who had all manner of racy, real-life tales to illustrate how the concept worked. Within the field of psychoanalysis, fetishism is a perversion in which sexual excitement or gratification is impossible without the presence of a fetish—usually a nongenital part of the human body, such as a foot, a hand, or a plait of hair; an inanimate object, such as a glove, a shoe, or lingerie; or something with a particular sensual quality, such as leather, rubber, or velvet. Often, the mere sight of the fetish can induce orgasm. And the fetish can be virtually anything. For one patient of Freud's it was the shine on the nose of the person for whom he felt attraction.

The sexual fetish, Freud believed, was not randomly chosen, but drew its power from an association with an early sexual experience. Thus, a penchant for fur might be symbolic of the pubic hair glimpsed when a child first saw an adult's genitals. And Freud helped one patient trace his foot fetish to strong memories of a boyhood experience involving a governess who had perched her injured foot (slim, daintily slippered) up on a cushion during lessons. In any case, the sexual fetish is always a stand-in, a substitute, for an experience from real life. Also among sexual fetishists there generally develops a need to possess the fetish; they become chronic, feverish collectors of the fetishized objects, which ultimately take the place and assume the role of the "normal" object of love.

The economic sense of fetishism was developed by Karl Marx in *Das Kapital,* in which he posits, often in unexpectedly lilting and dreamlike phrases, that all commodities are fetishes; that the instant an object becomes a commodity, a special kind of fetishism attaches itself to it. He speaks of commodities as having "mystical" and "enigmatic" characters, as "abounding in metaphysical subtleties." He says of an ordinary table that once it has entered the realm of the commodity, it "evolves out of its wooden brain grotesque ideas, far more wonderful than if it were to begin dancing of its own free will." He says that in order to understand commodity fetishism it is necessary to "take a flight into the misty realm of religion," that

> [t]here the products of the human brain appear as autonomous figures endowed with a life of their own, which enter into relations both with each other and with the human race. So it is in the world of commodities with the products of men's hands.

In this sense, the fetish of the commodity is the value that people collectively ascribe to it. When we endow commodities with a specific value, a character tied not incidentally to price, a fetish begins instantly to writhe within the object, to take it over, until we behave as though the object dropped from heaven or sprang from the skull of Zeus fully formed, its little pristine price tag already dangling from it like an original appendage—when, in fact, this value or price is artificially imposed, an abstraction *masking* the true identity of the object, the true story behind it. The whole idea of a thing being worth, or *equal* to, two ounces of gold, or forty bucks, or a loaf of bread, or whatever, is strictly a human conceit layered onto the object in question. There is nothing more objectively real about the value inhabiting each product than there is about the spirit inhabiting a scrap of tree bark—except that we all (mostly) agree to behave as though such value *is* objectively real, and we revere (and maintain) it daily by acts of exchange.

This is how we fetishize commodities. One set of associations gets burned off in the peremptory flame of price. So that a green apple is not a tart, shining globe of fruit; it is not a sign of autumn, a wonder of nature, a fingerprint of God. Rather, it is fifty cents, a product, a crop, a livelihood. And a gray cottage with a sloping lawn and a bay window and a few rows of corn out back becomes not a home but an investment, property, real estate. And pork bellies and antimony are not, respectively, the stuff hotdogs are made of and number fifty-one on the periodic table; they are Commodities with a capital *C,* nearly pure abstractions; we can own them, buy and sell them, without ever seeing or touching them, without even knowing what they are; they are not so much *things* as they are the bodiless, ethereal essence of value, value in its loftiest, wispiest form: divorced from the tangible, existing solely on our earnest fantasies.

Of course, once an object passes back out of the realm of commodities, its identity may shift again. If we buy something with no thought of resale—an apple, say—its exchange value goes dormant; then it takes on whatever new character we assign it. It might then smell sweet and delicious, remind us of pie, glow like a jewel in a bowl in the sun. A house, once lived in, might have its investment character, its identity as a piece of real estate, layered over by an animus of laughter, sorrows, coziness, family. And accidental delivery of a contract of pork bellies to your doorstep would certainly render them no longer abstract vehicles for accruing wealth; the forty thousand pounds of pig by-product would pretty swiftly become something else: a nuisance, for example.

But in all of these cases, the result is simply one fetish, one powerful imagined identity, replacing another. Nowhere is the mask shed; nowhere does what Marx called the true nature of the object rise to the surface. That has already been rinsed away, atomized, by the original act of inducting it into the field of commerce and profit. That, the truth beyond the fetish's glimmering mirage, is the relationship of laborer to product; it is the social account of how that object came to be. In this view every commodity, beneath the mantle of its price tag, is a hieroglyph ripe for deciphering, a riddle whose solution lies in the story of the worker who made it and the conditions under which it was made.

The charm fetish, the sexual fetish, the commodity fetish: all spring from one root and share certain basic qualities. It is perhaps not insignificant that the same Latin word that spawned "fetish" led also to "confect," "affect," "counterfeit," "manufacture," "artificial," "factitious," and "facsimile." Indeed, each of the three types of fetish acts as a facsimile of, or substitute for, something else. The charm fetish is a kind of literal representation of the supernatural or divine. The sexual fetish is a substitute for what Freud would have called the usual love object: in his opinion, a person of the opposite sex. And the fetish of the commodity—the belief in its innate, independent value—is a fabrication, a material mask, concealing what is really a relationship between people.

The other quality common to each of the three is this: what renders the object a fetish is entirely the faith of the beholder. A piece of specially boiled bark from the bohamba tree is no less an inducement for crops to grow—and a shine on the nose or the creak and smell of leather no less a trigger for orgasm—than are portions of the earth created with inherent property values. The fact that we in this country take the last for granted is a function not of its being absolute truth but of how deeply we have fetishized land as a commodity.

If it is a stretch for us to see beyond the commodity character in things, to lift the mask and recognize things, even for a moment, as being commodities only because we fancy them as such—that may be because we have commodified so *much* of life; it is hard to find a starting place, to think of anything so sacred that it lies really and truly beyond the reach of commodification. Yet not so very many centuries ago, our land itself—the brooks and prairies and tidepools and cliffs and gullies and deserts and pine forests of this country—was not property, had no monetary value, could not be bought or sold or owned. The people who then inhabited this continent had no more thought of owning the land than they had of owning the air, or the rain, or sunshine, or God. Land as property was introduced here by the colonialists; they got the idea established, and then eventually we came along, those of us who got born a few hundred years later, and by now it seems just like fact to us, true from the beginning and forevermore.

Anything we can control, even marginally, we can commodify. So of course today we've made commodities of things like trees and rocks and animals, even animal feces. We can pay for the service of having bees come and pollinate our orchards. We can pay to have

someone else's horse mate with ours. We cannot purchase sunshine but we can buy or rent space where it is
likely to fall, and we can buy equipment to harness its
strength for energy, just as we can harness wind and
water and then sell the energy they produce. Water,
unless in the act of falling from the sky, is owned as
part of someone's property, or else as a beverage
product that may be bought in bottles at the store.
Even air is now a commodity, with prices fixed to the
"air rights" above property, and to "air time," and of
course, to the all-important airwaves. On some of
those airwaves, radio and television evangelists are busy
doing their best to peddle no less than the personal
blessings of God. And on most of those airwaves, other
hawkers are summoning us to traffic in further goods
and services, which promise variously to ensure fresh
breath, natural-looking curls, inner peace, total enjoy-
ment, your friends' envy, their admiration, all their
love, and fewer calories. According to the hawkers,
there is little, if anything, that we can't have commodified, little we can't get boxed and beribboned.

This barrage of information in which everything appears as a commodity no doubt plays a large part in
reinforcing the mask, the idea that everything in its
purest form may appear in terms of its price. But the
single greatest obstacle to our ability to see commodity
fetishism as a construct we have imposed must be our
legacy, as a country, of commodifying our own selves.
Pounded into two and a half centuries of our history is
the enslavement, and consequent ownership, of human
beings—the branding, chaining, advertising, auction-
ing, weighing, inspecting, quantifying, buying, and
selling of people. And in the relatively short span of

time since that practice ceased, we have found other ways to commodify human bodies and functions that continue, really in ever more bizarre forms, into the present, so that today we can buy, rent, or sell, legally or not: sperm, eggs, sexual intercourse (as well as the enactment of virtually all manner of sexual fantasy, including the violent and murderous), plasma, organs, babies. We can even rent a uterus and all the reproductive workings of a woman's body for nine months in order to obtain a baby; this is called surrogate motherhood and is condoned by the courts; in 1990 the going price for such a service was about ten thousand dollars.

And it isn't only in such extreme ways that we commodify aspects of ourselves. Commodification occurs as well in regard to the more usual kinds of labor that most of us do. It is quite common practice to commodify one's time, for example, which is another way of saying one's worth, as measured in sixty-minute blocks. Usually, the more explicit the correlation between one's worth and standardized blocks of time—as in jobs that require punching a time clock—the lower the status of the job and, by association, the worker. Even where there is no time clock, this hierarchy is often plainly entrenched: the secretary at the desk out front is paid an hourly wage, while the administrator just beyond the closed door earns a yearly salary.

Certainly, this does not always apply; the high-powered lawyer bills by the hour, and the sweatshop worker is guaranteed nothing for hours worked but, rather, is paid piecemeal. Of course, the commodification of the lawyer's time is not seen as demeaning to the lawyer's self-worth; apparently if one's price is high enough, commodification transcends degradation. In the case of sweatshop workers, many of whom are in fact locked into a kind of indentured servitude, they are often treated more like dairy cattle or laying hens, regarded as something closer to property than to people, and the few dollars or cents they are paid for each stitched sleeve or assembled toy are more like the cost of maintaining one's equipment than employee wages.

In truth, there are very few among us who work and earn money who escape commodification. After all, what is it we get paid *for?* Most of us sell our time, our knowledge, our physical strength or dexterity, our expertise, our appearance, or our credentials. "Under capitalism," wrote Marx a hundred years ago, "labor becomes not the worker's own life-activity, the manifestation of his own life, but a commodity the worker must sell in order to live." Marx believed this sort of labor was shackling, that it robbed people of their freedom and their true sense of self-worth. But what he identified as an ill of industrialization and capitalism had in fact been going on for millennia. "Some men," wrote Aristotle in the fourth century B.C., "turn every quality or art into a means of making money; this they conceive to be the end, and to the promotion of that end all things must contribute."

Not everyone is subject to this predicament. There are the unemployed, both the very poor and the very wealthy. There are those who work, but without monetary value being assigned to their labor—the parent whose full-time job is caring for a house and family, for example. (In this case, and that of the poor unemployed, the price of escaping commodification may be quite high.) Then there are those who work and earn money while themselves remaining just outside of the sphere of commodification. Farmers, for example, growing soybeans and plums; artists producing watercolors and operas; craftspeople making wicker baskets and woolen blankets—all of these people sell the fruits of their labor and not the labor itself; they commodify their produce but not their time or bodies or minds. Finally, there are children. Virtually all of us enter this world uncommodified, and experience ourselves only in this way, in clean skins, as yet innocent of worth, for the first twelve or fifteen or eighteen years of our lives—the time before we begin the process of hiring ourselves out. Children as a rule don't think of themselves or their actions as being translatable into monetary worth. Yet most children, somewhere near the end of childhood, are expected to make this semiotic leap, more or less effortlessly, as a condition of functioning in adult society. The wonder is that so many manage this transition without crisis or resistance.

I had a friend in school named Mary McDonald. When the time came for everyone to feel the pressure of deciding "what we would be," meaning what we would do in order to earn money and thus pay rent and buy groceries and generally manage to sustain ourselves—that time when even those of us who had worked before were now feeling the odd shift of being about to consign ourselves to full-time, adult workerhood—I remember her one day declaring with great clarity and exasperation, "I think someone should just pay me a salary for being Mary McDonald!"—which proposition struck me as being at once absurd and strangely reasonable. She spoke neither from arrogance nor laziness; it was not that she did not want to work. Simply, the notion that her ability to support herself, literally to survive, should be contingent upon the quantification and commodification of herself through her labor was an affront to her human sensibility. Only because most of us, by the time we have reached the brink of adulthood, have been successfully taught to forget or reject such a sensibility does her idea seem preposterous. In fact, it is not unlike that expressed in Section 6 of the Clayton Antitrust Act, passed by our own Congress in 1914, which states plainly, "The labor of a human being is not a commodity or an article of commerce."

Mary McDonald and the Clayton Antitrust Act notwithstanding, we know this ideal to be far from the truth. Human labor, like soil and apples and cake and daisies, like gold and frozen orange juice and pork bellies and antimony, like newspapers and coffee beans and tall glass tumblers, can be and is reduced to a commodity on a daily basis, as something that may be bought and sold. In that regard, we, like all the products we gather and clutch to us, wear masks.

Here we all are in a fever-dream, trapped in our grotesque fetish masks. Some of these are cat-eyed, peacock-feathered, encrusted with pink sparkles or jet sequins, held to the face on slender sticks. Others are cardboard, eye slits cut crookedly with utility knives, held over the face with rubber bands stapled to the sides. On each one, ornate or plain, a white tag flutters from the left temple, and on this: a dollar amount. See us all, revolving through our neighborhoods as if in attendance at an eternal masquerade: people, bikes, strollers, dogs, shoes, garbage pails, umbrellas, trees, cars—nothing of value without a mask. All the stories obscured.

Plumweseep

Nights, after he's come back from the woods, shed his orange coveralls in the laundry room, showered, put on clean clothes, and eaten some stew or maybe some take-out Chinese, Brent Boyd puts his little Ellen to bed. Joy will already have bathed her ("batht," they say in the New Brunswickian way, with a short *a,* to rhyme with "laughed") and gotten her into her pj's and slippers, and the three will have had their evening sprawl on the black leather couch in the den, lit by the shimmying triple glow of woodstove, television, and fishtank. Joy will already have teased Brent about his mismatched socks, and Brent, whose woods habit is to dress for warmth and not style, will have studied the one green and one blue foot at the ends of his legs and replied that the socks do match—in thickness. And Ellen will have dipped near to sleep, lying across her mother's prone body, engaging in her nightly ritual of thumb-sucking while simultaneously rubbing a handful of Joy's brown hair across her own nose.

When Ellen's murmurings appear to be gaining, rather than losing, momentum is when Brent will declare, "Okay, c'mon," and bring her upstairs, where they will settle themselves, father and daughter, side by side on Ellen's white captain's bed, both of them flat on their backs—Ellen because she's supposed to be dream-bound, and Brent because after ten hours in the woods and another three, maybe, on the road, it's the position that most appeals. And from that position, father and daughter will gaze up toward the end of Brent's arms, at the picture book held there. Ellen's favorite book is anything she knows by heart, and the nightly parade of old favorites keeps him on his toes lest he miss a single sacred word.

There on the captain's bed, beneath the turning pages, they are both swaddled in layers of family, in the felt echoes of the loving hands that fashioned so many of the objects in this room. Here is the turquoise tulip quilt Brent's mother made, under which Ellen is now tucked. Here are the powder blue curtains Joy's mother sewed, softening the now-black panes of Ellen's bedroom window. Under the window sits the toy box Grampy Boyd built this past Christmas, and on it the Holly Hobbie girl Grammy Boyd painted in pink and blue. Here are the baby photos in picture frames, and the vase of dried flowers left over from an aunt's wedding, and here also is Ellen's most special possession: here is her Sooky Doll.

Sooky Doll is perhaps three inches tall. She's a hard, rubbery thing in a bright green dress. Her most striking feature is her hair, a blue-green shock of some stiff synthetic that sticks straight up from the top of her head—so far that it nearly doubles her height. She had been a gift from a baby-sitter when Ellen was only four months old, by which age she had already formed a powerful attachment to her mother's hair. When separated from Joy, the little girl latched on to Sooky Doll's blue-green locks for comfort; she'd twirl and stroke them across her face while sucking her thumb, fingers firmly entangled in the surrogate strands.

"Sooky" is a Cape Bretonism, a word from Joy's childhood on the tip of Nova Scotia, where the verb "to sook" meant to get one's way by acting pouty or whiny. Joy's father used to call her his Little Sooker, and the way she thinks of the word today has more to do with the memory of his teasing affection than with its original definition. Brent and Joy find it not a little amusing that of all Ellen's toys, the one she is most attached to is this rather frightful little green-frocked figurine. Of course to Ellen, Sooky Doll is no laughing matter. It's a totem, a charm, sweet with the strongest magic: a little piece of her mother.

But the magic has limits. Sometimes at night, when they are all home together, the spirit of warmth and comfort seems to drain from the doll's stubby body, and Ellen wants only the real thing. Then, midway through bedtime stories, when her woods-weary daddy as often as not begins to snore, she'll slip quietly out from under the covers and creep across the hall into the big bed, leaving Brent to dream on Minnie Mouse sheets while she nuzzles her mother's true locks until morning.

Lancaster

With night and day all topsy-turvy, dressed up in each other's clothes half the week like a couple of mischievous twins playing tricks, sleep doesn't always come to Ruth Lamp when she bids it. In the early morning hours, when the clock always seems to slow, to come almost to a standstill, and the top of the universe seems to lift a little bit higher, when the sky is at its blackest and the stars all edge just a touch farther away, Ruth lies awake in bed with a light burning. She's alone in the house tonight except for Shenna. An

insomniac dog is a kind of oxymoron: snores issue with
wolfy vigor from the patch of hallway outside Ruth's
bedroom, to which spot Shen, with all her bulky en-
thusiasm, is nightly relegated.

The farmhouse is not large. Downstairs there are
kitchen, laundry room, Ruth's sitting room, and the
boys' sitting room (the last two easily told apart; the
one being spotless and serene, with light seeping
through long, curtained windows onto a cream-
colored rug; the other being close and dim, appoint-
ed with a woodstove, deer-patterned wallpaper, a
mounted eight-point buck's head, arrows and shot-
guns, and a wall clock whose hands rotate around the
image of a deer). Upstairs the house narrows to accommodate only two bedrooms, Ruth's and Robert's,
the latter frequently, as now, vacant.

Ruth's bedroom is on the light side of the house.
With windows on three exposures, she has nearly pan-
oramic views of the farm; she can see her dirt road,
the gully, the barn, the garden and the hill behind the
house where some jeans and towels flap on the clothesline she's rigged, and the pair of lawn chairs and table
she's set higher up, under a bony, bare apple tree.
Come spring, it'll flower, grow a sweet-smelling cap
of floppy petals. Come spring, she'll sit and have a
cool drink there, under an awning of milky pink blossoms and bees.

All of this now is only in her mind's eye. Before her
eyes is simply her own bedroom. Lacy veils drawn
across each window contain the light from her reading
lamp and cast it back into the room, over the hand-
me-down mahogany bedroom suite, the framed pictures of her children, the flowered wallpaper and flow-

ered sofa, and her old Carmen Hohner accordion. She hasn't played in years. The bellows now are surely shot, their paper folds dried out and cracked. Still, she can remember how her fingers go, the patterns they would spell over the buttons and keys to squeeze out all those songs.

She does not pack it away. Even when she moved from Forest Rose out to the farm, she did not consign it to storage. Even though she knows it's unplayable now, she keeps it out, on the floor in the corner by the dresser, where she can see it from her bed.

Her mother paid ninety dollars for it back in 1948, when Ruth was twelve and wanted an accordion so badly it stung. A visiting evangelical minister and his wife had come to their church, and Ruth had fallen in love with the wife's beautiful voice and the way she accompanied herself on a strange contraption she held something like a muff and worked open and shut, her fingers flitting over a bank of little black buttons. This, Ruth learned, was an accordion, second in fineness only, in Ruth's doting preadolescent eyes, to the minister's wife herself. Ruth told her mother she longed to play the accordion when she grew up, and her mother, still earning only twenty-five dollars a week doing housework, did the astonishing, wondrous thing of somehow saving enough money to go downtown to Bruney's music store on South Columbus Street and buy Ruth her own. The instrument had an imitation-marble gray-and-black facade, and the name CARMEN in block letters that stuck out, so that when you rubbed your fingers across the surface, you could pretend you were reading Braille.

Ruth did play and sing in church, on Sundays as well

as during revivals, when she'd play every night for two weeks straight, squeezing out favorite hymns like "Precious Memory" and "What a Friend We Have in Jesus." Then in high school she learned to love country-western and bluegrass music, and she even got a gig at the local radio station, WHOK. A group of them would play a live jamboree in the studio every Saturday, and it nearly broke her mother's heart, Ruth knew, to have her play that worldly music. Then she turned seventeen, got married, and went off to Columbus. She brought her Hohner with her there but hardly ever played it anymore, just sometimes for her children, but only when her husband and mother-in-law weren't around; neither of them approved of or enjoyed it. There in the city she played it less and less, so that it became nearly petrified, frozen, like a snapshot or memento of itself, of another place and time.

It seems that way now, in the middle of the blackest, coldest chunk of the night, sitting alert and mute there in the corner by the dresser, its bellows squashed breathless, its catches fastened shut, no longer a source of music but a token of memories, a reminder of all kinds of faith.

Pluma

When the hottest part of the day begins to wane, at one or two or three o'clock, depending on how pushily the fog noses itself in again on any given day, Basilio Salinas rakes the coffee at La Palma back into a heap. *Tshhhhhk, tshhhhhk.* The wooden paddle corrals the dry beans, tumbles them together in the center of the patio.

Music comes through the woods, tinny and indistinct. Some of the pickers down the mountain have got a radio. The dogs now are hot and lazing around the sides of the two wooden structures that flank the patio: the new palm bunkhouse and the caretaker's house. Gudelia Surita stands in the open doorway of the latter, gazing out at Basilio and, behind him, the sky. A vulture glides softly, alone, describing a wide black circle in the blue. Gudelia is wearing a red skirt and a long white T-shirt and around her neck, on a piece of string, a square inch of chocolate-colored fabric with a tiny regal image of the Virgin stitched in gold. This was a gift from her godmother, who lives in *el centro*. It is a special charm: it protects the little girl from bad dreams.

Gudelia is the only one of the Surita children who still lives in Pluma. Her older siblings have all gone off to find work in the city of Oaxaca: one in a day-care center, one in a cafeteria, one as a cement pourer. Her father is down the mountain now, picking. Her mother is just behind her, out of sight within the dimness of the kitchen room, which smells of cactus ashes and also of damp. There is no window, but the fourth wall of the kitchen comes only halfway to the roof, and along that gap and in the open doorway dangle a few clear plastic bags of water, also a kind of charm, used to ward off mosquitoes and evil spirits.

Gudelia is a member of Basilio's family, too: not his blood kin but his family of workers. Watching him rake coffee is like watching her mother tend the fire, like watching the dogs bite at their fleas, like watching the sun come up: part of the rhythm of every day. Gudelia takes one lime from the dozens that she and her mother gathered earlier from low trees in the woods and piled on the narrow table that stands against the outside wall of the house. So much of what they have comes to them this way, directly from the earth into their hands: limes, beans, firewood, water, crabs. Gudelia pierces the rind with her two top front teeth, which are still her baby teeth, and black with rot. She spits out a bit of tough green skin, then uses her fingers to peel the rest.

Basilio, done raking, fetches the large rectangular gold can from the side of the Surita's house. The can's label, red with a drawing of a pig and the word *Paraíso,* identifies it as having once contained Paradise-brand lard. With this can he transfers beans into burlap sacks. No one remembers who brought the Paradise can to the patio. It has been the coffee scoop for as long as anyone can say. The scooping makes its own nice sound: a steady scrape of bean and metal and cement.

In *el centro* the church bell rings a few times, as it does at loose intervals throughout the day. The peals reach La Palma muted and cool, mixed in with the workers' distant radio and Basilio's scooping. Two tiny white worms wiggle out of the lime Gudelia is eating. She shakes them to the ground, stamps them under one flip-flop, goes back to sucking at the fruit in her hand. The afternoon is peaceful. The dogs give up their bellies to the breeze. Basilio sets down the Paradise can and secures the mouths of the burlap sacks. At night the skittering sound on the roof will be the small feet of rodents, coming to steal the coffee, but they won't get any from these tight sacks.

Beneath the corrugated metal Gudelia sometimes

hears them. Their tickling tread, too, is part of the rhythm of the day. All night long on her *petate* by her mother and her father, she lies amid the familiar, dreaming sweet dreams only, with the Virgin round her neck.

Essential to the fetishism of the commodity is the erosion of objects' singularity.

Here in the Someday Café, I sit at a rickety wooden table on which are laid: a newspaper, Sunday-fat; and a tall glass tumbler filled with steaming coffee.

Here in the [$300,000], I sit at a [$24.00] on which are laid: a [$1.50]; and a [$.60] filled with [$1.25].

It's the true Esperanto, money; it's the ASCII file in which all things material and immaterial may be transposed. The Someday's plate-glass windows, its hanging plants and recorded jazz, its juicy-looking oil paintings, its scones, and yard-sale-ish tables and chairs, even the Irish setter—all could be discussed in terms of price. The art on the walls and the baked goods are tagged, their prices visible to the human eye; those of the plants and the CDs and the dog and the furniture are implicit only, but no less real, so that if we wanted to, for the sake of a mathematics exercise, say, we could make logical, practical equations involving all of these disparate items, such as how many CDs equal one dog, and how many dogs equal one painting, and that sort of thing.

Actually, we engage in such comparisons as a matter of routine: *If I give up smoking,* we say, *in three months I will have saved enough to buy a new refrigerator; if we take the bus instead of a cab, we can get popcorn at the movie;*

that necklace could be the down payment on a house; those braces cost a year's tuition. The monetary system allows us to strip objects—and sometimes ideas and people— bare of their original identities and then refurbish them with new roles and relative values. Under the rubric of money, a grand reductionism ensues: we find we *can* compare apples and oranges. This common language serves not to illuminate distinctions but to obliterate them. The nineteenth-century German philosopher Georg Simmel wrote:

> [Money] becomes the frightful leveler—it hollows out the core of things, their specific values and their uniqueness and incomparability in a way which is beyond repair. They all float with the same specific gravity in the constantly moving stream of money.

To function in society, we have little choice but to enter into this contract. We agree to behave as though monetary values were fixed and inherent within objects. We agree not to think about the actual cost of production, or the social relationship of the labor that went into production. We agree to believe in the fetish of the commodity, and to trust in the supernatural power of dollars and cents. And because we believe, and our neighbors believe, and strangers believe, and all the employers and employees and landlords and tenants and bankers and lenders and borrowers and grocers and farmers and bus drivers and governments and armies and doctors and credit card companies and plumbers and ministers and ballerinas believe, the circuit is complete: our faith is rewarded. Money is the great common denominator, lubricating the operations of the world. It lets us get milk at the corner store and it lets us negotiate treaties across the ocean. If it makes us forget to wonder about the stories of how things come to be, well, we might assure ourselves, that's a small price to pay.

Money did not originate as a mask or frightful leveler. Its inception came about strictly for convenience sake, as in: it is more convenient to conduct trade without lugging actual sheep or bushels of corn around with you. If some smaller object could be made to stand for the actual material wealth, exchange could be expedited. Also, if that smaller object would keep indefinitely, and still stand for the same amount of wealth down the road, exchange could be liberated from rigid time constraints. Because before they dreamed up money, people could only barter directly, sheep for corn and so on, which imposed an awful reliance on chance coincidence—that our neighbor would have the item we wanted at the same time we had the item she wanted. With a standardized, long-lasting medium of exchange, people were able to store wealth and make purchases when it suited them, long after the sheep had died and the corn turned black.

How difficult it must have been in the early days, though, to relinquish your concrete goods and place your trust instead in a kind of totem. In the very beginning, the required leap of faith may not have been so large, for what was used as the medium of exchange was generally a commodity with intrinsic value itself. In Ba Bunda, salt packets served as money; in Tibet, bricks of tea did the trick; in Alaska, fishhooks; in Nigeria, copper wire. Elsewhere and throughout history, people have also used silk, dried fish, beaver pelts, cognac, and tobacco. Such things were not merely representational, but had their own concrete use-values; even if their role as the accepted currency were suddenly to evaporate, the holder would be left with something both functional and tradable.

The real test must have come with stone and bone and mineral currency—the metal bell money of Zambia; the tin crocodiles and roosters of the Malay Peninsula; the dolphin jawbones of the Marshall Bennett Islands; the cowrie shells of West Africa; the whale teeth of the Fiji Islands; the brass rods of the Nigerian Tiv people; the miniature brass shoes and hoes and billhooks of China; the clay, glass, and porcelain tokens of Thailand. These things must have seemed just like fetishes: mute and inert human-crafted objects that were yet alive with a kind of magical power. They had no utility of their own, but could procure things, could command goods and services as if through silent spells, or like a modified djinni: one wish granted per customer and then the fetish changes hands. Still, this leap of faith might yet not have been very strenuous. Money was passing further into the realm of abstraction, but only within communities that were relatively small and homogeneous, among people who were bound to know one another or at least one another's kin. Faith in currency is really an extension of faith in everyone else—in your trading partners, in your neighbors—to collectively uphold and honor the notion of that currency. Such a faith is perhaps not difficult to summon among people who live together closely, who know one another well.

Precious metals gained ascendancy over other types of currency about four thousand years ago, and until very recently they remained the favored exchange medium. At times people experimented with tokens of glass, wood, clay, feathers, leather, and even sealing wax, but none of these ultimately could rival the superior qualities of metal coins (most commonly silver, gold, copper, iron, and a natural alloy of gold and silver called electrum). Metal doesn't wear out easily. Its supply is relatively stable and confined, and does not, like that of so many other commodities, fluctuate wildly with the amount of rainfall or sunshine or disease or war. It is portable, durable, recognizable. Also it is divisible, which has its pros and cons: at times the practice of "shaving" coins threatened to undermine the uniformity of their value—but then merchants had only to equip themselves with a pair of scales to make sure they were receiving a fair sovereign or shekel or shilling.

Finally, and most important, metal is homogeneous. It can be punched, pressed, or cast into identical coins. Perhaps the most crucial feature of currency is its uniformity; the system hinges on the condition that each token of currency possess no unique value of its own. This is no less true today than it was thousands of years ago. The exception proves the rule: the "first dollar" taped sentimentally to the wall over the cash register in a diner; the lucky penny found faceup on the sidewalk with your birth year on it. Such special cases aside, money works because it is so perfectly interchangeable, so wholly without singularity.

The fetish-like qualities of coinage are conspicuous in their very guises, which from earliest times have been designed and fashioned with a level of painstaking, ceremonious care that mocks and transcends sheer practicality. Coins have been cut into squares, ovals, hexagons, octagons, diamonds, doughnuts, bean shapes, dolphin shapes, cup shapes, flower shapes. They have borne images of olive sprigs, ears of barley, palm trees, lilies; they have depicted likenesses of Persephone and Athena, Pegasus and Hercules, pharaohs and emperors, Cleopatra and Brutus, Christ and the Virgin, saints. They have shown bows and arrows, beetles, lions, rhinoceros, elephants, horses, doves. They have displayed signs of the zodiac, the two-faced Janus, the seal of Solomon, the swastika. The study of numismatics might easily be mistaken for a study of sorcery, of religious icons, of the potent jumble of scraps at the bottom of Merlin's bag.

Our own contemporary paper dollar is not without its rather cultish features, perhaps most prominently concentrated in the left-hand medallion on the back of the bill, whose unfinished pyramid has inspired a variety of speculative interpretations. William Barton, who helped design the bill in the late eighteenth century, described this pyramid rather blandly as representing the material power of the country and its continual striving for progress, but this hasn't stopped people from superimposing on the image all sorts of more tantalizing meanings linked to everything from ancient Egyptian symbolism to the enigmatic Brotherhood of Freemasons. The curious eye atop the pyramid, in its triangular frame with the radiant nimbus, is supposed to have been the contribution of Benjamin Franklin, and represent the all-seeing Eye of Providence, an acknowledgment that all material wealth is controlled by the divine. (Benjamin Franklin, incidentally or not, was a Freemason, as were many of the Founding Fathers.) The luminous "ANNUIT CŒPTIS" curving over the disembodied eye means "He [God] has favored our undertakings"; the more earthly "NOVUS ORDO SECLORUM," on the ribbon undulating below the pyramid, means "A new order for the ages"; the date on the structure's base, MDCCLXXVI, translates to 1776, the date of the Declaration of Independence. And to the right of all this floats the unabashed clincher, appearing, for some reason, in boring old English: "IN GOD WE TRUST."

There's much more, of course; the dollar is decked with symbolic minutiae: the eagle with its shield; its talons gripping olive branch and arrows; its beak gripping another ribbon with more Latin ("E PLURIBUS UNUM," or "One united out of many"). There are the thirteen stars and another ring of light. There are the tiny red and blue fibers woven throughout, and the curlicues and scrolls and leaves and berries, the seals and brackets and borders and infinitesimal geometric webbing lavished front and back across the paper rectangle—all of it identical on each dollar; all of it, in its very uniformity, contributing to the bill's fetish-like aura.

And why such ornate and elaborate fuss? Certainly, the more complicated the sketchings, the more difficult to counterfeit, but still—why all the mysticism? The Latin? The Roman numerals? The references to the Almighty? Why such codified and ritualized detail, such minute intertwining of wealth and spirituality, when the object of a currency system—making it easy for people to get their hands on some horseshoes or muslin or lard or whatever—is and has always been, after all, quite mundane, quite simply profane?

Because the faith is not. The faith necessary to make the system work is nothing less than tremendous. The alchemists who for centuries labored to find the secret of turning "base" metals into gold would understand just how tremendous. They would smack their foreheads in rueful recognition—for that faith is the priceless formula that eluded them all of their lives: what they failed ever to realize is that the secret of alchemy lies in manipulating not the metals but people's perceptions.

We have reached a point today where people's perceptions effectively make gold out of paper, out of plastic cards, even out of invisible, intangible things like wire transfers and telephone transactions. People's perceptions have even been known to make gold out of ordinary playing cards. This happened in Canada late in the seventcenth century, when metal coins were in such short supply that the French government ordained decks of playing cards as substitutes for money in its western colonies. Nothing more than a stamp of the treasurer's seal and a couple of governmental signatures rendered each card currency, but for three quarters of a century, the Canadian people's faith sustained the cards' monetary value.

This is not to suggest that people's faith in money, once established, is unshakable. To take such faith for granted would be a mistake—as has been illustrated in times of financial crisis: witness America during the Civil War, when confidence in the government faltered. People started hoarding precious metals, and the Treasury stopped redeeming notes for specie. In 1861 Congress authorized issue of "Demand Notes"—the infamous greenbacks, backed by nothing except faith in the government—and their value promptly proceeded to roller-coaster in accordance with how the Union army was reportedly faring on any given day.

Witness also Germany before the Second World War, when a wheelbarrow piled high with bills suddenly could not redeem a single loaf of bread. Faith in government and the economy had come apart; faith in one another was crumbling, too. The spellbindingly lovely veil of belief in the inherent value of money had been dragged from people's corneas. Everyone stood wounded and blinking at an emperor with no clothes; paper was revealed as being worth nothing next to bread; mayhem and ugliness and panic ensued.

In times of financial crisis, whenever faith waivers or the supply of metal coins simply runs short, people have a natural tendency to revert to barter, as well as to more concrete substitutes for currency. During the Civil War, people used postage stamps, encased in brass with mica fronts so that the denomination was visible; they also were more keen to receive private notes, issued by local merchants and tavernkeepers, than they were to accept the federally endorsed but nebulous greenbacks. In Colonial New England, people often used nails and musket balls as practical exchange media; in the South, tobacco was legal tender for a few centuries. In wartime, people have treated cigarettes, cognac, silk stockings, and ration coupons as currency. Patriotism is apparently a negligible factor in governing people's faith: should a particular country's economy falter severely, its citizens commonly look to another, more stable country's currency, even if it means trading on the black market for the foreign cash. And early Americans quite contentedly mingled the British shilling, the Spanish piece of eight, the Portuguese crown, the French écu and louis d'or, and the Dutch ducatoon with their own individual colony's currency, which was generally less stable and less widely acceptable than the more established foreign specie.

With faith in the abstraction so fragile and tenuously achieved, it is no wonder that in reifying money we must very nearly deify it. The economy may be no more than a notion, but it is probably the single notion in which the entire world collectively believes. No religion unites people so comprehensively. No one version of God, or morals, or truth, is so widely embraced. No language is so widely translated, spoken, understood. Money's power, its viability, is like an all-encompassing game we have forgotten we are playing, like a sprawling dragons-and-knights pageant enacted by all the neighborhood children at twilight: it exists only so long as everyone agrees to pretend. As soon as more than a couple of children get called in to supper, the fantasy breaks up; porch lights come on; the fort turns back into a sycamore tree. But so long as we engage in it, the rules of the game remain real and binding.

And we are falling deeper into the game all the time. It used to be that money, however ethereal and theorctical it may have been, was at least backed by something solid: namely, gold. For a long time people took this backing quite literally, to an extent that seems rather sweet now. For example, at one time, if the United States had made a loan to France, say, the appropriate amount of gold would actually have been wheeled on trolleys into the "French Room" at the Federal Reserve. The funny thing about this, of course, is that *gold* is valuable (except in a few things like dentistry and as a barrier against radiation in outer space) only in people's imaginations. Its usefulness as a standard of exchange stems in part from certain qualities intrinsic to the metal: its rarity, chiefly (only a hundred thousand tons of gold have ever been mined), and its homogeneity and durability and all of that—but these characteristics were not primarily responsible for elevating gold to its most-valued status. It was people who did that, human beings all over the world, in a massive act of collective imagination, the mutual acceptance of a fantasy on a very grand scale.

Then, a little earlier this century, a strange thing happened. Money got severed from gold's backing— not then to be transferred to silver or copper or cattle or wine or any of the other goods that had backed it over the preceding four millennia, but to become, for the first time, fiat: truly and undisguisedly free-floating, abstract, and relational. Government still decreed money legal tender, but now made no offer to redeem its notes for a standard commodity of exchange, or indeed for anything at all. The fantasy game of money rose to a new, breathless height of abstraction.

Yet people continued to work for the stuff, this paper with the pyramid and the eye and the Latin; they did and still do perform labor for it. Without ever a hesitation the game has stayed in play. Shopkeepers continue to hand out wares for the stuff, and mechanics will fix your car for some of it, and inns give you a night's lodging, and fishermen turn over barrels of cod and halibut, and tailors hem your trousers, and teachers teach your children, and machines dispense gum and colas and condoms—all for some pieces of this paper, these green rectangles invoking the name of God. And people are accepting ever more abstractions of the abstraction: first the use of personal checks proliferated, and then, exponentially, so did credit cards. Tokens of tokens, written promises to pay. By now we needn't even be there to make our promises in person; we needn't sign our actual names or shake the hand or meet the eye of anyone, but can punch in our credit card numbers over phone lines, and transfer and deposit and withdraw sums via a computer screen and modem. And it works, it all comes off without a hitch. Everyone's faith is perfect, so everyone's faith is sustained.

"Money," warned Henry David Thoreau, "comes between a man and his objects." Before an object's indoctrination into the realm of money, he suggested, we may somehow know it better, see it more faithfully and completely. Afterward, we are somehow at odds, alienated from the items we buy and sell. Because if money in some sense brings people together, it works a kind of malevolent spell on things, alters them, erodes their vital essences.

What troubled Marx so gravely was that when we usher an object into the world of commodities, when we render it in money form, we conceal the social character of the labor that went into it; we bury the fact of the workers, their relationships to the product, and our relationships to them. Instead, we see only a relationship, one as taut and tidy as an equation, between a product and a certain amount of cash. The labor that went into the product gets submerged, encoded in that cash amount, and we erase the singularity of both the object and the worker. Money is the fetish that swoops in and supplants the story of real human hands; this was Marx's concern. But there are other stories in things that are not the stories of labor.

We can think of Thoreau tramping through his "unpretending sprout-lands," or paddling around on his pond ringed by trees, by those "slender eyelashes which fringe it," and all of them unfettered by price tags, all of them revealed to him in profound simplicity, their true natures more simply wondrous than any fetishism we might layer on through commodification. Thoreau, like Marx, was bothered by that perverse brand of myopia which makes everything appear in money form. He wrote of this in his journals, of the peculiar and pervasive worship of gold, and the way it blinds people to what is real on earth. One entry reads:

> Remarking to old Mr. B——— the other day on the abundance of apples, "Yes," says he, "and fair as dollars too." That's the kind of beauty they see in apples.

For Marx, the missed vision would have been that of the laborer and the labor, but the things with which Thoreau was oftenest concerned, things like apples and grasses and elms, he beheld not in the light of their production at the hands of any workers (unless perhaps we speak of a single, immortal Worker) but, rather, in the light of how much he *loved* and was stirred by them.

We cannot call his vision any finer or truer than Marx's; nor can we call Marx's any finer or truer than Thoreau's. Nor, for that matter, can we judge either of theirs superior to viewing things in their money form. The different ways of perceiving rear up and clash with one another, but they also relent and mingle and carry on with room enough for them all.

There are stories in glass and paper and beans (and apples and diamonds and mulch) that have nothing whatever to do with their production, nor with their birth in nature, nor with their cash values. Some of these stories are invented by novelists and playwrights and poets. Some are invented by advertisers. Some spring from your and my own memories and fantasies and private associations; we layer on meanings inside our heads; we cannot help it. We gather stories as we gather minutes and goods. And *all* of the stories infuse the objects with fetish spirits. Marx spoke as if he could discern between an object's true nature and its artificial one, the fetish image we slip over its honest nakedness; but who are we, with mortal eyes, to say which story is truest to life? There are myriad ways of seeing an object; all we can do is tip our hats to this fact and try on the different lenses.

We are accustomed to having objects elevated, imbued with meaning and significance, in literature (as in film, dance, painting, theater). We are taught in high school English classes to look for the special significance of certain props: the pickle dish in *Ethan Frome,* the conch shell in *Lord of the Flies,* the brass ring in *The Catcher in the Rye,* Mr. Gruffydd's pencil box in *How Green Was My Valley.* We are taught that within the sphere of literature, unlike that of daily life, it is natural and proper for an object to represent more than its literal self, to be swollen with a life beyond its own.

In *The Glass Menagerie* we discover a cupboardful of tiny, transparent animals, a crippled girl in a violet kimono polishing them. A unicorn with a snapped-off horn, a shop window filled with colored glass bottles "like bits of a shattered rainbow." In Tennessee Williams's production notes to his play, he is careful, almost exhaustively so, to make his sense of glass understood precisely, to articulate all that glass must convey. "It expresses the surface vivacity of life with the underlying strain of immutable and inexpressible sorrow. When you look at a piece of delicately spun glass you think of two things: how beautiful it is and how easily it can be broken." "The lovely fragility of glass" is the image of the girl in violet, who becomes, like a piece of her own glass collection, "too exquisitely fragile to move from the shelf." So fetish-like is the power of glass over the girl that when a piece of her collection breaks, it precipitates a wound to her own human heart.

In *Cyrano de Bergerac* we see paper as leaves of books cherished by a baker, as sheets of poetry left as payment for cream puffs. Butter-stained sonnets and ripped stanzas, volumes dismembered and fashioned into paper bags. Edmond Rostand has imagined a pastrycook who cares more for verse than cash. The cook is plagued by his practical wife, who sees no value in the "scribblings" offered by the poet-customers of her husband. She takes it upon herself to salvage what worth she is capable of seeing by using the paper to package the pies and such that constitute their livelihood. She of course is plagued in turn by her husband, who persists in shelling out "free" gingerbread and almond tarts for poetry. The tension between their points of view is played for comic effect; while the two tussle over which of the roles is of greater value, paper oscillates giddily between being the preserver of language and the preserver of cakes.

In *A Tree Grows in Brooklyn,* coffee is a poor child's single luxury; a thin brew strengthened with chicory, softened with a dash of condensed milk. A bittersweet liquid to savor the smell and heat of, but not to drink; rather, a treasure to let grow cold and then pour down the sink, a thing to waste most deliciously. As Betty Smith writes it, coffee is more than a beverage, more, even, than a comfort, a thing to have "when you had nothing at all and it was raining and you were alone in the flat." It is a link to the world of the rich, a suggestion of wealth and casual extravagance, because it is the one thing that the child is permitted to squander. "*I* think it's good that people like us can waste something once in a while," says the child's mother, silencing a pair of scandalized aunts, and she looks on with a queer kind of satisfaction as daily the child chooses to empty her allotted cupful down the drain.

Fragility, poetry, luxury. A sampling only—in literature the same humble object may be heightened a hundred different ways. But accustomed as we are to accepting such transformations in literature, we don't usually think of them as happening in real life. Yet they do, constantly; objects get swollen with meaning, enameled with symbolism; the most pragmatic among us take part in this practice—not out of any secret whimsy or penchant for anthropopathism, but unwittingly, simply because it is not within us *not* to. We do not construct our symbols as neatly or intentionally as might novelists or poets, but our symbols are no less influential on the stories that we live. Each of us has our own private lexicon, unique as fingerprints, through which we make sense of the world; in everyone's personal dictionary of symbols, the entries—for coffee, for tumblers, for newspapers, and everything—all read just a little bit differently. But often the similarities outweigh the differences, enough so that when we speak to each other, we sometimes know just what the other means, even when we are being subtle, metaphorical, abstract.

Advertisers, like artists, are adept at recognizing the fetish-like power of the stories, the masks, that we layer over things. Artists exploit this power to give their works resonance, to thicken them with meaning, texture, allusion. Advertisers exploit this power to make people desire their products. They would develop in us a need to possess, would turn us, like Freud's sexual fetishists, into chronic, feverish collectors of the desired objects.

But this power is useful to advertisers and artists— to anyone who wishes to communicate with a large audience—only when the stories are held in common, shared. Advertisers know that their products may be subject to people's personal, and not necessarily predictable, interpretations of and symbolic associations with them. Their products will ultimately be assessed and defined within each consumer's psyche. (A print ad for American Express, featuring the Paris design house Hermès, acknowledges this with disarming frankness: large copy smack in the center of the page reads, "We give birth to the PRODUCT. The customer gives LIFE TO IT.'') Just as Williams and Rostand and Smith take time in their works to establish their lexicons, to put forth the specific characters of glass and paper and beans that they mean us to understand, so advertisers try to obviate ambiguity and a multiplicity of interpretations. They take care to instruct us how, exactly, we are meant to construe the images and symbols they use.

And they do; we get it; it works. We can manipulate and digest even conflicting information effortlessly. We read an ad in the weekly shopping circular touting the low bargain price of a boxed set of eight jelly glasses, and another ad in a glossy magazine exalting the dearness of a single, imported crystal champagne flute, and our minds are perfectly capable of sorting it out: that in the one, cheapness is what creates desirability, and in the other, expensiveness. We encounter a two-page spread, paid for by an international paper company, detailing its deep commitment to recycling and to the environment; then turn the page and confront an ad for a service that will mail you an original newspaper preserved from the date of your birth. And again we have no trouble processing the apparently contradictory messages: that we are meant to appreciate the first company because it recycles newspapers, and to appreciate the second because it hangs on to them. We see a man on TV open his eyes and smile, roused and invigorated by the aroma of a mug of fresh coffee, and a few minutes later we see a woman curled up in sock feet on a couch to unwind with a cup of the same beverage; and we understand automatically that the one is a stimulant and the other a relaxant, even though chemically they are identical;

our brains may even remember which package design is associated with which mood, and tell us to desire the corresponding brand next time we find ourselves in either of those circumstances.

Frequently, in the service of the stories they wish to create, advertisers dream up fictional origins for their products, and imaginary people who produce them. These people have cozy names, like Uncle Ben and Aunt Jemima and Mrs. Butterworth, and beaming faces, like those of Juan Valdez and the Pillsbury Doughboy and Mr. Clean. They are happy to make their products for you; their work is almost like play— you can see that when you watch the Keebler elves busy in their treehouse, and Sprout and the Jolly Green Giant frolicking among their crops—or at any rate, deeply satisfying to them. Some products require not even the activity of fictional workers, but are instead self-created: the chocolates that willingly dunk themselves in candy coating, the tuna fish that practically begs to be canned, the toilet paper that descends, giggling, from fluffy clouds. From talking margarine to dancing raisins, we see products appear as fully animate, autonomous objects, divorced from any suggestion of human labor. All of this constitutes a nearly hyperbolic extension of what Marx foresaw: the real stories of labor getting lost, commodities seeming instead to drop, prefabricated and prepriced, from the blue.

But lately, some advertisers have given a shrewd twist to their marketing strategies, coming almost full circle in their use of stories and symbols. Here's the new plan: ditch the elves and puppets, the actors and painted sets; offer the truth instead. Increasingly, the new sales tactic is to remove the mask, entice the customer with a glimpse behind the scenes. Saturn airs TV spots that consist of mini-profiles of some of its factory employees. Lands' End comes out with a catalog that intersperses full-color pages of polo shirts and seersucker shorts with black-and-white, documentary-esque "articles" on various workers; the catalog's cover proclaims this issue a salute to "Cotton People." Ads for Irish knit sweaters reveal that the garments are handmade in a "cottage industry"; ads for painted metal Christmas tree angels announce that the ornaments have been punched out of recycled oil drums and handmade by "contemporary Haitian artists." The very glorification of the word "handmade" suggests a certain novelty in the linkage of a product to a worker, as though this were not the norm, as though most products generally arrive on the planet unassisted by human efforts.

The urge to reveal more and more of the real origins of a product, to take the consumer on a sort of backstage tour, is gushing over onto packaging containers now, too, so that cartons of Florida Natural orange juice, for example, or Ben & Jerry's ice cream, or boxes of Annie's instant macaroni and cheese, or tubes of Tom's toothpaste, may feature encapsulated biographies of the companies, their workers, even their philosophies on matters such as business, the environment, and social issues. It has also become popular for companies to promise that some of the money you pay for the privilege of obtaining their product will go to what they consider a good cause—whether the Christian right, urban development programs, or the Yanomami people of Brazil: consumerism as a way not only to acquire goods but to reach out, share, help your immediate or global neighbors.

All of this at first appears to be a far cry from such mythical product representatives as Ann Page and Betty Crocker and Chef Boyardee. (A note on the Annie's macaroni and cheese package actually begins, "Hi! My name is Ann Withey. An advertising agency did not create me. I am a real person who lives on a farm . . .") It's as though some companies have tapped into a new level of advertising, a kind of meta-advertising, earnest, disarming, self-referential. The stories in which these companies enframe their products are presented as the truth, artless and uncontrived. But of course, true or not, a great deal of art and contrivance goes into the crafting of these stories, these apparently intimate, ingenuous revelations. Space and time, in print and on the air, still cost money, and the only reason anybody spends money on this kind of advertising is the same reason anybody spends money on the other kind of advertising: to create in people's minds a feeling about a product that will make them want to buy it.

Is there a basic difference between the two kinds of advertising? In one case, the product gets adorned with elves, or naked ladies, or majestic landscapes, and then, as if supernaturally possessed, the product itself begins to radiate a sense of fun, or sex, or power. In the other case, the product gets adorned with portraits of workers, statements of policy, educational briefs, and then the product itself is transformed into an agent of social action, a vessel of wholesomeness, of moral integrity. As used to sell a product, the images of actual employees serve exactly the same purpose as the images of elves. Either way, the product gets inhabited by a spirit not originally its own. Either way, what we wind up with is a fetish, and something, something, obscured.

Children understand that money is a game. Children, who are so expert at losing themselves in play that they continue to follow their own made-up rules to their games, half believing in them, long into the following day; who avoid sidewalk cracks, and seal bets with hooked pinky fingers, and go obediently mute if someone calls "Jinx!" on them; who believe that a monster sometimes lives in the laundry hamper, and that someday they will probably find a hidden door leading into olden times, and that the umbrella handle really once did sing a short song to them that time, no, it wasn't a dream—children yet somehow remain not entirely susceptible to, not completely convinced about money.

Other currencies make more sense to them. A child will trade a blue river rock for a stick of chewing gum. A child will trade her father's old wristwatch for a look at your scar. A miniature glass pear for a green pencil stub. Three baby pinecones for a bite of your sandwich. Your milk money for a ride on the handlebars. And until children finally stumble into the grown-up game, until they catch on that this game is as inviolably real and important to the grown-ups as any game of house, or outer space, or jungle explorers is to them, they may continue to prefer nickels over dimes because of things like the former's smooth edge or greater heft, or because that man with the ponytail looks more interesting than the one with cropped hair.

Surely if children were to peek into the heart of our

financial centers—the trading floors of the stock and commodity exchanges—they would recognize the atmosphere instantly. And wouldn't they think it funny to see all those grown-ups acting just as if they were in gym? Even on the approach, winding down some corridor toward the big room, the acoustics are uncannily like that of a school gymnasium where the big kids are playing a particularly exciting game of floor hockey or volleyball: a muffled and constant swell of voices, intermittently softening to a tense, expectant drone, pierced at frequent intervals by bursts of excited yelling and punctuated every fifteen minutes by the flat, blaring squawk of the time clock, marking the period. Once the trading floor is reached, the analogy seems no less apt, except that gym was never quite this wild or noisy or crowded or, well, *primal*. All kinds of conduct not usually acceptable in the adult business world are legitimized on the trading floor: people push and elbow, step on toes and breathe on necks and drip sweat on each other; the sheer physical contact is formidable.

Also, the team uniforms in school weren't half so snazzy. The traders, and brokers and runners and out-trade clerks and pit observers and everybody, are clad, according to role and station, in a fantastic collage of color-coded jackets: aqua, kelly green, magenta, maroon, gold, pink, crimson, lavender, orange, violet. Some are two-tone and some are checkered. Some have decals on the back and some are striped or even tie-dyed. Some, in deference to how sweaty it gets in the thick of the trade, have whole panels made out of the same kind of thin mesh as those colored pinnies they handed out in gym class to tell the teams apart.

The atmosphere is heightened at the New York Stock Exchange by the presence of varicolored lines and circles on the wooden trading floor; they mark trading zones and routes for foot traffic, but look an awful lot like foul lines and three-point circles. The Chicago Mercantile Exchange, the ''World's Largest Marketplace,'' describes the magnitude of its physical space by boasting that the Cubs and White Sox could hold infield practice on the lower floor and still have room left over to seat spectators. At the Coffee, Sugar and Cocoa Exchange in New York, traders in a desperate rush to get into a given pit sometimes drop to all fours and crawl between each other's legs, as if participating in a bizarre relay race. Large trading firms have even been known to seek out ex-football players to hire as brokers, because of the particular advantages they bring to the trading pits, with their large physical bearing and athletic skills.

In the pits, bodies throng and press together; between moments of active trading they sometimes lean and slouch into one another in a kind of weary camaraderie; a moment later the shouting may resume, and the pushing, and the waving, and the mysterious hand signals the traders use to tell each other what they want to buy or sell, the way a catcher tells a pitcher what kind of ball he ought to throw. Rather than break for lunch, many traders grind away all day at wads of chewing gum, and gulp Gatorade and coffee and Coke, and empty packets of M&M's and vending machine cookies into their mouths, tossing the empty plastic wrappers on the floor. During lulls the odd paper airplane might fly through the air, as might the locker room humor. Most of the exchanges have dress codes (some stricter than others) proscribing such transgressions as blue jeans and T-shirts, skirts that end more than two inches above the knee, sneakers and shorts and bandannas and fatigues, sweatpants and flannel shirts and thongs; but lots of traders somehow manage to defy the spirit of the rules even while following them to the letter, and the overall effect is more chaotic and irreverent than one might expect at the heart of an institution so hallowed.

Not infrequently, in the heat of the trade, people exchange vicious insults in full-throated, red-faced roars. But when the last bell rings and trading halts, it's all understood to be in the spirit of the game; the same two traders who seemed irreconcilable earlier in the day may go out for a burger and a couple of beers. On the other hand, one who does not play by the rules within the pit will be branded unsportsmanlike; he will be deliberately ignored, shut out of trades and eventually his job, since fellow traders can easily collaborate to render another ineffective. The rules, the codes, are everything. The thrill is that the game is real, and the mounted electronic quote displays that ring the trading floors like giant scoreboards instantaneously broadcast transactions and affect events, not only in the trading room but all over the earth.

Modern commodity exchanges originated in early markets and medieval fairs, where foodstuffs and raw materials might get auctioned off during the day and picked up by the customer that very evening, or by the end of the week, when the fair closed. In those days, the people making bids to buy were generally the same people who intended to take delivery of the goods, haul them home, and put them to personal use. It was only the advent, in much more recent times, of things like railroads and refrigeration, standardization of grading and improved telecommunications, that made it possible to begin to trade in the abstract—that is, trading not for the sake of bringing any commodity home with you for your personal consumption, but for the sake of retrading it and making a profit along the way. Pretty soon, people began to circumvent contact with actual commodities altogether, and instead dealt exclusively with slips of paper called futures contracts.

Futures trading first developed in this country about a hundred and fifty years ago. For a long time it remained somewhat disreputable. By the late 1880s, approximately two hundred bills had been introduced in Congress trying to ban futures trading as a form of illegal gambling. None of the bills passed, but the climate of skepticism that produced them is not difficult to understand. For the first time, people were trading contracts instead of raw products. They were dealing in rights to property rather than in the physical property itself. Such an abstraction was initially hard to swallow; it had the feel of a con game, or at any rate of something shaky and indefinite, perhaps even immoral, and seemed to represent a potential threat to the farmers and entrepreneurs who relied on the commodity exchanges to keep their honest businesses afloat.

Human beings have a long tradition of adjusting and modifying our attitudes toward the morality of various kinds of economic activity, generally in such a way as to reflect favorably upon those in power. Thousands of years ago, even the notion of accruing interest, which we accept today as a practically organic function of money, was condemned as the vilest sort of profiteering. Aristotle stated flatly that "money was intended to be used in exchange, but not to increase at interest." Early Christian doctrine also censured the extraction of interest, likening it to extortion. Not until the Middle Ages did the practice become acceptable, and even then it was frowned upon if the interest was collected on a loan taken out of personal need rather than to finance a business venture. As for our own country's early resistance to futures trading, or "playing the market," precedent can be found at least as far back as St. Thomas Aquinas, who wrote, "To sell dearer or to buy cheaper than a thing is worth is itself unjust and unlawful." He condoned trade when it was undertaken to meet the needs of life; he condemned it when undertaken to acquire profit.

However, the rise of mercantilism, and the commensurate power shift in favor of those who engaged in such practices as collecting interest and trading for profit, saw the ethical teachings of people like Aristotle and St. Thomas and, indeed, Christ slip from popularity. The pursuit of wealth conveniently shed its immoral connotations. By the latter part of the eighteenth century, in his seminal work on free-market economic theory, Adam Smith was writing of financial self-interest not only as natural and respectable but as beneficial to society. This is the moral attitude that prevails in our country today, where success in business constitutes upstanding citizenship, and leaders in the world of finance are closely and unabashedly linked with the leaders of the nation. In *The Merc*, the official history of the Chicago Mercantile Exchange, Bob Tamarkin writes, "There's hardly an office wall of a

Merc or [Chicago Board of Trade] official that doesn't display him or her with an autographed photo of a U.S. president or congressman.''

In the radiant nimbus of all this social virtue, trade advances, vivid and voracious, the ultimate live-action game. Every day tens of thousands of men and woman flock together on the floors of various marketplaces, decked out in their psychedelic jackets, to trade futures and options on everything from chickens to Eurodollars to stock indices. Computer software companies offer interactive programs for individual investors and commercial hedgers who want in on the game. An automated, electronic after-hours trading system makes it possible to trade futures and options internationally around the clock. The great temples of trade may now remain alert, humming and pulsing, all through the night. Money, or the idea of money, stays in play at every hour, unmindful of darkness, unneedful of light.

Almost lost in all of this are the commodities, the *things* that began it all: the fat lambs, the rapeseed, the peat, the dried cocoons and the greasy wool, the raw mink and the fox skins, the live hogs and the butter, the rubber, the onions, the shrimp and the apples, the natural gas and the scrap metal, the cheddar cheese and the recycled garbage, the platinum and the frozen orange juice, the shellac and the spices. Each of the items has hands behind it, and shoulders and backs and brains and souls, and there must live in each one tales of breakfast and blood and soil and toothache and laughter and nightmare and boredom and prayer.

But on the trading floor none of that is real. The commodities themselves are nonexistent, except in name——or not even name, but symbol, code, abbreviation. The idea of the commodity is important inasmuch as it represents an occasion for transaction, an opportunity to buy or sell, and eventually, many steps down the road, an amount of money lost or gained. But no essence of cocoon or hog or garbage is present in the actual exchange. The material commodity is hardly relevant in the wake of its own fetish.

Interlude

P*erson*

In my father's arms I ride, long past my bedtime. I am quite little: four or five. Over his shoulder I see the rest of my family, and the channels of shadow and streetlamp that traverse the park.

We have just come from the church across the street, where we have seen a play. I did not understand it but I liked it, especially the songs and the costumes. Some of the songs were sad and some were funny. One woman wore a hot pink leotard and chewed gum very fast. One man wore a police cap.

Now it is late, but we are in no rush. No one in this park is in any sort of rush at all. The night air rides our bodies, warm and easy as skin.

The fountain in the middle of the park is dry. In its well someone is eating fire. In between swallows, he says things that make the crowd around him laugh.

On a bench two men play tall drums. Somewhere else a radio plays a different song. Someone dribbles a basketball, slowly, in the darkness. Pricks of red light are cigarettes, glowing and dimming at the ends of people's unseen hands.

My father turns toward the fountain, so I am facing out now, away from our family and the fire-eater, looking at a quiet stretch of empty bench and unlit path. A man is wetting against a tree. He finishes, zips his fly, bends to get his bottle.

This man walks toward us, not in a straight line. He pauses to drink from his bottle, then continues. He isn't wearing shoes. When he is standing right behind my father's back, he squints up at me and says, "How you doing?" His voice comes grinding from his throat like nails pouring from a tin can.

I do not answer. I tuck my face against my father's shoulder; my father, feeling this, turns.

"Beautiful night we having," says the man.

"It sure is," my father agrees, easily. He says it just as if this man were not a stranger to us.

"Okay!" says the man. "O-*kay!*" Already he is moving on.

"Have a good night," my father says.

The man turns back and acknowledges the good wish with a wave of his bottle, but his message is for me, and I have lifted my head now and am looking at him when he delivers it: "Your daddy's got a lot of love to give."

*E*vening

In space, the earth turns itself counterclockwise and sends a valley dipping into shadow. Day lilies shrivel their petals together like hands knotted in prayer. The sun fails to reach the lower floors of buildings, and in an office, in a kitchen, electric lights are switched on. A lake swiftly drains of blue; it appears stolid now, impervious, cloaked in steely drab. Birds hush. Time clocks get punched, paychecks cashed, tips counted. The stock market closes; men loosen their ties from around their throats, women change their shoes. On a hillside a lizard grows cool on a cooling rock. Shopkeepers face their "Closed" signs out, crank their awnings up. Unsold items continue to sit, patient as air, on the shelves.

In factories and classrooms, on construction sites and piers, newspapers get folded, slid into trash bins, tossed onto piles of recycling. Other papers, eight or ten hours fresher, are purchased, tucked under arms, into attaché cases and grocery bags. In train and bus stations commuters salvage discarded editions for the ride home. Homeless people gather tabloids and broadsheets to make fresh bedding for the night. Men and women tear out recipes, classifieds, crossword puzzles to save; other pages they use for wrapping meat, stuffing into cracks along windowsills, or as mats on which to rest muddy boots.

In cities and villages the cafés fill up and empty out, refill and reempty in a steady stream all through the hours of the waning sun. The customers linger less at this time of day. In ones and twos they pay for their coffee, occupy the tables and chairs, regard the darkening street. Then they finish their drinks and disappear again without speaking. They leave only their glasses behind, along with crumpled napkins and dull smatterings of change.

Light ebbs further from the sky. Clouds along the horizon appear briefly fantastic: like pink ribbon candy, purple and orange fish bones, smears of molten yolk from a giant smashed egg. Then the earth tilts another notch and the clouds are evacuated of light. Another valley goes into a bath of shadow, another lake turns inward-looking and gray. More fingers switch on electric lights, set candles burning, pull curtains closed. More feet hasten along sidewalks and graveled roads and dirt paths toward home. Work ends; darkness kindles and catches; people disperse. They retreat to privacy, to the places where their lives begin.

Plumweseep

No matter the prowess of Brent's machine in altering the earth's facade, he still must bow to nature, all year round. Late summer and fall bring the threat of forest fires, which, when the fire index is high enough, can bar him from the woods during daytime hours; then he must adapt his schedule and go to work at night. Winter brings temperatures so far below freezing that he occasionally has to use cold couplings to get the harvester going, and tow the porter awhile before it'll concede to start; also, certain things break more easily in the brittle cold, and then he has to warm the frost off the tools in his cupped palms before he can make the repair. But nature's greatest moment of incorrigibility comes in spring, when everything goes runny and Brent is barred from woodswork entirely. Any day now, just as other creatures are emerging from hibernation, flying north, coming to term, the harvester and porter will be forced into dormancy; for two months they will cut and truck no tree.

Brent is unsentimental about all of this. He does not regard his role in the woods as either virtuous or villainous. To do so would imply a moral framework that has no place in something so vast and unsimple, so devoid of moral absolutes, as the forest.

For the forest is not an entity. A forest has no goal. A tree has a goal. A bush, a blade of grass, a bird, the spruce budworm, Brent—all of these have goals, and all of their goals, plaited together like the strands of a heavy velvet cord, compose the long, unfinished story of the forest, but the forest itself has no collective goal. One tree crowds another out of sunlight and root space; the budworm decimates the spruce; a fox sinks its teeth into the throat of a rabbit; Dave hunts partridge among the cranberries and thorn plum bushes; Brent razes a black spruce swale.

A hiss of static, then a voice crackles over the short-wave radio in the cab of the harvester. It's Dave, calling from the porter, out nearer the road. "You got some spectators."

Simultaneously, Norm the district engineer and four other men appear through the brush. They stand a good twenty yards off to the side of the harvester, all of them in caps and boots and bare-fisted, a couple of them perched up on stumps for a better view. Brent smiles and waves rather formally out the window, then launches into his crowd-pleaser routine, the two-fer. He moves the harvester forward and hugs the grip around two slender trunks at once, slices them down, turns them horizontal and delimbs them, then cuts them to length together. This is actually a less time-effective method of harvesting, but looks spiffy, and out across the swale the men are smiling, open-mouthed, shaking their heads.

Brent goes into reverse, then sidles the boom head up to another tree, this one quite broad-based, over two feet wide, and demonstrates his other trick. The harvester blade can slice through a maximum of twenty inches in diameter, but Brent can take down fatter trees by going through halfway and then coming around and doing a back cut. Severed, the tree falls; its crown comes arcing down, smashing past branches on other trees, landing with a resounding bounce. Undeniably, the bigger trees are more fun to fell; Brent likes the way they crash.

Woodswork today remains a dangerous business. Modernity has alleviated some risks but contributed others, what with power saws and heavier, mechanized equipment. And the men today don't work side by side so much as they did in the past; they're more often spread out and isolated, autonomous within their sealed woods vehicles. But then, what they have given up in terms of camaraderie in the woods, they gain in other places; thanks to paved roads and automobiles, today's woodsworkers may return each night to their hearths and families; they may bathe and read to their children, eat supper with their wives, sleep in their own beds.

For his part, Brent has never once felt fearful of either the woods or the big forestry machines. He loves them both, always has, is perhaps most at home among them. He finishes processing this last tree now by sending its length through the drive wheels to strip it, then chopping it into logs. Done, he shuts off the engine.

The spectators shoot glances at one another, shake their heads some more, spit in the snow. Brent knows just how they feel. It's something primal, something harkening back to the sandbox. The men begin to wander up toward the now-quiet machine. Brent swings open his door, steps politely out on the tire to greet them.

"Slick rig you got there."

"How much wood can you cut with that?"

"How big is the blade?"

"How much fuel does she burn?"

He fields their questions, all of them structured around numerical responses, while they look the machine over with ineffable appreciation, an almost mournful reverence.

"Still can't keep up with your father, though," Norm observes. The men had run into Howard on their way over; apparently, being stuck with a moment to spare, he'd been unable to keep from tinkering under the hood of his truck. At last report, he'd been sighted with a great pool of oil spreading out across the road from beneath his engine.

Brent laughs his short, elastic chortle. "I know," he agrees. "It's like working under the whip."

This seems to remind everyone that the hour is growing late. The men thank Brent and vanish again through the brush. Brent slips once more into his cab. The sky is steeling itself for evening, turning up the wattage of its darkening blue, and the sun lolls, dully visible behind a thick sweep of cloud, like a pat of butter on cold mashed potatoes, not melting. The tiny licking sound around the swale has shushed, things having frozen up again for the night, but underneath an ice membrane the liquor of the earth continues to course, more fluid now day by day.

Time passes, minutes ticked off by falling trees. Dave is gone, the porter parked and dark, its last toted load stacked at roadside. Howard's ruts are freezing solid for the night. On the main road, headlights of homebound cars shine white, like the eyes of huge, speeding owls cutting intently through the night.

Brent loves these woods. He is a man who dreams of building his own log cabin someday on a wooded lot by some water—over on the banks of Washademoak Lake, or maybe back where he was born, perched like a bird on the sapphire finger of Belleisle Bay. He is a man who stops to regard forest animals—a couple of bull moose scraping antlers in a frosty clearing at dawn, a russet fox flashing through the grass behind his grandfather's house—with the wordless gaze of a pilgrim whose destination has just come in sight. He is a man who keeps a battered Audubon bird guide in the glove compartment of his half-ton, one who pauses to look up the specific sort of woodpecker he notices in the woods one day, who learns for himself (because he likes to know) that the name is "pileated," and the habitat dead wood—that, in other words, this bird ought normally to feed on the insects and grubs that crawl through the rotting architecture of trees that have fallen, trees that in this case Brent will remove from the woods, for trucking to mill, for exchange for cash, which will be further exchanged for diesel fuel, ice cream, socks, a tricycle for Ellen, and some crab apples that Brent will pickle and wind up exchanging as gifts.

He is a woodcutter who loves the woods. Ask him if he feels like an anomaly and he'll bounce the question straight back, his voice easy and light, inflected with real curiosity: *There's so many different people in the world, how could any one of us be an anomaly?*

At last Brent shuts things down, drops from the harvester. Around him the earth is minty, starlit, where the woods have been carted away. He cannot see past the dense tapestry of trees still standing, but he knows that just beyond the swale, on the rise over Plumweseep Cross, house lights will be burning in the shape of a neatly subdivided E. And in one of those houses, a woodstove will be going, a pot of stew warming for supper, a little child chatting to her mother in her own special dialect: half-English, half-birdsong. It calls him home.

Lancaster

In the early morning hours, Ruth Lamp dips into her dinner bag. Tonight she's packed an orange, an apple Danish, cut-up raw carrots, a Tupperware with some leftover turkey in it, and a small, thick plastic bottle of a sort of cherry gelatin beverage called Squeeze-It, which Ruth drinks to help ward off osteoporosis. She usually packs a dinner at home, but sometimes she forgets. Anchor Hocking has a small cafeteria, but at night it's dormant except for a few vending machines. Instead, she can usually place an order with someone heading over to the pool hall across the street, which is a funny kind of establishment, dark and mysterious— they don't allow women to set foot inside—but they cook up decent little burgers, and chicken-on-a-bun and things, and it's convenient to the plant.

Ruth absently rolls the orange around under her palm and scans her desk, organizing her thoughts about what needs doing next. She is preempted by the jangling summons of her desk phone, which she picks up. "Ruth," she announces, then listens, frowning. "Torn bottoms? . . . Okeydoke." She holds the receiver button down a minute, dials another number, waits a second, and then her work face clears away, or is supplemented, enlivened, by a melting warmth, and the fine lines on her face spread like tiny beams of light as she smiles into the phone. "Hi, *Joe!* Hi, sweetie." Her deep voice crackles, lively and varied as water tumbling through a brook. Joe Barrett—Indian Joe, they call him affectionately—is a particular friend of hers down in the furnace room. "Hey," she says, "I just

got another quarantine for three-two for torn bottoms
. . . I didn't see any either . . . Hon, I don't know
. . . They put a new mold on? I bet that's when it
was . . . Okay."

Ruth whisks the pencil stub from her ear, jots, replaces it, and switches gears. "You get off soon, don't
you?" she asks Joe. "You and Sally going out partying
tonight? . . . Over at the Holiday Inn . . . Yeah,
I'll be in here 'til five in the morning . . . What?
You'll buy me a 7Up? Well then, you know what I
drink, then, don't you!" and she laughs, a low, gravely
staccato. "Two 7Ups? Okay, thanks, sweetie. Bye-
bye." Such snippets of conversation provide a kind of
succor during the factory nights. They are terribly
small, terribly important, these morsels of human contact.

The sluer office door opens and in walks a serious-
looking man with biceps bulging through his T-shirt
and a long, skinny braid running halfway down his
back. He's a hand trucker, which is sort of like a
gofer, someone who works the floor, keeps it clean,
moves around equipment according to which shops are
in operation on what jobs. Hand truckers, roller boys,
tow motor operators, millwrights, checkers, and, of
course, selectors and packers are just some of the
workers who populate this end of the floor.

"Anything you need from the storeroom, Ruth?"

"Hi, Chris. Yuh: gloves, thanks."

He returns with an armful, and she unloads them
into the second drawer of the filing cabinet.

Almost as soon as he leaves, a couple of women
come in, wanting gloves for the new shift. "Ruthie,
what lehr am I on?" asks one, a little breathlessly. Her

girth is something like the Michelin Man's. Ruth shows her the shift list.

A minute later a man with long white sideburns and a white mustache comes in. "Ruthie, you're not excusing anybody for tomorrow, are you?"

"Hiya, Bobby. You know, I'm being real slow and haven't gotten to the list yet, but I'm pretty sure I will be."

"I was just wondering, because I have a bowling tournament . . ."

She makes a note.

"Thanks, Ruthie."

He's followed by another man, in cowboy boots and a baseball cap. "Can I get off on Monday?" he wants to know. "My wife's real sick. She went in to the doctor, to the hospital—I think she has a bladder infection. She couldn't even walk this morning."

Ruth duly notes it.

Another man asks to take a vacation day so that he can bring his son to the children's hospital up in Columbus; he's got something wrong with his spine, it seems, only they don't know what. "And he's got real chunky, too, Ruth," the man says, peering over her shoulder as she marks the date. "He's gained a heap of weight real quick."

Next comes an earnest young man holding a bottle of Dad's Old Fashioned Root Beer in two hands. He asks to be excused the next night so that he can attend his uncle's funeral: the uncle drowned four months back, but his body was only just found. Ruth knows all about it; it was in the *Lancaster Gazette*. Together, she and the young man consult the little yellow booklet of union rules she keeps in the file cabinet, only to find that uncles' funerals are not covered in the contract as excused absences.

Absenteeism is a chronic problem. If it were up to Ruth, she'd address the problem through an incentive program—a bonus, say, or maybe a day off, after three months of perfect attendance. As it stands, a whole year's worth of perfect attendance gets you only a certificate and a box of free glassware, or else an Anchor Hocking T-shirt, which in Ruth's eyes amounts to little better than an insult. Poor attendance is treated rather more decisively, with a "point" meted out for every absence not excused by a doctor's note: more than three points within a hundred-twenty-day period results in progressive disciplinary steps, from a warning note for a first offense to increasing periods of suspension.

All night long the workers' requests will pile in. When not discussing their own tales of hardship, they catch Ruth up on news of other people's misfortunes: how so-and-so is coming along with the radiation treatment, and whose husband has got Alzheimer's real bad, and how this one had a breast removed, and that one lost a leg to gangrene, or a cousin to heart failure, or a child to leukemia. Her friend Indian Joe alone has had a year of misfortune: his house burned down, a chainsaw accident left a scar on his chin, his son lost his hand, and his mother died. It often strikes Ruth that there seems to be more illness and strife in Lancaster than in most places, at least among the people she knows. Everywhere she turns, it seems, someone else has been diagnosed with cancer, another person has died.

About two A.M., midway through her carrots and

fourth cup of coffee, the door opens and a slight, wiry man in a Chicago Bears T-shirt pops in. He mischievously declares he won't be showing up anymore after tonight.

Ruth, already shuffling a sizable pile of requests from workers who wish to be excused, lowers wary eyebrows. "You have vacation time?"

"Nope. I'm *never* coming back," he asserts, grinning like he's about to whip a bunch of flowers out from behind his back.

"Ah!" Ruth remembers. "You're going to the tank!" She thumps her desk, pleased. "When did you put in for that?"

"Back in February."

A transfer to the tank, or the department upstairs that regulates the mixing and melting of batch, is a definite promotion—a person's wages may rise only a dollar or two an hour, but fewer people work up there than in Select and Pack, and the likelihood of moving into a salaried position is greater. As is morale.

She beams at him—"The *tank*"—and her steady, opaque eyes seem brimful of thoughts, pictures, connotations. It's just plain good to see someone moving up off the plant floor.

Ruth herself won't be leaving Select and Pack until she leaves the plant for good, a day she dreams of often. Grateful as she is for her job at Anchor Hocking, thankful as she is for all it's made possible, she's getting itchy to retire. Too many people stay on the job too long—when she walks down that ramp the final time, she means to walk down it a healthy person. A year from this June she'll turn sixty: a good turning point, she figures, a good time to move on. She's not sure how she'll support herself then—her retirement pay from Anchor Hocking won't amount to two hundred dollars a month. Ruth had been hoping the company might bring back what she calls the silver bullet, or early retirement plan, although the latest rumors make this look unlikely. But when the time comes for her to leave, she'll know it, and she'll trust things to work out for her then, as they always have.

The office quiet once more, Ruth glances outside the murky window over her desk. In a minute she'll make the rounds again, go visit each shop, see how the various jobs are going, but for a moment she takes the long view. The few windowpanes set up high against the outer walls of the factory are more translucent than transparent, and partly obscured anyway by towering stacks of wooden pallets, pillars, machinery. If Ruth could see them from the sluer office, they would appear right now as little more than cubes of black. But she cannot see them; life inside the plant is timeless, untethered: free-floating, the way bodies are supposed to be in outer space, without any gravity to claim them. Instead, all she sees are the line workers, and the yellow backing-up lights of the tow motors pulsing in syncopation with their plaintive electronic bleats, and, way back, the Creamsicle-hued glow of the furnace room. Occasionally she'll happen to glance out the window just as a gather of molten glass is shooting down from one of the tanks; it's like spotting falling stars.

Ruth is always amazed when she encounters a fellow worker who's never once taken a moment to visit the furnace room. As far as she's concerned, it's the best thing about the plant. To watch the molten gathers drop from the tanks up above down into the chutes, and the shears chop them off, and those fiery globes sink into their molds—well, she could stand back there indefinitely, taking it in, her eyes bright and solid as buttons. Nightly she waits for incidents to occur that necessitate her going back there.

The date is not long off, she suspects, before computers will make that part of her job obsolete. All information will one day get fed back to the furnace room automatically, and the men there will have only to look at pixels on a screen to know exactly which lasagna dishes are not passing the thermal shock test, or how many Moments platters came off the lehr in the last hour with streaks. Then there'll be no cause for Ruth ever to tread down the aisles between lehrs, toward the noise and billowing steam and thundering pistons of the great glass machines, to see the glass being born and shaped, and bring her mouth close to someone's ear and explain, in a human way, modulating the message with a twist of humor or a stern glance, what's wrong with the ware coming down the line. To her it's plain cold, the way technology always seems to lead to a loss of human contact.

Already tonight she's been back there three times. First it was those pesky whiskeys cropping up with torn bottoms, and then she had to check on a job change with the beer tankards—switching from plain to rim-tempered—and then it was a matter of some butter dishes coming off the lehr with dented handles, which turned out to be a problem with the way one of the molds was coming down. Every time she goes to the furnace room, no matter how many times she's done it before, it's like entering another world, an

unearthly place, the stuff of fairy tales, stage sets, hal-
lucinations. No doors, not even a curtain, separate it
from the rest of the floor, but somewhere around the
mouths of the long metal lehrs, where each piece of
newly formed glass enters its long, cooling birth canal,
a certain gritty darkness falls.

Water vapor gushes and shimmies between the six-
teen glass-forming machines, which rotate and revolve
like infernal carousels, their metal parts making the
sound of gnashing teeth. Black oil drips from the thick
metal arms and gears. The floor is strewn with
Speedy-Dry, a fine, crunchy, cat-litter-like substance,
which absorbs oil and provides traction over slicks.
Work lights glow mutedly through the vapor, like
streetlamps through mystery-novel fog; they are out-
shone by the gobs of molten glass themselves, which
pierce the darkness with their strange, jeweled light as
they drop like fiery moons and revolve in metal molds,
get machine-pressed and blown, cool to garnet and
cobalt, then are refired back to primordial, eye-sting-
ing orange. This is the throbbing, unpausing heart of
the glass factory. No matter where she stands in Select
and Pack, Ruth's eyes can always find the furnace
room; she can always catch a breath of its awesome
power, its nightmarish radiance, a glimpse of that mysterious landscape where liquids are turned into solids,
fiery elements harnessed to become punch bowls and
pie plates.

She makes her rounds out on the plant floor. It is
near three A.M. Ruth has that sneezy, itchy feeling she
often gets by this time of night, the combined effects
of carton dust, tow motor gasoline, and oil fumes
from the furnace. She delivers a fat roll of extra bar

code labels to a couple of packers (''Are you trying to keep us out of trouble, or what?'' they josh her gamely over the machinery's racket), and starts back to the sluer office to fetch her cardigan and a few Anaprox (when she's tired, she gets chilled, and the clubbiness is wont to settle more achingly into her joints), when she hears herself being paged again. She starts for the lehr where her presence has been requested, thinking maybe it's another breakdown; earlier tonight they had a mechanic over on that lehr fixing a slipped belt, but when she arrives it turns out to be fishbowls.

A quality control technician has identified flaws throughout a whole batch—they're stippled with tiny pits like grains of sand. Ruth walks a sample bowl over to the end of the lehr where three women stand shoulder to shoulder, picking up warm fishbowls as they float to the end of the belt and sticking bar code labels to their bottoms. Ruth shows them the pittedness they failed to catch, points out the whole stack of ware that'll need to be reselected, then shouts grimly past their earplugs, ''I've got three of you working this shop—that's too much, I can't afford it.''

Theirs is a staggeringly monotonous job; she knows, having stood in their place herself. Sometimes the sheer quantity and sameness of ware coming off the lehr could strike a person as unnatural, stomach-turning. A person could go mad trying to pick out singularities in each stiff, expressionless clone. Safer to dim your mind, lock your senses in a holding pattern, than to bring your full personhood to the task. But glass rules here; Ruth must uphold that. The workers nod, looking frankly more sleepy than chastened, but they begin to select more aggressively now, suddenly culleting more than half the bowls they handle.

The next step is to notify the furnace room, and Ruth heads back there with her long, faintly brittle stride, emerging between two massive, mesmerizing, revolving machines, like a couple of flaming black mandalas. In the summer it can get to a hundred forty degrees back here—the men come out at the end of their shifts with shirts soaked through and scallopy white lines of salt where their sweat has dried. Tonight, though, the heat feels good to Ruth (she never did get her cardigan), and she breathes in the thick, hot-oil aroma, and feels on her face the misty caress of all the billowing vapor, and enjoys, as always, being back here.

She comes upon one of the men working the shop that's producing the fishbowls. He's guzzling a cream soda before one of the barrel cam machines, watching it go round and round with its perpetual load of soft orange batch. Tall as she is, Ruth has to go on tiptoe to give him the message about the pitted bowls. She shouts in his ear, and he shouts back some, and they nod, and both linger then a moment, staring helplessly at the machine as if it's some riveting puppet show, or an elaborate, animated Christmas display down at the River Valley Mall.

Back in the sluer office, Ruth peers in consternation at the willful air conditioner, wheezing out chilly blasts. "Floyd, what's that thing up there doing? We'll have to get a stepladder to turn it off." Her coworker puts down his apple, lopes over, kneels up on her desk, and squints at the thing, his whistle belying the stern set of his jaw. "Don't know," he determines, climbing down. Ruth shakes her head, puts on her sweater, and goes to refill her coffee mug. She pours nondairy creamer until the powder entirely coats the surface of the liquid, then brings it back to her desk, stirring, and pops a couple of painkillers out of their plastic-and-foil casing.

A minute later the furnace room supervisor comes in, oily black gloves sticking out of a back pocket, hackles up, a rejected fishbowl worn like a boxing glove over one fist. "I don't think they're that bad, Ruthie," he protests.

Ruth swivels her chair slowly around, takes the bowl, and holds it grimly to the light. She scans it keenly through her eyeglasses, which reflect the fluorescent tubes and bounce back glare at the man.

"They're just being real persnickety tonight," he asserts, taking a few steel-toed steps toward her, hulking over her desk and inadvertently blocking her light.

"Well," says Ruth, abruptly handing back the bowl, "you can ask Sharon—she quarantined the whole lot."

The man receives the bowl, but seems reluctant to leave without scoring his point with Ruth. "You fill that with water and see if you notice." He steps away and then circles back, leaning over her with a wink, lowering his voice. "Anyways, the fish don't care!"

Ruth joins him in a short, barking laugh and sends him amicably on to Sharon, but after the door shuts behind him, she snorts. "When the customer unpacks that bowl and puts it on the shelf, it's not going to be filled with water," she mutters. "And 'the fish don't care'—I *love* that."

Over at his desk Floyd whistles a sweet, skippy tune through his teeth, possibly but not definitely in commiseration, and concentrates on some task involving a calculator and pen. The clock says three-forty. Pam'll be back from her night at home to relieve Ruth in less than an hour. It's always like that—the hours inching by as slow as molasses in January until all at once you look up and they've raced past, run out. Ruth slaps her desk, but softly, as if at an abrupt, delicious thought. "I swear," she says, "the older I get, the ornerier I seem to get." It feels like a blessing, a gift, and she laughs again, a little burst of pure delight. Sometimes she does surprise herself.

Orneriness and faith—or orneriness *of* faith—whatever the mix that makes it possible for her to decide, Ruth is suddenly quite certain she *will* retire next June, silver bullet plan or no. June: the month she came into this world, the month of the longest day, the month of commencement. She'll walk down that ramp a final time, feeling herself to be an instrument once again, trusting in where she's going—for she can sense it in her bones, in her fingertips: the best part of her life has yet to come.

Pluma

Home again Basilio Salinas walks, below the cemetery, which even now has acquired some new offerings: a fresh bundle of wildflowers and, resting by one of the wooden crosses, a bit of food, some favorite meal of a relative on the first anniversary of his death. The souls of ancestors rustle among the tall grasses on the hill. Truly, time here does shift and bend, move forward and backward, spiral and unwind. Notions of precisely clockable time are of little consequence. No one wears a wristwatch. Labor is performed when conditions— sunlight, weather, good health—allow. No one ever clocks in or out, and divisions between work and rest, family and colleagues, home and business, all blur. Simply, when his stomach is empty, when the beans are sacked, and the light is ebbing from the sky: home, then, Basilio walks.

He enters the yard to see his children. Yolanda is absorbed in trying to teach Juan Diego how to run and fall down. She demonstrates repeatedly, taking a few running steps and flinging herself quite gaily upon the ochre dirt. The toddler claps his hands each time but fails to follow suit, an error his older sister appears to find increasingly hilarious. Silvestre sits on a rock, chewing a piece of *pergamino*—a dried, golden bean still in its parchment skin—and taking in all these antics with the slightly lofty bemusement befitting an elder brother. Behind him a couple of hens peck for insects in a pile of *abono*. The floppy-throated dog lies at his feet.

"La Yolandita." Basilio calls her by her pet name, and she leaps from the ground, her face and dress streaked with dirt, and runs to him. Her braids shimmy and smack against her back. He hands her the *plátano macho*. Beaming and saucer-eyed, Yolanda conveys it toward her mother in the kitchen.

"Chive," says Basilio, and Silvestre jumps up from his rock, spits out the bean, and extends two arms proudly for a large bunch of plantains. Basilio remembers how they used to call Silvestre "old man" because he was so toothless and wrinkled as a baby. Now, at six, he is already handsome, with his impish eyes and silky black sideburns, his mother's quick laughter and his father's serious attitude toward work. He wraps his arms around the huge bunch of fruit and follows his sister across the yard with it, ducking a pair of brown pants on the clothesline strung across the front of the house. Various articles of clean laundry are always about to lend the yard some character—aprons and blouses hang from tree branches; diapers and underthings lie strewn across bushes, like huge limp flowers.

"Diego." Basilio simply nods at the two-year-old and carries the last bunch of plantains himself toward the house. A wooden table, covered with a crocheted cloth, stands with some straight chairs in the yard under a tin overhang, which, like virtually all the roofs in town, has developed a pattern of red and blue stripes: rust on metal. This humble portico serves as the dining room. Isidra sits here now, nursing Enriquetta.

"Buenos, Chilio," she says, peacefully, her dumpling cheeks expanding further with a smile.

"Buenos." Basilio sets the fruit on the table. Juan Diego, suddenly whimpery to find himself stranded by his siblings, goes toddling toward the kitchen, but Genoveva comes out just then and intercepts him, wiping her hands on her skirt and laughing at his fretful baby face. He attaches himself to her leg and she limps toward the table.

"From *Tía* Lupe," Basilio tells his wife, gesturing toward the plantains.

"Ah? Great."

"Where's Lucío?"

"Washing beans."

Coffee, once pulped, must soak in water for a day or two. Then it gets rinsed of *miel,* or "honey"—any mucilaginous cherry goo still clinging to the beans. Only then, in nothing but its parchment skin, is it ready to be dried in preparation for its trip to the coast.

"Chive," calls Basilio. The boy zips out of the kitchen doorway. "Let's go find *Tío* Lucío."

"When do you want to eat?" asks Genoveva.

"Ahorita," he says, with classic imprecision. *Right now, in a minute.* But in the gesture, the breath before speaking, the amount of light in the sky, and the way he holds his shoulders—in these nonverbal clues lie the better answer to her question. Down they go, father and son, past the little shed where the black turkey is kept locked up (otherwise he would eat the drying coffee cherries), and down the path that winds through the two and a half hectares of El Corozo. Genoveva watches them, effortlessly gauging. Then she detaches her younger son from her leg and recedes back into the kitchen. The men will not be long.

Tonight is not a meat night. The Salinas family eats meat about twice a week, usually either *res,* which is scraped from the skull of a cow, or some fish from the coast. They buy meat on Saturday or Sunday, at the market in *el centro,* where vendors from nearby towns, the coast, and the city of Oaxaca come every week to set up their awnings and stalls. On market days everything is busy. *El centro* reeks of gasoline from all the trucks, and empty silver beer cans roll around in the streets, and, most Sundays, a priest comes up from Candelaria and holds an afternoon service in the big pink cement church. Not only residents of Pluma Hidalgo come to shop, but also people who live in the neighboring hills and those who work all week on the *fincas.* Some come by truck, but most walk, leaving their homes at sunrise to get home again before dark.

Usually, the Salinas family buys just what it needs for the week: corn and beans, perhaps some tomatoes and grapes, a bit of cheese and meat. The meat vendors generously rub salt into their product before wrapping the slabs in plastic for the customers to take home; even so, with no refrigeration, the meat must be consumed in the early part of each week. Tonight the Salinas family will dine on their more regular meal of beans, tortillas, avocado, the couple of eggs their own hens yield daily, and cheese—the local version of which is chalk-white and damp, with tiny perforations running throughout, and extremely salty.

Now Basilio disappears with Silvestre down the hill, and Juan Diego joins his mother in the kitchen room. Enriquetta has fallen asleep at her mother's breast. Isidra buttons her blouse, deposits the baby in the small outdoor hammock made of rope and two sticks, and gives this a gentle swing before she, too, goes inside.

"Yola," says Genoveva, "go keep the flies off the baby." She sends her daughter out of the kitchen with a little push, and the two women, sisters by adoption and now also by marriage, set about readying supper. With only the open doorway and one window (a flap of corrugated metal that has been cut away on three sides and propped open with a stick) for light, the kitchen grows dark long before night settles down on the land. El Corozo has had electricity, and three bare lightbulbs, since 1987, but it isn't working this week. Pricks of light show through tiny holes in the walls, inventing strange constellations for the smoke-blacked room. A few larger holes in the ceiling let in shafts of light, which fall like pale coins on the dirt floor. Genoveva has lit one candle, and the cooking fire spreads a sighing roseate glow.

Just beyond the door, Yolanda is chanting under her breath a song about a little cat. She has learned it at *kinder,* and finds it accompanies well the motion of fanning flies and the swaying of the hammock. *"Mi gatito tiene dos orejitas, una cola larga, y bien suavecito . . ."*

Inside, Genoveva adjusts the temperature of the cement block that serves as a stove by removing one burning stick from under the pot of beans and setting it down at the other end of the block, where no food is cooking. A large basin near the stove is heaped with fine gray powder; each morning when the women clean the previous night's ashes from the stove, they save them, to be added to the *abono* later. Genoveva sidesteps one of the scrawny brown pullets that has wandered into the house and spreads a few tortillas to warm on the *comal*—the traditional curved white cooking stone that serves as a wok or frying pan, and on which everything from eggs to coffee beans gets cooked and toasted. She and Isidra made the day's tortillas on it this morning. One day's supply amounts to forty or so of the thin cornmeal disks, for the men alone eat seven or eight apiece at one sitting.

"Mi-ou, mi-ou, mi-ou," chants Yolanda outside, rocking the hammock in rhythm. In the kitchen Juan Diego is becoming weepy again. He bumbles around the feet of the women, sniffling. Genoveva clucks at him in mock exasperation, then slips him a piece of cinnamon bark to chew on and pours him a drink of water from a plastic jug. Three such jugs sit on a wooden ledge in the kitchen; they get replenished several times a day from the birthplace of water down the mountain, where Basilio and Silvestre have gone to find Lucío.

She clucks her tongue again, this time at herself: she should've asked them to fill up the empty jug.

Juan Diego, well appeased, sits on a low wooden stool and chews his cinnamon bark while his mother and aunt move surely, speechlessly, through the dim kitchen and his sister chants the kitten song just outside, in the soft blue-and-amber light. Soon his father and uncle and brother will climb again up the hill, sweaty from their labor, perhaps, even though the earth has cooled with the coming of dusk. They will take off their shirts, wash the sweat and *miel* from their chests and hands with water from the rain barrel behind the house—Silvestre imitating the way his father, with a handful of water, rakes hair off his forehead—and then they will come and sit at the table, and everyone will eat beans and tortillas, eggs and avocado and cheese.

Someday soon Juan Diego will begin to help the women lay the beans out to dry every morning, and pack them up every afternoon, as Yolanda and Silvestre already do. Someday not long after that, he will begin to accompany his father and uncle down the steep path to where the coffee grows, and to the nursery, and the pulper, and the tub where they rinse the beans. Someday after that, he may go to work on UCI's *parcela,* and one afternoon not very much later, on a Sunday afternoon when the priest comes to town, he will marry some young woman he's known all his life in the big pink church in *el centro.* And perhaps he will bring his wife back to El Corozo, where they will live with his brother Silvestre's family, and the two of them together will tend the nursery and the *abono* and the half-moons and the harvest. Or else he may work his wife's family's *parcela,* and live there instead, but still tend to the same plants in the same way that his father did before him, and come home in the evenings smelling of the same smells, weary in the same joints, anticipating the same suppers. And a little while after that, he will be carried to the cemetery, the same one that sits across the road from him now, the same one where the bodies of other Salinas men, all of them coffee growers, have been laid for more than a hundred years, and there he will be laid beneath a wooden cross and flowers.

Or perhaps this will not be his story. Pluma is changing, if slowly. Electricity has come, and paved roads, in patches, and two new schools that did not exist when his own parents were young. Perhaps Juan Diego will be one of the few to go on beyond secondary school; perhaps somehow there will be money for him to study in Pochutla or Oaxaca or even Mexico City. Perhaps in any case he will head for the city, will leave coffee, be the *hijo* who prunes himself from the tree, who sets out somewhere and chooses what he will do with his hands, his thoughts, his life.

But for now, too little to wonder such things, he sits on his low kitchen stool, chewing his cinnamon bark, the air around him reeking so delicately and familiarly of *abono,* dried coffee pulp, woodsmoke. He hears the men come treading through the yard, and the splash of water as they busy themselves at the rain barrel out back. His mother and aunt are carrying plates of food out to the table. Yolanda leaves her post and climbs onto a chair; Isidra gives the hammock a push with her fingertips. By seven the sky will be fully dark; by eight the family will be in bed for the night, readying their bodies to rise again with the next dawn. In the trees the insects have begun their throbbing, invisible song.

Along the ground the fog sighs and settles. Halfway around the earth, morning comes.

C o d a

Someday Café

A gain in the Someday Café, I sit with the paper and a cup of coffee. The couch I am sitting on smells of wet dog, and the plate-glass windows are streaked pale gray, as though it has recently rained sugar water. Around me other people sit, too, at little tables or in armchairs patched with duct tape, alone with their newspapers or in pairs, talking. The scraps of their conversations float together to make a dadaist poem.

> —*So how come you didn't call me back, fink?*
> —*Obviously, it would be very complex.*
> —*Maybe we could lighten your hair a little bit.*
> —*I look forward to my death.*

At the rest of the tables people sit alone, reading. A woman in mudcloth and bifocals, a man in a suit and bow tie, a girl peeling an orange under the table—all of them locked in a closed circuit with their coffee and newspaper, engrossed in the solitary act of keeping in touch with the world. Someone turns a page and stretches; someone rubs an eyebrow; someone raises her glass to her mouth, takes a swallow. Then each returns to the print, to the visible stories at hand.

My own hand is locked around the warm glass tumbler, utterly plain and functional—except for the little anchor pattern branded onto the bottom. I click my fingernail over the logo's tiny ridges. There is one more story to tell.

This glass has journeyed from Lancaster, Ohio, from Anchor Hocking's Plant 1 on Pierce Avenue, across from the pool hall where women are not allowed. It has been formed in the furnace room, has shimmied down one of the lehrs and been selected and packed by hand, under the supervision of one Ruth Lamp, before journeying on by rail to the distribution center, and then by truck all the way to Chelsea, Massachusetts, just across the Mystic River from Somerville. The owners of the Someday Café make jaunts there as needed, to a big warehousey place called New England Store Fixture, to replenish their supplies.

Coffee arrives at the café by way of UPS, which

delivers cartons of vacuum-sealed beans every five or six days. I'm drinking the Mexican roast, supplied by Aztec Harvests. This coffee was picked and pulped and raked and bagged at the hands of Basilio Salinas and other UCI farmers around Pluma Hidalgo. It was trucked down the mountain to the pink-and-lavender compound at Rincón Alegre and milled there, then sent by sea to Long Beach, California; by rail to San Francisco; by truck to an Alameda warehouse; and by truck again to Batdorf and Bronson Roasters in Olympia, Washington. The owners of the Someday Café, who went to college with the chief roaster at B&B, buy all their coffee from this small establishment across the continent. There it gets roasted in a small one-story building off Columbia Street, where gray light streams through glass-brick windows and the roasting beans make a noise like rain.

And the thin, bone-colored paper of my *Boston Globe* harbors remnants of the New Brunswick forest—balsam fir, a little jack pine and hardwood, but mostly spruce—perhaps even fibers of certain black spruce trees that once populated a swale near Plumweseep. Portions of these trees, felled by Brent Boyd and sold to Irving, made their way down to the city of Saint John, where they got cooked and washed and bleached into pulp, then felted and pressed into newsprint. Irving, one of the *Globe*'s newsprint vendors, conveys reels of this paper south on railcars, which chug right into the newspaper's main plant, on Morrissey Boulevard in Dorchester. This is where the ads and articles are applied, where ink meets the page, and meaning gets made, at the rate of sixty thousand printed copies an hour. About three each morning, a handsome green-and-gold delivery truck pulls away from the loading dock, Somerville-bound; before dawn it deposits several bundles at the convenience store across from the café.

Glass, paper, beans. These are the stories I would tell. Yes, it's also true that the glass is included in the price of coffee; that the coffee costs a dollar twenty-five; the daily paper, thirty-five cents. True, too, that the glass may signify practical utility; the coffee, modest sophistication; and the paper, an interest in current events. But beneath any such latterly applied layers of identity, each of the items carries something more basic—a thing quite separate from price, wholly innocent of my desires: its lineage.

Somewhere in this glass is Ruth, strolling among the lehrs with her clubby gait; tithing from every paycheck; planting a hill of beans out on her teacup; chatting to her wolf. Somewhere in this coffee is Basilio, scooping beans with the Paradise can; Silvestre and Yolanda helping to pulp the cherries; Gudelia shaking a worm from her lime; the dogs slouching across the patio, paws clicking delicately on the drying beans. Somewhere in this paper is Brent, greasing his drive wheel in the bitter cold of morning; looking up pileated woodpecker in his Audubon field guide; making homemade pickles and mousse; reading books with Ellen at the end of the day. And those are slim glimpses—elsewhere in these objects lie many more stories, of innumerable workers never met: accountants and truck drivers, secretaries and sailors, roasters and postal workers, commodity traders and floor moppers. Their labor hours, their lives, like so many strings attached.

These objects are brimming, teeming. In my hand, on my lap: a dazzling convergence of strangers.

I set the drink gently on a table, fold the newspaper slowly aside.

Beyond the window, as though across a proscenium, a pageant of the commonplace conducts itself. The beginnings of rush hour traffic slide about the square— cars and buses, a dump truck piled with dirt, a van with the words "Doggie Day Care/Doggie Pajama Parties" on its side. The larger vehicles all declaim their contents in artful lettering. One truck says it's carrying water; another, potato chips; another, heating supplies. The buses and taxis have all been costumed in bright advertisements for cigarettes, mints, phone companies, sitcoms. Far above them a jet, like the bravest ant ever, creeps along an unseen curve, delivering people or goods to a faraway place.

Foot traffic passes in the foreground, just on the

other side of the glass. Everybody has something to carry: a garbage bag bulging with empty cans, a brief-case, crutches, a doughnut. A man goes by with a duffel bag on his head. A woman goes by with a hairdo like a pineapple. A flock of pigeons migrates with sudden purpose from one side of the square to the other. Behind the bus station, from a third-floor porch, a few white garments stretch their drying sleeves earthward.

Inside the Someday, the poem ravels on, each line supplied by dint of diction and decibel.

> —*I did my bibli-um-ography.*
> —*Hey, is there any toilet paper?*
> —*It's much easier than Sanskrit.*
> —*I'm dying to tell someone the truth.*

Applause, like a cloudburst, spatters from the stereo. A new song begins.

The window imperceptibly transforms itself into a mirror. Outside, streetlamps cast their sallow glow. Some people from the street come in; some people from the café go out. The slow pageant continues; there is no proscenium. It plays everywhere all the time, without intermission. Everyone has a bit part—all of the people, as well as all of the things: tables and lamps, scones and duffel bags, drying laundry and garbage trucks, bow ties and oranges.

Everywhere you rest your eyes, invisible stories blossom.

Bibliography

Aiton, Grace. *The Story of Sussex and Vicinity.* Kings County
    Historical Society, 1967.

Allen, Glen. "A Delicate Balance: Canadian Forestry Prac-
    tices Are Under Fierce Attack." *Maclean's,* December
    16, 1991.

A Long Road Ahead. Ministerial Task Force, Logging Sector
    Employment in the Northeast, 1987.

Anderson, Benedict. *Immagined Communities.* Verso, 1991.

Anderson, Kenneth. *The Pocket Guide to Coffees and Teas.* Peri-
    gee Books/ G. P. Putman's Sons, 1982.

Appadurai, Arjun. "Introduction: Commodities and the Pol-
    itics of Value." In *The Social Life of Things: Commodities
    in Cultural Perspective,* ed. Arjun Appadurai. Cambridge
    University Press, 1986.

Aristotle. *Politics.* Modern Library, 1943.

Barry, Tom, ed. *Mexico: A Country Guide.* Interhemispheric
    Education Resource Center, 1992.

Bayley, Stephen. *Taste: The Secret Meaning of Things.* Pantheon Books, 1991.

Bedford, John. *Looking in Junk Shops.* David McKay Company, 1961.

Benjamin, Walter. *Illuminations.* Harcourt Brace Jovanovich, 1968.

Bernard, Sharyn. "Glass Acts." *The Weekly Newspaper for the Home Furnishing Network,* March 27, 1995.

Bloch, Maurice, and Parry, Jonathan. "Introduction." In *Money and the Morality of Exchange.* Cambridge University Press, 1989.

Brecher, Jeremy. "After NAFTA: Global Village or Global Pillage?" *The Nation,* December 6, 1993.

Bürgin, Dr. Eugen C. *Coffee.* A Casa Do Livro Eldorado (Rio de Janeiro; no date).

Capek, Milic. "Time." In *The Encyclopedia of Religion,* ed. Mircea Eliade. Macmillan Publishing Co., 1987.

Cassidy, Picot, ed. *In Mexico.* EMC Publishing, Chancerel Publishers, 1988.

Castle, Timothy James. *The Perfect Cup.* Aris Books/Addison-Wesley, 1991.

Cavendish, Richard, ed. *Man, Myth and Magic: The Illustrated Encyclopedia of Mythology, Religion and the Unknown.* Marshall Cavendish Corporation, 1995.

Connick, Charles J. *Adventures in Light and Color: An Introduction to the Stained Glass Craft.* Random House, 1937.

Cook, Olive. "The Art of Collecting." In *The Thirtieth Saturday Book,* ed. John Hadfield. Clarkson N. Potter, 1970.

David, Gregory E. "Let Us Prey: Having Swallowed 31 Companies in 25 Years, Ruthless Newell Remains on the Prowl." *Financial World,* June 21, 1994.

Davis, Pearce. *The Development of the American Glass Industry.* Harvard University Press, 1949.

DeMont, John. "The Irvings March on Maine." *Canadian Business,* September 1991.

Eidelberg, Ludwig, M.D., ed. *Encyclopedia of Psychoanalysis.* Free Press, 1968.

Ellis, William S. "Glass: Capturing the Dance of Light." *National Geographic,* December 1993.

English, Horace B. and Ava C. *A Comprehensive Dictionary of Psychological and Psychoanalytical Terms.* David McKay Company, 1958.

Fisher, Peter. *History of New Brunswick.* New Brunswick Historical Society, 1825.

Freedman, Milton. *Money Mischief: Episodes in Monetary History.* Harcourt Brace Jovanovich, 1992.

Freud, Sigmund. *Introductory Lectures on Psycho-Analysis.* W. W. Norton and Co., 1966.

Fulford, Robert. "The Forest and Canadian Culture." *The Forestry Chronicle,* Vol. 68, No. 1, 1992.

Galbraith, John Kenneth. *Money: Whence It Came, Where It Went.* Houghton Mifflin, 1975.

————. *Economics in Perspective.* Houghton Mifflin, 1987.

Green, Philip. "NAFTA Thoughts for the Left." *The Nation,* January 3, 1994.

Hall, Kevin G. "Mexican Rebellion Imperils Coffee Harvest." *Journal of Commerce and Commercial,* January 20, 1994.

————. "Coffee Growers Press Mexico to Join International Cartel." *Journal of Commerce and Commercial,* February 15, 1994.

Hallowell, A. Irving. "Temporal Orientation in Western Civilization and in a Pre-Literate Society." *American Anthropologist* [N.S., 39, 1937].

Harvey, David. "Money, Time, Space and the City." In *Consciousness and the Urban Experience: Studies in the History and Theory of Capitalist Urbanization.* Johns Hopkins University Press, 1985.

Hattox, Ralph S. *Coffee and Coffeehouses: The Origins of a Social Beverage in the Medieval Near East.* University of Washington Press, 1985.

Heidensohn, Klaus, ed. *The Book of Money: A Visual Study of Economics.* McGraw-Hill Book Company, 1978.

Hunter, Dard. *Paper-Making: The History and Technique of an Ancient Craft.* Crescent Press, 1957.

Illy, Francesco and Ricardo. *The Book of Coffee: A Gourmet's Guide.* Abbeville Press, 1989.

Jobes, Gertrude. *Dictionary of Mythology, Folklore and Symbols.* Scarecrow Press, 1962.

Katona, Christie and Thomas. *The Coffee Book.* Bristol Publishing Enterprises, 1992.

Kelly, Keith J. "Stop the Presses! Paper Costs Up Again." *Advertising Age,* May 29, 1995.

Kerr, Laura E. *Campfire to Courthouse.* Fairfield Heritage Association, 1981.

Kishler, Patsy. *Who, What, Where, Why, When and How of Immigration to Fairfield County, Ohio.* Fairfield County Chapter of the Ohio Geneological Society, 1986.

Kolpas, Norman. *A Cup of Coffee: From Plantation to Pot, a Coffee Lover's Guide to the Perfect Brew.* Grove Press, 1993.

Kopytoff, Igor. "The Cultural Biography of Things: Commoditization as Process." In *The Social Life of Things: Commodities in Cultural Perspective,* ed. Arjun Appadurai. Cambridge University Press, 1986.

Knappert, Jan. *The Encyclopaedia of Middle Eastern Mythology and Religion.* Element, 1993.

Knaster, Roland. "Unconsidered Trifles." In *The Saturday Book, Eleventh Year,* ed. Leonard Russel. Macmillan Co., 1951.

Kristal, Leonard, gen. ed. *The ABC of Psychology.* Facts on File Publications, 1982.

Landman, Isaac, ed. *The Universal Jewish Encyclopedia*. Universal Jewish Encyclopedia, 1939.

Lang, Jennifer Harvey, ed. *Larousse Gastronomique: The New Edition of the World's Greatest Culinary Encyclopedia*. Crown Publishers, 1988.

Lent, Henry B. *From Trees to Paper: The Story of Newsprint*. Macmillan Co., 1957.

Lingle, Ted. "Specialty Coffee Report." *Tea and Coffee Trade Journal*, April 1994.

Lustig, Nora, ed. *North American Free Trade: Assessing the Impact*. The Brookings Institution, 1992.

McCracken, Grant. *Culture and Consumption: New Approaches to the Symbolic Character of Consumer Goods and Activities*. Indiana University Press, 1988.

MacIsaac, Merle. "Stop the Presses I Want to Get Off." *Canadian Business*, November 1994.

MacKay, Donald. *The Lumberjacks*. McGraw-Hill Ryerson, 1978.

McKearin, George S. and Helen. *American Glass*. Crown Publishers, 1941.

McKibben, Bill. "An Explosion of Green." *The Atlantic Monthly*, April 1993.

Maggs, John. "US, Canada Agree to Begin Lumber Talks." *Journal of Commerce and Commercial*, December 19, 1994.

Marx, Karl. *Capital*. Penguin Classics, 1990.

————. *The Communist Manifesto*. Bantam, 1992.

Mintz, Sidney Wilfred. *Sweetness and Power: The Place of Sugar in Modern History*. Penguin Books, 1986.

Monroe, A. E., ed. *Early Economic Thought*. Harvard University Press, 1924.

Moore, Thomas. *Care of the Soul*. Harper Perennial, 1992.

Mulloy, Michael. "Five Experts Talk Coffee Prices: Where We've Been and Where We're Going." *World Coffee and Tea*, October 1994.

Munn, Nancy D. "The Cultural Anthropology of Time: A Critical Essay." *Annual Review Anthropology,* Vol. 21, 1992.

Nassau, Robert Hamill. *Fetichism in West Africa: Forty Years' Observation of Native Customs and Superstitions.* Charles Scribner's Sons, c. 1904.

New Catholic Encyclopedia. McGraw-Hill Book Company, 1967.

Northend, Mary Harrod. *American Glass.* Tudor Publishing Co., 1926.

Onions, C. T., ed. *Oxford Dictionary of English Etymology.* Oxford University Press, 1966.

"Outlook 1994: Canada Makes Comeback Try." *Pulp and Paper,* January 1994.

"Outlook 1995: Canada Repositioned for Profit." *Pulp and Paper,* January 1995.

Parkes, Henry Bramford. *A History of Mexico.* Houghton Mifflin, 1938.

Partridge, Eric. *A Short Etymological Dictionary of Modern English Origins.* Macmillan Publishing Co., 1958.

Paul, Cynthia A. "Promos Galore from Anchor Hocking." *The Weekly Home Furnishings Newspaper,* August 16, 1993.

Perry, John D., Jr. *The Coffee House Ministry.* John Knox Press, 1966.

Pollitt, Katha. *Reasonable Creatures: Essays on Women and Feminism.* Knopf, 1994.

Radford, Edwin and Mona. *Encyclopaedia of Superstitions.* Hutchinson and Co., 1969.

Reinfeld, Fred. *The Story of Paper Money.* Sterling Publishing Co., 1957.

Riding, Alan. *Distant Neighbors: A Portrait of the Mexicans.* Knopf, 1985.

Roberts, Gerald, ed. *Guide to World Commodity Markets.* Kogan Page/Nichols Publishing Co., 1985.

Roseberry, William, ed. *Coffee, Society, and Power in Latin America.* Johns Hopkins University Press, 1995.

Saint John Fundy Region Development Commission Town of Sussex Community Profile, Saint John, N.B., 1991.

Saltman, David. *Paper Basics: Forestry, Manufacture, Selection, Purchasing, Mathematics and Metrics, Recycling.* Litton Educational Publishing, Van Nostrand Reinhold Company, 1978.

Sanderson, George, Esq. *A Brief History of the Early Settlement of Fairfield County, Being the Substance of a Lecture Delivered Before the Lancaster Literary Institute with Additional Facts.* Thomas Wetzler, 1851.

Schafer, Charles and Violet. *Coffee.* Yerba Buena Press, 1976.

Schapira, Joel, Davide, and Karl. *The Book of Coffee and Tea.* St. Martin's Press, 1975.

Schapiro, Mark. "Muddy Waters: The Lore, the Lure, the Lowdown on America's Favorite Addiction." *Utne Reader,* November/December 1994.

Schultze, Fritz, Dr. Phil. *Fetichism, A Contribution to Anthropology and the History of Religion.* Humboldt Publishing Co., 1885.

Scoville, Warren C. *Revolution in Glassmaking.* Harvard University Press, 1948.

Shawn, Wallace. *The Fever.* Noonday Press-Farrar, Straus and Giroux, 1991.

Shermach, Kelly. "Coffee Drinking Rebounds; Specialty Blends Lead Way." *Marketing News,* September 12, 1994.

Silk, Leonard. *Economics in Plain English.* Simon and Schuster, 1978.

Simmel, Georg. "The Metropolis and Mental Life." In *On Individuality and Social Form,* ed. D. Levine. Chicago (no publisher), 1971.

Singer, Peter. *Marx.* Oxford University Press, 1980.

Smith, Anthony. *The Newspaper: An International History.* Thames and Hudson, 1979.

Spillman, Jane Shadel, and Frantz, Susanne K. *Masterpieces of American Glass.* Corning Museum of Glass, Crown Publishers, 1990.

Springer, John S. *Forest Life and Forest Trees.* Harper and Brothers, 1851.

Starr, Frederick. *In Indian Mexico: A Narrative of Travel and Labor.* Forbes and Co., 1908.

Stephens, Mitchell. *A History of News: From the Drum to the Satellite.* Viking, 1988.

Talboy, Gary. "What's So Special About Organic Coffee?" *Tea and Coffee Trade Journal,* January 1991.

Tamarkin, Bob. *The Merc: The Emergence of a Global Financial Powerhouse.* HarperCollins, 1993.

Tannahill, Reay. *Food in History.* Crown, 1988.

Teale, Edwin Way. *The Thoughts of Thoreau.* Dodd, Mead and Company, 1962.

Thompson, E. P. "Time, Work-Discipline, and Industrial Capitalism." *Past and Present,* No. 38.

Thoreau, Henry David. *Walden and Other Writings.* Modern Library, 1937.

Village of Sussex Corner—Draft Community Plan. Proctor, Redfern, Bousfield and Bacon, Consulting Engineers and Planners, 1972.

Visser, Margaret. *Much Depends on Dinner: The Extraordinary History and Mythology, Allure and Obsessions, Perils and Taboos, of an Ordinary Meal.* Grove Press, 1987.

————. *The Rituals of Dinner.* Grove Weidenfeld/Grove Press, 1991.

Walbank, Alan. "Joys of the Junk Shop." In *The Saturday Book, Fourteenth Year,* ed. Leonard Russel. Macmillan Co., 1954.

Waugh, Alec. *In Praise of Wine and Certain Noble Spirits.* William Sloane Associates, 1959.

Weeks, Lyman Horace. *A History of Paper-Manufacturing in the United States, 1690–1916.* Lockwood Trade Journal Co., 1916.

Williams, Richard L. *The Loggers.* Time-Life Books, 1976.

Zerwick, Chloe. *A Short History of Glass.* Harry N. Abrams, 1980.